Television's Female Spies and Crimefighters

Television's Female Spies and Crimefighters

600 Characters and Shows, 1950s to the Present

KAREN A. ROMANKO

McFarland & Company, Inc., Publishers
Jefferson, North Carolina

LIBRARY OF CONGRESS CATALOGUING-IN-PUBLICATION DATA

Names: Romanko, Karen A., 1953– author.
Title: Television's female spies and crimefighters : 600 characters and shows, 1950s to the present / Karen A. Romanko.
Description: Jefferson, North Carolina : McFarland & Company, Inc., Publishers, 2016. | Includes bibliographical references and index.
Identifiers: LCCN 2016001620 | ISBN 9780786496372 (softcover : acid free paper) ∞
Subjects: LCSH: Women on television. | Women heroes on television. | Criminal investigation on television. | Spy television programs—History and criticism. | Detective and mystery television programs—History and criticism. | Superhero television programs—History and criticism.
Classification: LCC PN1992.8.W65 R66 2016 | DDC 791.45/6522—dc23
LC record available at http://lccn.loc.gov/2016001620

BRITISH LIBRARY CATALOGUING DATA ARE AVAILABLE

ISBN (print) 978-0-7864-9637-2
ISBN (ebook) 978-1-4766-2415-0

© 2016 Karen A. Romanko. All rights reserved

No part of this book may be reproduced or transmitted in any form or by any means, electronic or mechanical, including photocopying or recording, or by any information storage and retrieval system, without permission in writing from the publisher.

Front cover image of Barbara Feldon from *Get Smart*, NBC 1965–1970 (Photofest)

Printed in the United States of America

McFarland & Company, Inc., Publishers
  Box 611, Jefferson, North Carolina 28640
  www.mcfarlandpub.com

For TV's female trailblazers
and for Bob, my partner in crime

Table of Contents

Preface: What's in This Book — 1

Introduction: A Brief History of Female Spies and Crimefighters on Television — 3

Television's Female Spies and Crimefighters by Character Name and Series Title — 15

Appendix: The Most Rewatchable Television Shows on DVD (Female Spies and Crimefighters Edition) — 229

A Note on Sources — 235

Index — 237

Preface:
What's in This Book

From Emma Peel with her "kinky boots" to Amanda King and her poppy seed cake, from Julie Barnes with her hippie pad to Honey West and her pet ocelot, television's female spies and crimefighters leave an indelible impression, but there hasn't been a reference work devoted to them until now.

Television's Female Spies and Crimefighters: 600 Characters and Shows, 1950s to the Present covers television series which feature female spies, private investigators, amateur sleuths, police detectives, federal agents and crime-fighting superheroes as lead or noteworthy characters. The focus is on live-action shows which aired in the United States on network TV, cable, or in syndication, wherever produced, from television's inception through August 2014. For series which aired fewer than 25 episodes in the U.S., the coverage is selective, emphasizing shows with distinctive female lead characters.

Every show in the book receives at least one entry under series title, arranged alphabetically, and the listing includes the range of years in production, number of episodes, and country of origin. Under the title is a listing of series credits, including creator, production company, original U.S. network, and main cast, followed by a synopsis of the series, covering notable plot points, important or fun facts, and sometimes critical commentary. Among those plot points, facts, and critical comments, the occasional spoiler creeps in, so readers using the book as a viewer's guide should consider this a universal spoiler alert.

Female characters whose names are highlighted in bold within the title entry also have entries under their own names (last name first) to provide more in-depth coverage, while female characters not receiving separate entries are listed with a cross-reference to the series title. Thus, readers are able to reference characters by either series title or the character's name.

For the series *Cold Case*, for example, the main entry is under:

Cold Case **(2003–2010, 156 episodes, USA)**

An entry on *Cold Case* lead character **Lilly Rush**, a homicide detective in the series, adds valuable detail, including descriptions of representative episodes, under:

Rush, Lilly (*Cold Case*)

Cold Case detective Kat Miller, a supporting character, is mentioned within the series entry, so she receives a brief description with a cross-reference:

Miller, Kat (*Cold Case*)
Member of a Philadelphia homicide team specializing in unsolved cases. See: *Cold Case* (2003–2010, 156 episodes, USA)

Cross-references are also provided for alternate series titles, such as:

The New Adventures of Wonder Woman
See: *Wonder Woman* (1975–1979, 59 episodes, USA)

Entries which begin with numbers are alphabetized as though the numbers are spelled out. The following entry for *21 Jump Street*, for example, is found under "T," as though it were "Twenty-one Jump Street":

21 Jump Street (1987–1991, 103 episodes, USA)

Covering 350 female spies and crimefighters who have appeared in more than 250 television series since the 1950s, this is a comprehensive reference to an important but overlooked aspect of television history.

Introduction: A Brief History of Female Spies and Crimefighters on Television

"Honey." A peculiarly sweet name for a person who works in the hardboiled profession of private detective, but when *Honey West* hit the small screen in 1965, "Honey" was the perfect name to signal that women were about to step out from behind the secretary's desk to become detectives in their own right. Honey West was the head of her own agency and ahead of her time. She was a woman in a traditionally male profession, but she made private investigating "women's work," using every tool at her disposal—intelligence, bravery, martial arts skills, and, yes, sex appeal—to solve mysteries and bring bad guys to justice. The actress who portrayed her, Anne Francis, was breaking new ground as well, starring as the lead in an action/crime series, a province usually reserved for men. Yes, the times they were a-changin', but the revolution would come slowly. *Honey West* lasted only one season.

Female detectives weren't exactly foreign to television prior to *Honey West*, but most were amateur sleuths and even then usually appended to a husband as part of an adorable sleuthing couple. Connie Conway (Lynn Bari) as *The Detective's Wife* (1950), Louise Baker (Randy Stuart) as the partner in life and intrigue of *Biff Baker, U.S.A.* (1952–1953), Pamela North (Barbara Britton), the distaff half of *Mr. & Mrs. North* (1952–1954), and Nora Charles (Phyllis Kirk), wife of *The Thin Man* (1957–1959), were all detectives by marriage, and often waited for crime to find them, usually with comic results. Pamela North, with her keen eye for detail and ability to read people, stands out as a true detective here, perhaps because the source novels for *Mr. & Mrs. North* were co-authored by Frances Lockridge, who contributed a woman's viewpoint to her writing partnership with husband Richard.

One exception to the dearth of professional female detectives on TV during the 1950s was Casey Jones in *Decoy: Police Woman* (1957–1958). Portrayed by Beverly Garland, Casey tackled undercover assignments for the New York

City police department, posing as a blackmailer, nurse, or gun moll to catch crooks in the act. *Decoy: Police Woman* lasted just one season and appeared only in syndication, but gave a hint of better things to come for female detectives as lead characters on television.

Other than Jones and the adorable wives, women in detective shows of the 50s were usually secretaries, receptionists, girlfriends, or some combination thereof. One standout among the clerical set was "Sam" (Mary Tyler Moore and later Roxane Brooks, both uncredited at the time), an answering-service operator for private eye Richard Diamond (David Janssen) in *Richard Diamond, Private Detective* (1957–1960). Sam called "Mr. D." with important messages, often catching him in the nick of time to avert danger and possible bodily harm at the hands of assorted bad guys. She was shown only from the waist down to emphasize her shapely legs, setting the bar low for working women in crime series, but it would be raised substantially just one year later with international help.

As the 60s dawned, our progressive cousins across the pond set a high example for female derring-do with both Dr. Cathy Gale and later Mrs. Emma Peel on *The Avengers* (1961–1969). Cathy Gale, portrayed by Honor Blackman, was an anthropologist-turned-amateur-operative, who assisted John Steed (Patrick Macnee) with his way-out cases, while proving she was adept at both mental and physical gymnastics. Although the Gale episodes didn't make it to U.S. television during the 60s, her character was reportedly one of the inspirations for the TV incarnation of *Honey West*. The heir to Gale's catsuit, Emma Peel, continued the good doctor's judo-chopping, high–IQ approach to the spy-fi biz, but with actress Diana Rigg's own inimitable style and sensibility. The Rigg episodes of *The Avengers* did reach American TV sets starting in the spring of 1966, further feeding the mid–60s spy craze, and showing that female spies could hold their own without the need for a steel-plated bowler hat like Steed's.

But back in the States the Gale/Peel lesson seemed to be lost on the creative folks behind *The Girl from U.N.C.L.E.* (1966–1967), who were confused (if not sexist) about what "girl spies" should be like. April Dancer (Stefanie Powers) was certainly a stylish secret agent who wore the latest mod fashions, and at times she was plucky and resourceful, able to free herself when suspended over a pit of hungry piranhas (which happens surprisingly often in the spy game). At other times, however, April was too demure for the intrigue trade, helpless and content to await rescue by partner Mark Slate (Noel Harrison). *The Girl from U.N.C.L.E.* never did find the right balance, and was canceled after one season.

Mission: Impossible (1966–1973) had a more substantial female spy with its Cinnamon Carter (Barbara Bain). Cinnamon was an elite operative with the Impossible Missions Force (IMF), which brought down governments, rescued prisoners, and foiled assassinations by means of long and elaborate deceptions/cons. A former top model, Cinnamon used her physical attractiveness to advantage, but was more than just pretty bait for evil men. She was also adept at role-playing, posing as a psychic, photographer, or lost princess, and proved her mettle under psychological torture, never giving up her colleagues to their adversaries. Though not the series lead, Barbara Bain made an indelible and positive impression with Cinnamon Carter.

Another iconic, albeit comic, female operative during the spy-crazed 60s was Agent 99 (Barbara Feldon) from *Get Smart* (1965–1970). Agent 99 made her partner look good, not only with her willowy beauty and style, but also with her competence and "smarts," which helped to compensate for bumbling Maxwell Smart's legion of deficiencies. She and Max, Agent 86, worked as undercover operatives for CONTROL, which battled an international organization of evil, appropriately named KAOS. If 99 had a flaw, it was that she was always mooning over Max (Don Adams), in one of those "opposites attract" romantic conundrums. But even eventual marriage to Max and the delivery of twins didn't keep 99 off the job for long, making her TV's groundbreaking "spy mom."

The rise of the counterculture in the late 60s led to the creation of one of television's truly unique female cops, Julie Barnes of *The Mod Squad* (1968–1973). Julie (Peggy Lipton), a down-on-her-luck "flower child," was recruited along with Pete Cochran (Michael Cole) and Linc Hayes (Clarence Williams III) to form an undercover squad able to go where the traditional police couldn't. Hippie chick Julie was (and still is) the most sensitive cop ever depicted on television, constantly wrestling with her conscience over whether she was doing the right thing by "working for the man." The boys weren't far behind Julie in the raised-consciousness department, but when physical action was involved, Pete and Linc tackled the baddies while Julie waited on the sidelines. Julie excelled, however, in her covert assignments, and helped to shine a light on subjects previously taboo on TV such as abortion, domestic violence, and unwed motherhood.

With the feminist movement in full swing, 70s television saw the arrival en masse of women as lead characters in action/crime series: *Police Woman* (1974–1978), *Get Christie Love!* (1974–1975), *Wonder Woman* (1975–1979), *Charlie's Angels* (1976–1981), and *The Bionic Woman* (1976–1978). With the exception of the groundbreaking *Get Christie Love!*, starring Teresa Graves as the first African American female undercover cop on the LAPD, all the series survived more than one season, showing that the viewing public was willing to accept women as protagonists in police procedurals, mysteries, and adventures.

Angie Dickinson's Pepper Anderson led the way as *Police Woman* in 1974. Pepper specialized in undercover assignments for the LAPD, posing as a prostitute, exotic dancer, or prison inmate, roles that tended to place her in suggestive attire, such as a dress so short no nurse could ever wear it and, well, be a nurse. But Pepper wasn't just about sex appeal. Dickinson imbued the character with intelligence and sensitivity, creating an indelible portrait of professional and personal life for a single woman in the 70s and inspiring real women to seek employment as police officers.

Charlie's Angels upped the sex ante even further, to the point that the media began to refer to the series as "jiggle TV." The Angels were three former policewomen who had been underutilized in their jobs, but a wealthy, unseen boss "took them away from all that," giving them exciting and glamorous lives as private detectives for his firm. Charlie's original Angels were Kate Jackson as intelligent and self-sufficient Sabrina Duncan, usually the most covered up of the three and referred to as "the smart one"; Farrah Fawcett as athletic and often scantily-clad Jill Munroe, also famous for her golden mane and brilliant smile; and Jaclyn Smith as sensitive and photogenic Kelly Garrett, the only Angel to remain with the series until the end. Tooling around Los Angeles in their Ford Mustangs, these and later Angels worked undercover as masseuses, roller derby queens, prostitutes, heiresses, and dancers, and no bikini op was left unexploited. Three female leads as private investigators had sounded so promising, and the actresses gave it their all, but the emphasis on the ladies' anatomical features made it hard to think of *Charlie's Angels* as a true step forward.

Wonder Woman and *The Bionic Woman* were female intelligencers in the superhero mold, albeit in different flavors—*Wonder* played it more campy, while *Bionic* went the sincere route. Diana Prince (Lynda Carter) worked for the Inter-Agency Defense Command, and when the agency's resources proved inadequate in the battle against crime and terrorism, she would spin into action as Wonder Woman, using her magic bracelets, tiara, and lasso to thwart Hitler clones and diabolical rock stars. Jaime Sommers (Lindsay Wagner), *The Bionic Woman*, came by her superpowers via cybernetic body parts after an accident, and used her exceptional abilities, such as massive strength and lightning speed, to fight evil around the world as an agent for the Office of Scientific Investigations. While not always the most realistic television, *Wonder Woman* and *The Bionic Woman* showed that women could be successful leads of action series, which, as it happens, are not always the most realistic television anyway.

The 70s also saw some successful additions to the venerable club of adorable sleuthing couples. *McMillan and Wife* (1971–1977) starred Rock Hudson and Susan Saint James as San Francisco Police Commissioner Stewart "Mac" McMillan and his hip, irrepressible wife Sally, who solved crimes together even though Sally wasn't on the police payroll. *Hart to Hart* (1979–1984) brought us Robert Wagner and Stefanie Powers as Jonathan and Jennifer Hart, a self-made millionaire and his sometimes journalist wife, who stumbled upon and solved murders in posh surroundings. Sally paid some lip service to feminism and Jennifer was independent-minded, updating this subgenre for 70s audiences, but mostly the shows were entertaining with couples who had amazing on-screen chemistry.

The 80s were a watershed period for female spies and sleuths on television. Series such as *Cagney & Lacey* (1982–1988) revealed the difficulties for women when they tried to work in a man's world. Others, such as *Scarecrow and Mrs. King* (1983–1987) and *Murder, She Wrote* (1984–1996), remained in cozier realms, but took a big leap forward by featuring married, divorced, and older female detectives and spies, where the earlier trend had been to depict young, single women as crimefighters.

Cagney & Lacey, a police procedural set in New York City, was almost synonymous with the word "groundbreaking." The series gave us two female leads, Tyne Daly as working-class Mary Beth Lacey and Sharon Gless as her more sophisticated partner, Christine Cagney, detectives in a squad room full of men. Mary Beth was a wife and mother, who had to juggle her home life, including three children, with full-time work in a demanding and sometimes dangerous profession. Christine, the daughter of a cop, was a strong and dedicated detective, even while battling alcoholism and her desire to be "just one of the boys." *Cagney & Lacey* depicted women as real cops and cops as real women.

In the same year *Cagney & Lacey* debuted, *Remington Steele* (1982–1987) brought us Laura Holt (Stephanie Zimbalist), another woman trying to make it in a man's world. Laura had started her own detective agency, but clients weren't interested in a female private investigator, so she invented a male superior, Remington Steele, a desperate deception that worked. Things got complicated, however, when a charming con man (Pierce Brosnan) assumed Remington Steele's identity. Independent and capable Laura repeatedly suffered the ultimate indignity when her own creation, now made flesh, received the credit for all her efforts, expertise, and long hours. Laura was a role model for young, professional women in the 80s, a surprising accomplishment for a character in a romantic mystery/comedy series.

Maddie Hayes (Cybill Shepherd) also had her own detective agency in *Moonlighting* (1985–1989), but she wasn't a private investigator at the start. She had planned to liquidate the struggling business, set up by her embezzling accountant as a tax write-off, but fast-talking agency honcho David Addison (Bruce Willis) convinced her to give the P.I. business a try for real. Maddie may have been a novice detective, much like Remington Steele earlier, but she never hesitated to offer her feminist views on a case, where David always gave the guy's perspective. During these discussions, which often took place in the car, Maddie and David talked over each other frequently, a series trademark. *Moonlighting* was a delicious battle of the sexes, if you didn't get a headache from a surfeit of yammering.

Like Laura Holt and Maddie Hayes, Stephanie "Steve" Oskowski was an independent-minded, professional woman of the 80s, although her profession—or perhaps the more accurate word would be "calling"—was that of a nun. Sister Steve (Tracy Nelson) worked alongside Father Frank Dowling (Tom Bosley) at St. Michael's Parish in Chicago, but in between masses and bake sales, they solved crimes, since, like all amateur sleuths, they were magnets for murder. But Sr. Steve's conservative black habit never got in the way of her investigations with "Frank" in the *Father Dowling Mysteries* (1987–1991). In fact, she sometimes chucked it aside altogether, posing as an aerobics instructor, a bartender, a truck driver, and even a prostitute, in attire appropriate for each of these undercover operations. To accompany her startlingly extensive wardrobe, Steve had an amazing array of skills, from lock-picking to mixology, from automotive repair to shooting pool, all apparently obtained from an ill-spent youth in the 'hood. For a woman with a conservative calling, Sr. Steve sure was a spunky original.

In the 80s, television began to recognize that it was not only single women who worked, but also married women and women with children who held down jobs outside the home, even dangerous ones. *Cagney & Lacey* had given us a dramatic portrait of a wife and mother, Mary Beth Lacey, who worked full-time as a police detective. *Scarecrow and Mrs. King* featured a divorced woman, Amanda King (Kate Jackson), who was raising two sons and needed to enter the workforce for some extra cash. Amanda had started her own small business of caring for people's dogs and plants, when a handsome stranger, code-named Scarecrow (Bruce Boxleitner), had thrust a package into her hands, unintentionally recruiting her into the spy business. Amanda was initially a part-time "civilian" operative, but worked her way up to a full-fledged agent, all the while juggling her domestic responsibilities, such as sewing costumes for school plays and coaching Little League games. The conflict between her professional and home lives was particularly acute, because she couldn't tell anyone, especially nosy mom Dotty (Beverly Garland), what she actually did for a living. But Amanda managed as a working mom, as Mary Beth Lacey had, although Mrs. King's situation was usually played for laughs.

Along with married detectives and spy moms in the 80s came older female sleuths, women whose brains were as sharp as ever, but whose feet now screamed for sensible shoes, especially if there was legwork to be done. Octogenarian Jane Marple (Joan Hickson) ran rings around long-suffering Chief Inspector Slack (David Horovitch) when it came to solving crimes in *Agatha Christie's Miss Marple* (1984–1992). Miss Marple may have seemed like a harmless old fool, whose interests didn't extend beyond knitting and gardening, but her cool blue eyes took in *everything*, and you underestimated her at your peril, especially if you had murder in mind.

America's Miss Marple, Jessica Fletcher, spent her days writing mystery novels rather than knitting, but Mrs. Fletcher (Angela Lansbury) had the same unerring propensity to stumble upon murders and solve them ahead of the police in *Murder, She Wrote* (1984–1996). Jessica, a widow, used her observational and analytical skills to catch killers in her small town of Cabot Cove, Maine, and later in New York, where even the big-city police seemed challenged in the deductive reasoning department. *Murder, She Wrote* showed that a woman in her 60s could be the successful lead of a crime series, albeit a cozy one, for a remarkable 12 seasons. Alas, the honchos at U.S. television networks appeared to forget that lesson as soon as they learned it.

The diversity of 80s female characters in crime series—single, married or divorced, with or without children, young, old, etc.—began to include women of color, but in supporting rather than lead roles. *Miami Vice* (1984–1989) focused on leads Don Johnson and Philip Michael Thomas, but featured two women of color in supporting roles, Saundra Santiago as Cuban American detective Gina Navarro Calabrese and Olivia Brown as Trudy Joplin, Gina's African American partner. Gina and Trudy specialized in sex-related assignments, especially early in the series when they went undercover as prostitutes to lure unsuspecting johns. Later they posed as the lovers of mobsters and drug dealers, sometimes forced into sex to maintain their cover stories.

Holly Robinson had a bit more variety in her role as black policewoman Judy Hoffs on *21 Jump Street* (1987–1991). Johnny Depp played the lead, of course, as Officer Tom Hanson in this *Mod Squad*–esque series about a band of young-looking cops who go undercover in high schools and colleges to solve crimes from the inside. Judy had her share of assignments, however, working undercover at a Catholic girls' school to smoke out an arsonist, posing as a model to flush out a pornographer, or infiltrating a girl gang to sniff out a killer. Since *Jump Street* was targeted at a younger demographic, Judy was presented as a role model.

After the progress of 80s, you would have expected the floodgates to open in the 90s for crime and mystery series with female leads, and they did, to a torrent of series that didn't survive an entire season on network television. *Angel Street* (1992), about a pair of female detectives à la *Cagney & Lacey*, with the twist that one was African American, lasted just four episodes on CBS. *Mann & Machine* (1992) featured a female cop who was actually a sophisticated (and beautiful) robot, but the series didn't make it to the mid-season point on NBC. *Sirens* (1993–1995), about three female rookie cops in Pittsburgh, was axed after 13 episodes on ABC, but did manage to eke out an additional season in first-run syndication. *Under Suspicion* (1994–1995) made it to 18 episodes on CBS in a gritty drama about the only female detective in a Portland police precinct. *Snoops* (1999) was another 13-episode wonder on ABC, this one about three glamorous female private eyes.

On broadcast avenues other than the big three networks, however, women seemed to fare better as leads and co-leads of 90s crime series, a trend that continues to the present day. *Prime Suspect* (1991–2006), a British import which appeared on public television, starred Helen Mirren as Detective Chief Inspector Jane Tennison. While the 80s had made progress in depicting women as police detectives, *Prime Suspect* went one step further by placing a woman *in charge of* a major murder investigation. This dark series pulled no punches in portraying Tennison's nasty reception by an all-male squad and the toll her work obsession took on her personal life. *Prime Suspect* won multiple awards over its lifetime, including a Peabody Award in 1993.

Although Fox is one of the "big four" networks now, in 1993, when it premiered *The X-Files* (1993–2002), it was only seven years old and searching for its place among broadcasting's big boys. *The X-Files* featured one of television's most intelligent and complex female detectives, FBI Agent Dana Scully (Gillian Anderson), who investigated weird, unsolved cases, while keeping an eye on her paranormal-obsessed partner, Fox "Spooky" Mulder (David Duchovny). Scully, a medical doctor, had to reconcile her training as a rational scientist with mounting evidence of UFOs and global conspiracies, while factoring her Catholic faith into an ultimately unsolvable equation. *The X-Files* ran for nine seasons, and was Fox's first series to break the Nielsen Top 20, making Mulder and Scully household names, and spawning two theatrical sequels.

La Femme Nikita (1997–2001) also found success off of the main networks with an edgy, sexy espionage thriller shown on the USA cable network. Peta Wilson starred as Nikita, a beautiful woman blackmailed into working for Section One, a spy organization of questionable motives and lineage. Nikita tried to retain a shred of humanity in the face of her heartless, bloody missions and the mind games of her manipulative overseers in Section One. A slow-burning romantic relationship with her cold handler, Michael (Roy Dupuis), added dimension and spice, while double-crosses, suicides, and sacrifices kept the plots twisting and turning for five seasons.

Pamela Anderson scored a hit in syndication with *V.I.P.* (1998–2002), a campy series about a woman, Vallery Irons, who worked at a hotdog stand in Los Angeles, only to become an accidental and famous celebrity bodyguard. Signing on as a figurehead with a failing protection agency, Vallery joined several beautiful women (not to mention a couple of beautiful men) to become Vallery Irons Protection (V.I.P.), a firm which guarded celebrities, accepted undercover assignments from the feds, and generally chased people around L.A., while looking gorgeous. Not the high point of female sleuthing on television, but at least Anderson and the gang didn't take themselves too seriously.

One exception to the lack of network love for female leads in crime series was *Profiler* (1996–2000), starring Ally Walker in a grim police procedural on

NBC. Walker portrayed Dr. Samantha "Sam" Waters, a forensic psychologist who had a psychic ability to "see" a murder after inspecting a crime scene, a picture-show running just for her, which moved her to the head of the class in crime-solving. But Sam's gift came with a curse, as most fictional gifts do, and that curse was named "Jack of All Trades" (Dennis Christopher), a serial killer obsessed with Samantha. After three seasons, the cat-and-mouse game ended, with Samantha the (Pyrrhic) victor over Jack, after which she retired from profiling. Her successor at the FBI's Violent Crimes Task Force, Rachel Burke (Jamie Luner), tried to fill Sam's shoes, but the dark spell cast by Sam and Jack had been broken, and the series was canceled after its fourth season.

As the new century dawned, ensemble police procedurals were all the rage. These dramas featured women in prominent and compelling roles as police detectives, private consultants, and forensics analysts, although men were usually the series leads, especially on the major networks. *Law & Order: Criminal Intent* (2001–2011), debuting on NBC, starred Vincent D'Onofrio as a brilliant, Sherlock Holmes–type detective, with Kathryn Erbe in the less flashy role of his cool and professional "Watson." *CSI: Miami* (2002–2012) on CBS brought us David Caruso as Horatio "H" Caine, a sunglasses-loving police lieutenant in charge of the Miami-Dade crime lab, while his second-in-command was Detective Calleigh Duquesne (Emily Procter), a by-the-book investigator. The long-running CBS series *NCIS* (2003–) continues to shine a spotlight on Mark Harmon as agent in charge and irascible father figure Leroy Jethro Gibbs, while Abby Sciuto (Pauley Perrette), a forensics specialist, and a changing cast of female junior agents try to keep Gibbs happy at the Naval Criminal Investigative Service. In *Numb3rs* (2005–2010), another CBS offering, the Eppes brothers, Don and Charlie (Rob Morrow and David Krumholtz), take center stage as an FBI agent and his genius/mathematician brother, while female agents and consultants, although talented and competent, provide backup. The list goes on.

Cold Case (2003–2010) was one exception to the seeming rule about female leads on major networks' ensemble police procedurals. Kathryn Morris portrayed Lilly Rush, a Philadelphia homicide detective who specialized in "cold cases," unsolved crimes which received renewed attention when a fresh lead was uncovered. Although an entire team investigated the cold cases, Lilly was the focal point of the series, her delicate features and porcelain skin harking back to an earlier era, perfectly suiting the tone of this series which spent so much of its time in the past. Detective Rush's looks, however, belied her toughness, born of a childhood full of parental neglect and used as an adult to bring justice to victims, long forgotten or ignored. The final, evocative scene of each episode featured an evanescent murder victim, who offered a seeming acknowledgment to Lilly, the detectives, a friend or family member. This tough and touching series with a female lead lasted seven seasons on CBS.

Spy TV got caught up in the ensemble procedural craze with *Alias* (2001–2006) on ABC. Jennifer Garner starred as intelligence operative Sydney Bristow, who made the mistake of confiding her secret identity to her fiancé, with tragic consequences. (Amanda King could have taught her a thing or two about keeping secrets.) Even worse, Sydney discovered that the outfit she snooped for, SD-6, was an enemy organization and not part of the CIA at all, so she turned into a double agent to seek revenge. Sydney worked with her father, Jack Bristow (Victor Garber), also a double agent, and ran into her mother, Irina Derevko (Lena Olin), a former Russian operative who had been presumed dead for years. Things were just as complex for Sydney outside her spy family, with her boss and nemesis, Arvin Sloane (Ron Rifkin), a man of constantly shifting alliances, and her CIA handler, Michael Vaughn (Michael Vartan), her on-again, off-again lover. Betrayal was as much a part of espionage procedure as surveillance on *Alias*.

Cable channel Lifetime, which targets a female demographic, made the police procedural its own, with five, count 'em, five women as main characters in *The Division* (2001–2004). Bonnie Bedelia led the way as Captain Kate McCafferty, who worked her way up through the male-dominated ranks to head a team of police officers in the Felony Division of the San Francisco Police Department. Given Lifetime's focus, the series paid a lot of attention to the characters' personal lives, which were particularly trouble-prone. Inspector Jinny Exstead (Nancy McKeon), for example, battled alcohol and drug addiction, as well as concomitant promiscuity, while trying to hold onto her job. But there was plenty of the usual mayhem—murders, kidnappings, and bombings—and the women worked, sometimes with male partners, to set things right, even foiling a Columbine-style high school takeover.

The first female detectives with disabilities appeared in the new century, but not on the main networks. PAX debuted its first original series, *Sue Thomas: F.B.Eye* (2002–2005), starring Deanne Bray as a character based on the real-life Sue Thomas, a deaf woman whose lip-reading ability landed her on an FBI surveillance team. Lifetime wasn't quite as realistic with its disabled character, Vicki Nelson (Christina Cox), a retired Toronto homicide detective with failing eyesight who was helped with her private investigations by a centuries-old vampire (Kyle Schmid) in *Blood Ties* (2007–2008). Both women's disabilities were caused by illness, unlike their male predecessors *Longstreet* and *Ironside*, who were the victims of violence.

After *Murder, She Wrote*, new series featuring older female sleuths did not take U.S. TV by storm, but a batch of high-quality British imports with middle-aged (and older) women did break through the lines via public television. *Rosemary & Thyme* (2003–2007) starred Felicity Kendal and Pam Ferris as two 50s-ish professional gardeners who stumbled upon murder in the undergrowth and solved mysteries, criminal and botanical. The venerable Miss Marple returned in *Agatha Christie's Marple* (2004–2013), a lavishly produced and sometimes off-canon adaptation of Christie's novels and stories, starring Geraldine McEwan and later Julia McKenzie as the octogenarian amateur sleuth who ran rings around local police inspectors merely by knitting and observing. *Vera* (2011–) brings us Detective Chief Inspector Vera Stanhope (Brenda Blethyn), who gives *Columbo* a run for his money in the rumpled raincoat department, and investigates complex homicides while grumping at her long-suffering staff.

Women of color made some slow progress in American television sleuthing after 2000. In its second season, Lifetime's *Missing* (2003–2006) added Vivica A. Fox as its lead character, FBI Agent Nicole Scott, who is cut from the same sassy supercop cloth as African American groundbreaker Christie Love. *Person of Interest* (2011–) had a much more nuanced black detective in Jocelyn "Joss" Carter (Taraji P. Henson), but gave her up in a hail of bullets after two seasons, while the two male leads stayed behind. Fox's *Sleepy Hollow* (2013–) has another strong black cop with Lieutenant Abbie Mills (Nicole Beharie), who manages to remain real while chasing demons around Washington Irving's not-so-sleepy hamlet.

Asian American women also made some headway as mystery/espionage leads and co-leads, delivering on the promise of early television pioneer Anna May Wong, who had starred in *The Gallery of Madame Liu-Tsong* (1951) as an art dealer involved in foreign intrigue. In the new millennium, Vietnamese American actress Maggie Q performed her own stunts and fight scenes as the title character in *Nikita* (2010–2013), a reimagining of USA Network's earlier spy hit *La Femme Nikita*. *Elementary* (2012–) updates the Sherlock Holmes story with a female Watson (Lucy Liu), an Asian American doctor who becomes a sober companion for Holmes (Jonny Lee Miller) and his partner in crime-solving.

The current decade has started off promisingly, with a good-sized crop of female leads in crime and espionage series. *Covert Affairs* (2010–) on the USA Network stars Piper Perabo as Annie Walker, a young CIA field agent fluent in six languages, who finds excitement and danger around the world. Premium channel Showtime offers its subscribers *Homeland* (2011–), a political thriller with Claire Danes as Carrie Mathison, a CIA agent with bipolar disorder. *Unforgettable* (2011–2014) on CBS brought us Poppy Montgomery as NYPD homicide detective Carrie Wells, who had a rare medical condition which allowed her to remember everything she saw or heard. TNT's *Major Crimes* (2012–) stars Mary McDonnell as Captain Sharon Raydor, head of the LAPD's Major Crimes Division, a job which she inherited from Brenda Leigh Johnson (Kyra Sedgwick) of the successful predecessor series *The Closer* (2005–2012).

Cable channel TNT debuted a *Cagney & Lacey* for the 21st century with *Rizzoli & Isles* in 2010. Angie Harmon stars as Jane Rizzoli, a brilliant, working-class homicide detective for the Boston Police Department, who can't manage to escape her overprotective family members even at work. It's no surprise, given the ubiquity of coroners in current crime shows and books, that her partner in crime-solving is a medical examiner, Dr. Maura Isles (Sasha Alexander), whose encyclopedic knowledge prompts frequent eye-rolls from Jane. The women have a working relationship and friendship of opposites, but their complementary worldviews are needed to close cases. Maura's precise, painstaking scientific method unearths data that others have missed, while impatient, intuitive Jane makes deductive leaps that speed them toward the right conclusion. Jane's other fortes, bravery and strength, save her from two serial killers, but her dedication to the job also brings about a miscarriage. Both Rizzoli and Isles are professional crime-solvers first, and everything else second.

The road from Honey West to Jane Rizzoli wasn't a straight one, detouring at times and even doubling back on itself, but the way is paved now and built for speed. Still, TV's future female spies and sleuths, or those who would portray them, should travel with the guidebook written by the trailblazing women who came before them.

Television's Female Spies and Crimefighters by Character Name and Series Title

Acapulco H.E.A.T. (1993–1994, 1997–1998, 48 episodes, USA/Mexico/France)

Created by: Max A. Keller, Micheline H. Keller
Production Co.: Balenciaga Productions, M6 Films, CNC, Max Keller & Micheline Keller Productions, et al.
Originally Aired: In Syndication
Main Cast: Catherine Oxenberg, Brendan Kelly, John Vernon, Fabio Lanzoni, Lydie Denier, Alison Armitage, Michael Worth, Christa Sauls

Spies in bikinis! Hoping to cash in on the popularity of lifeguard series *Baywatch*, *Acapulco H.E.A.T.* brought us the Hemisphere Emergency Action Team or H.E.A.T., a group of great-looking undercover agents who pose as models and photographers for a beach fashion business (as often happens). Catherine Oxenberg leads the way as Ashley Hunter-Coddington, a former MI6 operative now code-named "Sarong," who works with Mike Savage (Brendan Kelly), once of the CIA, to herd this group of beautiful bodies into action against international terrorism and crime. Other members of the team include Catherine "Cat" Avery Pascal (Alison Armitage), a.k.a. "High Dive," a former cat burglar forced to join the unit to avoid jail time (there's always one of these), Krissie Valentine (Holly Floria) or "Spring Board," a computer expert and researcher, and Tommy Chase (Michael Worth), "Backflip," a profiler and martial arts practitioner. Cat and Tommy were the only members to return for a revamped (and delayed) second season, which finds them working as freelance operatives with Nicole Bernard (Lydie Denier), a former French spy, and Joanna Barnes (Christa Sauls), the new computer whiz.

Despite its name, H.E.A.T. was not as hot as the long-running *Baywatch*, and permanently cooled after its second season.

Adams, Lydia (*Southland*)

Los Angeles robbery-homicide detective who must adjust to a succession of partners.

See: *Southland* (2009–2013, 43 episodes, USA)

Adderly (1986–1988, 44 episodes, Canada)

Based on: The novel *Pocock & Pitt* by Elliott Baker
Created by: Elliott Baker
Production Co.: Global Television Network, JayGee Productions, Robert Cooper Productions
Originally Aired: CBS
Main Cast: Winston Rekert, Dixie Seatle, Jonathan Welsh, Ken Pogue

V.H. Adderly (Winston Rekert), an agent for International Security and Intelligence (ISI), is assigned to desk duty after losing the use of his left hand in an enhanced interrogation involving a medieval mace. Adderly isn't one to sit still, however, finding overlooked threats amongst the pushed papers in the Department of Miscellaneous Affairs, so he takes action to prevent the plots, job-title be damned. Assisting Adderly and sometimes covering for him is overqualified secretary Mona Ellerby (Dixie Seatle), who herself yearns to be unshackled from her desk. Occasionally she gets her wish, as in "The Perils of Mona" (1987), when her simple courier assignment becomes a chase, taking her to Europe in pursuit of enemy agents. Mona gets out of the office again in "Requiem" (1987), when she, Adderly, and their boss, Melville Greenspan (Jonathan Welsh), go undercover as ushers at an international film festival. This ostensibly routine assignment forces Adderly to fake his own death, because in his new paperwork hell, every folder should be filed under "D" for "Danger."

The Adventures of Shirley Holmes, Detective (1997–2000, 52 episodes, Canada)

Created by: Ellis Iddon, Phil Meagher
Production Co.: Credo Entertainment Group, Forefront Entertainment
Originally Aired: Fox Family Channel
Main Cast: Meredith Henderson, John White, Sarah Ezer, Blair Slater, Brendan Fletcher, Annick Obonsawin, Chris Humphreys

The great-grandniece of Sherlock Holmes is on the case in this youth-oriented mystery series from Canada (broadcast there without the word "Detective" in the title). Twelve-year-old Shirley Holmes (Meredith Henderson) attends the prestigious Sussex Academy in Redington, a (fictional) Canadian city, where mysteries abound. Shirley is just the person to solve them, with the observational and deductive skills inherited from her famous great-granduncle and her own shade of spunkiness. Assisting Shirley in sleuthing is fellow student

Bo Sawchuck (John White), who becomes Shirley's "Watson" after she clears him of arson charges in "The Case of the Burning Building" (1997). The Moriarty of the piece is Molly Hardy (Sarah Ezer), a scheming, power-hungry student at Sussex, whose machinations take her from new kid on campus to student council president in "The Case of the Ruby Ring" (1997). Shirley and Bo are not fooled, however, by Molly's innocent demeanor, and thwart her plans and those of all evildoers in Redington, as only a pint-sized Holmes and Watson could.

Adventures of Superman (1952–1958, 104 episodes, USA)

Based on: The comic book series by Jerry Siegel, Joe Shuster
Originally Aired: In Syndication
Main Cast: George Reeves, Phyllis Coates, Noel Neill, Jack Larson, John Hamilton, Robert Shayne

The man of steel leaped to the small screen for the first time in this classic 50s series, starring George Reeves as Superman and his alter ego, newspaper reporter Clark Kent. Clark works for *The Daily Planet* in Metropolis, where he gets the inside scoop on mysteries, crimes, and disasters which may require Superman's prodigious powers for resolution. Working with Kent at The Planet are **Lois Lane** (Phyllis Coates and later Noel Neill), an experienced newshound, Jimmy Olsen (Jack Larson), a cub reporter, and Perry White (John Hamilton), the newspaper's irascible editor. The first season of Superman has a noir sensibility, dark in both look and tone, focusing on mystery and crime, and directed at an adult audience. Lois Lane (Phyllis Coates) has her inquisitive nose buried deep in most of the mysteries and crimes during this "dark series" of *Adventures of Superman*. Later seasons, however, are lighter in nature, and with the shift to color episodes in 1954, the series takes on a more cartoonish feel, aimed at the young fans who were flocking to the show at the time.

Light or dark, the episodes lived on in reruns and now, in the digital age, are immortal, just like the man of steel himself. George Reeves died in 1959 of an apparent suicide, so he never got to see that *Adventures of Superman* would live so far beyond him.

See also: **Lane, Lois** (*Adventures of Superman*)

Against the Wall (2011, 13 episodes, USA)

Created by: Annie Brunner
Production Co.: Universal Cable Productions, Paid My Dues Productions, Open 4 Business Productions
Originally Aired: Lifetime
Main Cast: Rachael Carpani, Kathy Baker, Marisa Ramirez, Brandon Quinn, Mayko Nguyen, Andrew W. Walker, Chris Johnson, Treat Williams

Rachael Carpani stars as Abby Kowalski, a Chicago police officer who finds that her dream job comes with a catch. After five years with the force, she is promoted to detective, but the only opening available is with Internal Affairs. Abby accepts the position, but the decision doesn't sit well with her family, which bleeds blue through and through. Her father, Don Kowalski (Treat Williams), is a cop, as are her three brothers, none of whom are fond of IAD, the police who investigate the police. As Abby and her partner, Lina Flores (Marisa Ramirez), investigate officer-involved shootings, poor police response times, and coroner's office improprieties, Abby strives to keep peace with her unhappy family members. In the meantime, she juggles relationships with two men, one of whom is (you guessed it) a cop and her brother's partner to boot. The complications of Abby's life, including the question of which lover she should choose, were never resolved, since Lifetime pulled the plug on this one after one season.

Agatha Christie's Marple (2004–2013, 23 episodes, UK)

Based on: The novels and short stories of Agatha Christie
Production Co.: ITV Studios, WGBH, Agatha Christie Ltd.
Originally Aired: Public Television
Main Cast: Geraldine McEwan, Julia McKenzie

Agatha Christie's famed female sleuth returns to the small screen in this lavishly produced, modern adaptation of the Jane Marple novels and stories. Geraldine McEwan dons Miss Marple's shawl for the first three seasons, depicting the elderly spinster who loves to knit, but has a penchant for stumbling upon murders and solving them several steps ahead of the police. In "The Body in the Library" (2004), the authorities are compe-

The unassuming but whipsmart amateur sleuth Miss Jane Marple (Julia McKenzie) in *Agatha Christie's Marple* (PBS/Photofest).

tent, but confused until Miss Marple sorts out the motives and mistaken identities behind the appearance of a beautiful but quite dead woman in the library of her friend Dolly Bantry (Joanna Lumley).

Julia McKenzie slips into the sleuth's sensible shoes for the last three series, giving us a Jane Marple who prefers tweed suits to McEwan's long loose dresses, and one who is at the same time more diffident, but less apt to sit back and let the clues come to her. In "The Pale Horse" (2010), McKenzie's Marple investigates the death of a priest, leading her to a weird country inn run by three witches, while the police warn her off at every turn.

This adaptation played fast and loose with Christie's sacred texts, angering some purists, by adding lesbians where there hadn't been any, swapping out killers, and inserting the protagonist in some originally non–Marple stories. But with their high production values, intricate plots, and an iconic old lady who is smarter than everyone else in the room, these movies successfully translate and transmit Miss Marple to a new generation.

Agatha Christie's Miss Marple (1984–1992, 12 episodes, UK/USA)

Based on: The novels of Agatha Christie
Production Co.: British Broadcasting Corp., A&E Television Networks, 7 Network
Originally Aired: A&E
Main Cast: Joan Hickson, David Horovitch, Ian Brimble

Miss Jane Marple lives in the quaint village of St. Mary Mead, content to spend her days gardening and knitting, until murder comes to call. Though she may seem like a dotty old busybody to irascible Chief Inspector Slack (David Horovitch), Miss Marple sees clearly with her cool-blue eyes and not only hears, but listens, allowing her to combine observation with intellect to solve mysteries where the authorities can't. Miss Marple, brought to tweedy life by Joan Hickson, comes to the aid of an old friend when poison pen letters lead to murder in "The Moving Finger" (1985). "Nemesis" (1987) is the nickname given her by a recently deceased friend, who writes from the grave asking Miss Marple to solve an old crime without telling her what the crime is. Miss Marple doesn't carry a gun or use judo, but her mental gymnastics and the pretty pastoral settings in this series will satisfy fans of cozy British mysteries.

Agatha Christie's Partners in Crime (1983–1984, 10 episodes, UK)

Based on: The short stories of Agatha Christie
Production Co.: London Weekend Television
Originally Aired: Public Television
Main Cast: Francesca Annis, James Warwick, Reece Dinsdale

Tommy and Tuppence Beresford run a small detective agency during the roaring 20s as married partners in crime. Stylish and whip-smart Tuppence (Francesca Annis) loves an adventure, while boyishly charming Tommy (James Warwick) loves Tuppence, and both have a flair for their new line of work. As Tuppence buys hats, and the marrieds exchange witty banter, the occasional client stops by with a mysterious circumstance in need of urgent investigation. In "The House of Lurking Death" (1983), the Beresfords are called in when poison decimates a family at a country estate. Scotland Yard recruits the glamorous couple to infiltrate an upscale nightclub in search of counterfeiters, providing Tuppence with a dizzying array of sequined flapper couture in "The Crackler" (1984).

This short-lived series is a bit hard on contemporary eyes with its abrupt shifts between stark videotape and muddy film footage, diminishing the spiffing fun of Tommy and Tuppence.

The Agency (2001–2003, 44 episodes, USA)

Created by: Michael Frost Beckner
Production Co.: Radiant Productions, Studios USA Television, Universal Network Television
Originally Aired: CBS
Main Cast: Beau Bridges, Ronny Cox, Gil Bellows, Rocky Carroll, Gloria Reuben, Paige Turco, David Clennon, Richard Speight, Jr., Jason O'Mara, Will Patton, Daniel Benzali

Although spy shows don't often refer to the CIA by name, using fictional euphemisms instead, this series was unabashed in its focus on the inner workings of the Central Intelligence Agency after the Cold War era. The real-world events of 9/11 occurred only weeks before the series was to debut, prompting rescheduling of the pilot episode to November, because it dealt with an impending terrorist attack. A large and changing cast populated *The Agency* for its two seasons on the air, but a mainstay throughout its run was Paige Turco as Terri Lowell, a graphics designer and documents forger, who also carries out missions in the field. In "The Gauntlet" (2002), Lowell accompanies agent Matt Callan (Gil Bellows) to Belarus in search of an arms shipment, and she blows her cover to save Matt, leading to her own capture. Danger is everywhere for these undercover operatives, and Matt is killed on a later mission, while Terri lives to fight another day. Matt's replacement, A.B. Stiles (Jason O'Mara), heads to Spain with Terri and Lex (Richard Speight, Jr.), an agency tech expert, to investigate the murder of military wives in "Soft Kills" (2003). But things look bad again for Terri in "Our Man in Washington" (2003), when her kidnappers detonate a "bomb necklace" she's wearing, and the rest is left to our imaginations, as the series was not renewed for a third season.

Agent 99 (*Get Smart*)

Agent 99 works for super-secret government agency CONTROL alongside "top" operative Maxwell Smart (Agent 86) to battle the evil forces of KAOS. As portrayed by Barbara Feldon, Agent 99 is long, cool, and competent, while Don Adams's Max is none of those things. For some unfathomable reason, though, the sleek 99, whose real name is never revealed in the series, is enamored of her bumbling partner. In "Too Many Chiefs" (1965), Agent 99, sporting a stylish holster/belt accented by a lace hanky, reveals her jealous side when Max must guard a beautiful refugee in his apartment. Otherwise, it's business as usual, as in "Shipment to Beirut" (1966), when 99 goes undercover as a fashion model to thwart a smuggling operation and is almost turned into a mannequin for her trouble. "With Love and Twitches" (1968) finds the couple finally ready to wed, but 99's big day may be in jeopardy when an important map surfaces as a rash on Maxwell's body. Agent 99 and her unlikely hubby go on to produce even more unlikely spy-twins in the two-part "And Baby Makes Four" (1969), proving that 99 is a trooper 100 percent of the time.

A holster hankie is the finishing touch for stylish Agent 99 (Barbara Feldon) of *Get Smart* (NBC/Photofest).

See also: *Get Smart* (1965–1970, 138 episodes, USA)

Agents of S.H.I.E.L.D. (2013– , 22 episodes, USA)

Based on: The comic book feature "Nick Fury, Agent of S.H.I.E.L.D." by Stan Lee, Jack Kirby
Created by: Joss Whedon, Jed Whedon, Maurissa Tancharoen
Production Co.: ABC Studios, Marvel Television, Mutant Enemy Productions
Originally Aired: ABC
Main Cast: Clark Gregg, Ming-Na Wen, Brett Dalton, Chloe Bennet, Iain De Caestecker, Elizabeth Henstridge

The agents of Strategic Homeland Intervention, Enforcement and Logistics Division (S.H.I.E.L.D.) battle threats to the U.S. and planet Earth, such as a CEO who wants to control the planet's gravity, a street performer with pyrokinetic abilities, and an international organization of evildoers with its tentacles in everything (the aptly named, Hydra). It's just your everyday spy outfit, if you're a character in the Marvel Cinematic Universe, that is. Leading the way for S.H.I.E.L.D. is Agent Phil Coulson (Clark Gregg), who has been mysteriously resurrected after his death in *The Avengers*, the blockbuster movie hit from 2012. Coulson assembles a team of crack field operatives to investigate weird phenomena around the globe, and to dispatch any related threats, whether of this world or someplace more exotic. Melinda May (Ming-Na Wen), nicknamed "The Cavalry," is Coulson's right-hand woman, a veteran pilot and weapons expert, who is loyal to Coulson, despite her secret assignment to monitor him after his resurrection. Skye (Chloe Bennet), a computer hacker and orphan, is captured by the team, but later joins the unit at Coulson's behest, while continuing to investigate her mysterious origins. Jemma Simmons (Elizabeth Henstridge), the crew's life sciences expert, works closely with Leo Fitz (Iain De Caestecker), the engineering and weapons guy, in this uber-high-tech environment. Coulson's talented, but trouble-prone team chases bad guys while their loyalties are continually questioned and tested. In "Turn, Turn, Turn" (2014), they even learn that one of their own, Grant Ward (Brett Dalton), a specialist in black ops, is actually an agent of the dreaded Hydra.

Although this series is chock full of fancy gadgets, at its core, it's still about that most powerful of weapons—secrets.

Alcatraz (2012, 13 episodes, USA)

Created by: Elizabeth Sarnoff, Steven Lilien, Bryan Wynbrandt
Production Co.: Bonanza Productions, Bad Robot Productions, Warner Bros. Television
Originally Aired: FOX
Main Cast: Sarah Jones, Jorge Garcia, Jonny Coyne, Parminder Nagra, Sam Neill, Jason Butler Harner, Robert Forster

Science fiction thriller à la *The 4400*, wherein the prisoners and guards of Alcatraz Federal Penitentiary, all of whom mysteriously disappeared in 1963, suddenly reappear in modern-day San Francisco, without having aged and with no memories of the missing time. Emerson Hauser (Sam Neill) heads a secret government unit tasked with finding and capturing the returning prisoners, known as "63s," who are continuing their criminal ways but with a hidden agenda. SFPD homicide detective Rebecca Madsen (Sarah Jones) is drawn into the Alcatraz mystery while searching for a killer, and has a family member among the returning inmates. Rebecca works with Hauser and Alcatraz historian Dr. Diego "Doc" Soto (Jorge Garcia) to stop the inmates' crime spree and learn the secrets behind their return.

Due to the short run of this series, most of the secrets of the 63s are still safe today.

Alias (2001–2006, 105 episodes, USA)
Created by: J.J. Abrams
Production Co.: Bad Robot Productions, Touchstone Television
Originally Aired: ABC
Main Cast: Jennifer Garner, Michael Vartan, Ron Rifkin, Bradley Cooper, Victor Garber, Merrin Dungey, Carl Lumbly, Kevin Weisman, Lena Olin

Sydney Bristow works as a field agent for SD-6, a clandestine branch of the Central Intelligence Agency. The life of a spy seems to suit Sydney (Jennifer Garner) until she confides her secret identity to her fiancé, who is killed for Sydney's mistake. Sydney learns that SD-6 is not part of the CIA at all, but rather an enemy organization, and she agrees to work as a double agent for the real CIA to help bring down the group which murdered her fiancé. That is just the beginning of the twists and turns in this story about the family of spies and Sydney's own spy family, which includes her father, Jack Bristow (Victor Garber), also a double agent, and her mother, Irina Derevko (Lena Olin), a former Russian spy. Sydney's chief nemesis, Arvin Sloane (Ron Rifkin), head of SD-6 and later her boss in a CIA black ops division (don't ask), is obsessed with the search for artifacts created by the da Vinci–esque Renaissance inventor Milo Rambaldi. Sprinkle in romances, exotic locales, and so many betrayals you'll need a scorecard, and you have *Alias*.

See also: **Bristow, Sydney** (*Alias*)

Allen, Jaimie (*Dark Blue*)
Rookie cop who works with an undercover unit of the LAPD.
See: ***Dark Blue*** (2009–2010, 20 episodes, USA)

Alphas (2011–2012, 24 episodes, USA)
Created by: Zak Penn, Michael Karnow
Production Co.: BermanBraun, Universal Cable Productions
Originally Aired: Syfy
Main Cast: David Strathairn, Ryan Cartwright, Warren Christie, Azita Ghanizada, Laura Mennell, Malik Yoba

Science fiction series about people with enhanced natural abilities, known as "Alphas," who work with the Defense Department to fight crimes committed by others of their kind. Dr. Lee Rosen (David Strathairn), a psychiatrist and non–Alpha, leads this exceptional group, serving as neurological expert, counselor, and father figure. Five Alphas fill out the team, including Ryan Cartwright as Gary Bell, an autistic savant with the ability to track communication sources with his mind, and Malik Yoba as Bill Harken, a former FBI agent able to enhance his strength and endurance by amping up his fight-or-flight response. Azita Ghanizada portrays Rachel Pirzad, the "sensitive" Alpha, who can heighten any one of her five senses to track someone by scent or view evidence at a microscopic level. Nina Theroux (Laura Mennell) has the power to "push" people into doing her bidding, which allows her to get past security guards or erase inconvenient memories from witnesses. Together, the team battles Alphas who are unable or unwilling to control their abilities, such as the radical group Red Flag, which espouses the primacy of Alphas. Along the way, Rosen's group wrestles with the problems generated by their own Alpha abilities, such as social isolation, health issues, and lack of self-control.

Amanda (*Highlander: The Raven*)

A 1200-year-old thief who uses her immortality to battle evil.
See: *Highlander: The Raven* (1998–1999, 22 episodes, France/Canada)

The Americans (2013– , 26 episodes, USA)

Created by: Joe Weisberg
Production Co.: Nemo Films, Amblin Television, Fox 21 Television Studios, FX Productions, DreamWorks Television
Originally Aired: FX
Main Cast: Keri Russell, Matthew Rhys, Maximiliano Hernández, Holly Taylor, Keidrich Sellati, Noah Emmerich, Richard Thomas, Annet Mahendru, Susan Misner, Alison Wright, Lev Gorn, Costa Ronin

The Americans are no Americans at all, but a pair of KGB sleeper agents in suburban Virginia during the early 80s. Elizabeth Jennings (Keri Russell), whose real name is Nadezhda, was recruited by the KGB as a teenager, and later agreed to an arranged marriage with Philip Jennings (Matthew Rhys) a.k.a. Mischa, so she could serve the interests of the USSR. Elizabeth and Philip have two children, Paige (Holly Taylor) and Henry (Keidrich Sellati), who were born in the United States and have no idea about their parents' true identities. It is fascinating to watch how the Jenningses conduct their missions, which sometimes involve danger, injury, and odd hours, while trying to keep their secret from the children and maintain a seemingly normal middle-class life. Conflicts between American and Soviet values are also part of the bargain, as when Paige finds God and donates all of her savings to a local church, upsetting her parents. Further tension ensues when the KGB wants to recruit unwitting Paige for a second generation program, and Elizabeth grows to support the idea while Philip is reluctant. Elizabeth and Philip try, at times, to have a real marriage, but extramarital affairs get in the way, and so do mission parameters, as when Philip marries FBI secretary Martha Hanson (Alison Wright) so she will place a listening device in her supervisor's office. No one will mistake this Reagan-era family for the wholesome Keatons of *Family Ties*.

Amy Prentiss (1974–1975, 3 episodes, USA)
Created by: Francine Caroll
Production Co.: Francy Productions, Universal TV
Originally Aired: NBC
Main Cast: Jessica Walter, Johnny Seven, Art Metrano, Helen Hunt

Amy Prentiss is San Francisco's first female Chief of Detectives. At 35 years old, Amy (Jessica Walter) is young for the job, but she must execute the chief's normal duties, while dealing with a department full of men, many of whom doubt that she is qualified because of her youth and gender. While battling criminals and male chauvinism, Amy, a widow, must also navigate the waters of single motherhood with her daughter, Jill (Helen Hunt in an early role). Chief Prentiss is up to the task, however, bringing mad bombers, cat burglars, renegade cops and murderers to justice. Part of the *NBC Mystery Movie* "wheel" of rotating series, this *Ironside*-spinoff, though short-lived, is a TV trailblazer.

Anderson, Pepper (*Police Woman*)

Angie Dickinson stars as Suzanne "Pepper" Anderson, a sergeant with the Criminal Conspiracy Unit of the LAPD. Pepper specializes in undercover assignments, posing as a prostitute, jewel fence, or prison inmate—whatever is required to bring murderers, baby sellers, and rapists to justice. In "Blast" (1975), Pepper goes undercover as an exotic dancer to flush out the killer of a wealthy politician. "Flowers of Evil" (1974) finds her as a nurse in a retirement home, as she investigates multiple murders in a plot considered controversial at the time for its lesbian theme. Pepper seems to enjoy her often salacious assignments, gyrating as a jeans-wearing gym teacher in "Smack" (1974), while her boss and friend Bill Crowley (Earl Holliman) looks on approvingly. But Dickinson makes us take Pepper seriously, giving her intelligence and sensitivity to go along with the sex appeal, not only blazing a trail for females as drama series leads, but also inspiring real women to seek employment on the police force.

In 1987, the Los Angeles Police Department awarded Dickinson an honorary doctorate for her groundbreaking role as Pepper Anderson.

See also: *Police Woman* (1974–1978, 91 episodes, USA)

Angie Dickinson as groundbreaking 70s cop Pepper Anderson in *Police Woman* (NBC/Photofest).

Andrews, Jenny (*Team Knight Rider*)

A former Marine who fights crime in a gossipy Ford Mustang.
See: *Team Knight Rider* (1997–1998, 22 episodes, USA)

Angel Street (1992, 4 episodes, USA)

Production Co.: Warner Bros. Television
Originally Aired: CBS
Main Cast: Robin Givens, Pamela Gidley, Ron Dean

If you blinked, you might have missed this series about a pair of female detectives in an otherwise all-male precinct, à la *Cagney & Lacey*. The setting this time is Chicago, where college-educated, African American detective Anita

King (Robin Givens) teams with working-class, Polish American rookie Dorothy Paretsky (Pamela Gidley) to solve crimes, overcome their personal differences, and fight the prejudices of their male colleagues. In the four episodes which made it to air, the detectives deal with murders of various stripes: multiple homicide, drug-related, and cold case.

With that short a work history, Cagney and Lacey they ain't.

Angela's Eyes (2006, 13 episodes, USA)
Created by: Dan McDermott
Production Co.: NBC Universal Television
Originally Aired: Lifetime
Main Cast: Abigail Spencer, Lyriq Bent, Joe Cobden, Rick Roberts, Paul Popowich, Boyd Gaines, Alberta Watson

Angela Henson (Abigail Spencer) is an FBI agent with a special talent—she can accurately detect when people are telling lies. Angela honed her lie-detection skills on a painful past with parents who were professional liars, a.k.a. spies, now serving long prison sentences for treason. The young agent pursues her cases while battling trust issues in her personal life and combing through clues which hint that her parents may be innocent, a theory favored by her troubled brother Jerry (Paul Popovich). In the meantime, Angela donates bone marrow to her ill mother in "Eyes of the Father" and is shot at home by someone from her past in "Lyin' Eyes." A surprise twist about her parentage in series finale "Eyes on the Prize" is tantalizing, but does not reveal all the secrets promised by this prematurely canceled series.

Angell, Nikki (*Rendezvous*)

French singer and intelligence operative working at her own nightclub in Paris.
See: *Rendezvous* (1952, 4 episodes, USA)

Anna Lee (1994, 5 episodes, UK)
Based on: The novels of Liza Cody
Production Co.: Carnival Films, London Weekend Television
Originally Aired: A&E
Main Cast: Imogen Stubbs, John Rowe, Peter Wight, Brian Glover

Imogen Stubbs stars as title character Anna Lee, a young cop who leaves the sexism and bureaucracy of the Metropolitan Police force for private consulting at the Brierly Detective Agency. In her first outing for Commander Martin Brierly (John Rowe), Anna is charged with finding a missing person, a case which leads to murder, blackmail, pirated videos, and an undercover assignment for the novice P.I. ("Dupe," 1994). At home in her flat, Anna deals with colorful neighbor Selwyn Price (Brian Glover), a professional wrestler hoping to make a comeback, while on the job she follows a friend's philandering husband in "The Cook's Tale." Anna resigns from the agency after an argument with Brierly in the aptly titled "Requiem," never to return, forever stuck in the unemployment office that is series cancellation.

Arkin, Paige (*Graceland*)

DEA agent living in a confiscated Southern California beach house with other Feds.

See: *Graceland* (2013– , 25 episodes, USA)

Arno, Barbara, Celeste, and Ruby (*Cover Me*)

Female members of undercover operative Danny Arno's spy family.

See: *Cover Me: Based on the True Life of an FBI Family* (2000–2001, 25 episodes, USA)

The Avengers (1961–1969, 161 episodes, UK)

Created by: Sydney Newman
Production Co.: ABC Weekend Television, Associated British Corporation
Originally Aired: ABC
Main Cast: Patrick Macnee, Ian Hendry, Honor Blackman, Diana Rigg, Linda Thorson

Groundbreaking British spy-fi series known for its wit, style, and strong female characters. Through many incarnations and cast changes, Patrick Macnee is the one *Avengers* constant, portraying John Steed, dapper secret agent and crime fighter. Steed works with a succession of partners, the most notable of whom is Mrs. **Emma Peel** (Diana Rigg), a brilliant, sexy, sardonic, leather-suited, judo-chopping amateur agent. Her immediate predecessor, Dr. **Cathy Gale** (Honor Blackman), an anthropologist, is cut from the same cloth (or leather) in her intelligence, bravery, and martial arts expertise. Tara King (Linda Thorson), Mrs. Peel's successor, is less worldly than Steed's other partners, but is a bona fide, though inexperienced, agent. The various *Avengers* pairings investigate outré crimes and circumstances, such as killer robots, haunted castles, mind-transference devices, machine-gun-wielding nuns, and lethal pussycats. But evildoers are no match for Steed's steel-plated bowler hat, Mrs. Peel's IQ, or Cathy's indomitable spirit.

See also: **Gale, Cathy** (*The Avengers*); **Peel, Emma** (*The Avengers*)

Avery Pascal, Catherine "Cat" (*Acapulco H.E.A.T.*)

Former cat burglar forced to join an elite team of spies in bikinis.

See: *Acapulco H.E.A.T.* (1993–1994, 1997–1998, 48 episodes, USA/Mexico/France)

Bailey, Rachel (*Scott & Bailey*)

Detective Constable on the Manchester police department's Major Incident Team.
See: *Scott & Bailey* (2011– , 22 episodes, UK)

Baker, Louise (*Biff Baker, U.S.A.*)

Partner in life and intrigue of Biff Baker, a Cold War spy.
See: *Biff Baker, U.S.A.* (1952–1953, 26 episodes, USA)

Barnaby Jones (1973–1980, 178 episodes, USA)

Created by: Edward Hume
Production Co.: Quinn Martin Productions, Woodruff Productions
Originally Aired: CBS
Main Cast: Buddy Ebsen, Lee Meriwether, Mark Shera, John Carter

Barnaby Jones (Buddy Ebsen) comes out of retirement to find the killer of his P.I. son, working with widowed daughter-in-law Betty Jones (Lee Meriwether) and fellow sleuth Frank Cannon (William Conrad of CBS's *Cannon*), as this series opens. After solving the murder, Barnaby decides to plunge back into the detective business, with Betty as his secretary/assistant back at the office. Barnaby is the antithesis of the hard-boiled detective, with his mild-mannered folksiness and trademark milk-drinking, preferring forensics in his home crime lab to fisticuffs in a dark alley. Although Betty carries a lot of folders at the beginning, she graduates to full-blown detective work in later years, alternating cases with Barnaby and his young cousin once removed, J.R. Jones (Mark Shera). In "Academy of Evil" (1978), Betty goes undercover at a private girls' school to investigate a series of accidents plaguing the faculty, discovering danger and a malicious secret society. When Betty doesn't go looking for trouble, it finds her, as in "Killer without a Name" (1980), where she falls for a man targeted by police of a South American dictatorship. There's more trouble for Betty in series finale "The Killin' Cousin" (1980), where she is suspected of murdering two relatives for an inheritance. The episode was planned as a pilot to spin off a new series about a father-and-son detective team, but neither the spinoff nor *Barnaby Jones* made it to the Fall 1980 schedule. Still, elderly Barnaby ran longer than most. Raise your (milk) glass.

Barnes, Julie (*The Mod Squad*)

Hippie chick turned undercover cop, Julie Barnes hunts for criminals, along with partners Pete Cochran and Linc Hayes, while straddling the generation gap in the late 60s. Bright, caring, and sensitive to a fault, Julie, as portrayed by Peggy Lipton, leaves most of the chasing and tackling of bad guys to Pete (Michael Cole) and Linc (Clarence Williams III), while shining in covert assignments. In "Twinkle, Twinkle, Little Starlet" (1968), Julie goes undercover in an acting class to catch a killer obsessed with young blonde actresses. "Child of Sorrow, Child of Light" (1969) finds her posing as an unwed mother to foil a blackmail gang in an adoption scheme. With her hip pad, happening clothes, and counterculture conscience, Julie is the grooviest cop ever to make the TV scene.

See also: *The Mod Squad* (1968–1973, 123 episodes, USA)

The Baron (1966–1967, 30 episodes, UK)

Based on: The novels of John Creasey
Created by: Monty Berman, Robert S. Baker
Production Co.: Associated Television, Incorporated Television Company
Originally Aired: ABC
Main Cast: Steve Forrest, Sue Lloyd, Colin Gordon, Paul Ferris

Steve Forrest stars as John Mannering, a.k.a. "The Baron," an American antiques dealer who works as an undercover agent for British intelligence. Assisting the jet-setting Baron on his cases, which are often art-related, is glamorous British agent Cordelia Winfield (Sue Lloyd), who teams with Mannering in "Diplomatic Immunity" (1966) to retrieve a valuable Fabergé miniature. The work is dangerous, especially for the Baron's partners, and Cordelia finds herself captured or kidnapped on a number of occasions, as in "Enemy of the State" (1966), when she is arrested by an Eastern Bloc government. But the Baron is always there—to bargain for her release, engineer an escape—whatever it takes.

Bates, Lucille (*Hill Street Blues*)

Rookie cop who rises to sergeant at an inner-city precinct.
See: *Hill Street Blues* (1981–1987, 146 episodes, USA)

Batgirl (*Batman*)

A librarian who dons the cowl to help Batman and Robin fight crime.
See: *Batman* (1966–1968, 120 episodes, USA)

Batman (1966–1968, 120 episodes, USA)

Based on: The comic book series by Bob Kane, Bill Finger
Created by: William Dozier
Production Co.: Greenway Productions, 20th Century–Fox Television
Originally Aired: ABC
Main Cast: Adam West, Burt Ward, Alan Napier, Neil Hamilton, Stafford Repp, Madge Blake, Yvonne Craig

Campy, superhero action series starring Adam West as Batman/Bruce Wayne and Burt Ward as Robin/Dick Grayson. When summoned by Gotham City's Police Commissioner Gordon (Neil Hamilton), the dynamic duo springs into action, sliding down Batpoles to the Batcave, suiting up, and screeching off in the Batmobile to meet the villain of the week. Well-known actors lined up to play the colorful evildoers, including Cesar Romero as the Joker, Vincent Price as Egghead, Julie Newmar as Catwoman, Frank Gorshin as the Riddler, and Burgess Meredith as the Penguin. In the episode "Enter Batgirl, Exit Penguin" (1967), Yvonne Craig joins the series as Barbara Gordon, a librarian with a few secrets of her own, including a cape, cowl, and a Batgirlcycle. Batgirl unites with the caped crusaders for more Batadventures, which culminate in climactic fight scenes, punctuated by superimposed, comics-style action words.... POW!

Bauer, Kim (*24*)

Former trouble-prone teen who becomes a computer analyst at the Counter Terrorist Unit in Los Angeles.
See: *24* (2001–2010, 194 episodes, USA)

Baywatch Nights (1995–1997, 44 episodes, USA)

Based on: Characters from the TV series *Baywatch*
Created by: Michael Berk, Gregory J. Bonann, David Hasselhoff, Douglas Schwartz
Production Co.: The Baywatch Company, Tower 18 Production Company, All American Television, et al.
Originally Aired: In Syndication
Main Cast: David Hasselhoff, Gregory Alan Williams, Angie Harmon, Lisa Stahl, Lou Rawls, Eddie Cibrian, Donna D'Errico, Dorian Gregory

Spinoff from the long-running lifeguard series *Baywatch*, wherein two of the beach folk decide to give the P.I. biz a try, although they stay close to the ocean in their new line of work. Garner Ellerbee (Gregory Alan Williams) and Mitch Buchannon (David Hasselhoff) are the industrious dudes in question, joined in their investigations by the beautiful Ryan McBride (Angie Harmon). The first season focuses on standard detective fare, as the team pursues murderers, drug dealers, smugglers, and burglars, often by means of outré undercover operations. In "976 Ways to Say I Love You" (1995), Ryan overcomes her personal misgivings to go undercover as a phone-sex operator in hopes of catching a killer.

The second season shifts to a paranormal universe, with vampires, mummies, sea monsters, time travel, and UFOs. (Think *X-Files* at the beach.) Alas, this wasn't *The X-Files*. It wasn't even *Baywatch*.

Beaumont, Nicole "Nikki" (*Counterstrike*)

French con artist who joins a team of private operatives to fight crime and terrorism.
See: *Counterstrike* (1990–1993, 66 episodes, Canada/France/USA)

Beauty & the Beast (2012– , 44 episodes, USA/Canada)

Based on: The TV series *Beauty and the Beast* created by Ron Koslow
Production Co.: CBS Television Studios, Take 5 Productions, Whizbang Films
Originally Aired: The CW
Main Cast: Kristin Kreuk, Jay Ryan, Sendhil Ramamurthy, Max Brown, Austin Basis, Nina Lisandrello, Brian White, Nicole Gale Anderson

Loosely based on the 1987 series of the same title (give or take an ampersand), the 2012 edition reimagines Catherine Chandler (Kristin Kreuk) as a homicide detective who witnessed her mother's murder, but was saved from harm herself by a mysterious creature. Nine years later, a murder investigation leads Cat to Vincent Keller (Jay Ryan), a doctor and Army veteran, supposedly deceased, but clearly very much alive and living a shadow life in New York. Vincent had been the victim of a "supersoldier" experiment gone awry, which transformed him into "a beast" with heightened senses and extraordinary strength, but only when agitated. Catherine realizes that Vincent was her savior many years before, and the two form an alliance, which quickly becomes complicated by romantic feelings, old loves, and secrets from the past. Some of those secrets involve an organization called Muirfield, the group responsible for unleashing enhanced "beasts" upon the world and the former employer of Cat's deceased mother. Helping to protect Vincent's secret(s) are J.T. Forbes (Austin Basis), a university professor who once had ties to Muirfield, and Tess Vargas (Nina Lisandrello), Cat's partner on the force and best friend, the only person in New York who doesn't seem to have a connection to Muirfield. Definitely not your mother's (or Mr. Disney's) *Beauty*.

Beckett, Kate (*Castle*)

Kate Beckett (Stana Katic) is an NYPD homicide detective who is saddled with an immature, womanizing partner, Richard Castle (Nathan Fillion), a mystery writer and private consultant to the department. Kate is brilliant and driven, haunted by the murder of her mother, and unamused by the antics of this hedonistic interloper. As Castle begins to contribute actual value to the crime-solving team, however, Kate softens her stance, and even comes to see his value as a human being. In "After the Storm" (2012), Beckett and Castle embark upon an intimate relationship after four years of working together, while Kate confronts the man responsible for her mother's murder, a highly placed politician. Although dedicated and often intense, Kate has a fun side, and her fangirl past is revealed in "The Final Frontier" (2012), when she and Castle investigate murder at a science fiction convention in an episode rife with allusions to popular and cult TV shows. The pendulum swings back to suspense in "Dreamworld" (2013), when Beckett must race against time to save Castle from a deadly toxin after accepting his marriage proposal. Kate can't even catch a break on her wedding day in "For Better or Worse" (2014), when Castle seems to have been consumed in a fiery car crash. Stay tuned....

See also: *Castle* (2009– , 128 episodes, USA)

Belding, Fran (*Ironside*)

Plainclothes officer and assistant to police consultant Robert Ironside.
See: *Ironside* (1967–1975, 199 episodes, USA)

Bennett, Patricia (*Foreign Intrigue*)

European correspondent for *Associated News*, who has a penchant for running into saboteurs.
See: *Foreign Intrigue* (1951–1955, 156 episodes, USA)

Benson, Kate (*Special Unit 2*)

Chicago detective who deals with "Links," missing links between apes and humans.
See: *Special Unit 2* (2001–2002, 19 episodes, USA)

Benson, Olivia (*Law & Order: Special Victims Unit*)

Mariska Hargitay stars as Olivia Benson, a detective with the NYPD's Special Victims Unit, a precinct devoted to the investigation of crimes with a sexual component. Benson is herself a child of rape, so she tends to identify with the victims of sex crimes, sometimes allowing her empathy to cloud her professional judgment. In "Payback" (1999), Benson sympathizes with the perpetrators of murder and sexual mutilation, because they themselves had been the victims of rape and torture at the hands of the man they killed, a Serbian war criminal. Sometimes Benson's cases hit close to home, as in "Lowdown" (2004), when her former boyfriend is murdered, revealing his secret life as a gay man who had contracted AIDS. During her 16 years with SVU, Benson has even been a victim herself, running afoul of a serial killer in "Surrender Benson" (2013), who kidnaps and tortures her for days. She manages to break free, avoiding rape, but the aftermath, including further encounters with this psychopath, leave Benson with emotional scars that require psychological counseling. Still, she continues to pursue her work, rising to the rank of Sergeant, and bringing justice to the victims of sexual crimes.

See also: *Law & Order: Special Victims Unit* (1999– , 343 episodes, USA)

Beresford, Tuppence (*Agatha Christie's Partners in Crime*)

One half of an adorable married sleuthing team during the roaring 20s. See: *Agatha Christie's Partners in Crime* (1983–1984, 10 episodes, UK)

Bering, Myka (*Warehouse 13*)

Myka Bering is a Secret Service Agent with an exceptionally secret secret. Myka (Joanne Kelly) works at Warehouse 13, a repository for the world's supernatural artifacts, located in a remote corner of South Dakota. Partnered with fellow Secret Service Agent Pete Lattimer (Eddie McClintock), Myka searches the world for strange occurrences, always finding an "artifact" as the root cause, such as Man Ray's Camera, which steals the youth of supermodels, causing rapid aging in "Age before Beauty" (2010). At first, Myka, the detail-oriented, straight arrow clashes with Pete, the fun-loving manchild, but soon they learn that their styles are complementary, making them an effective team. Myka has a prodigious knowledge of books, gained at her father's bookstore, and her familiarity with the Bard comes in handy when Shakespeare's Lost Folio starts killing people in "The New Guy" (2011). Agent Bering survives ovarian cancer, the loss of a colleague, her boss's psychotic break, and all manner of Warehouse *mishigas*, finally realizing that she is in love with partner Pete in series finale "Endless" (2014).

See also: *Warehouse 13* (2009–2014, 64 episodes, USA)

Berrigan, Diana (*White Collar*)

FBI agent who works with a charming con man to solve white-collar crimes. See: *White Collar* (2009– , 75 episodes, USA)

Biff Baker, U.S.A. (1952–1953, 26 episodes, USA)

Production Co.: Revue Productions
Originally Aired: CBS
Main Cast: Alan Hale, Jr., Randy Stuart

Espionage series set in the early years of the Cold War, starring Alan Hale, Jr., as Biff Baker, an import-export dealer who spies on the side, and Randy Stuart as Louise Baker, his partner in life and intrigue. Traveling on jaunts behind the Iron Curtain and around the world, Biff and Louise stumble into trouble, discovering counterfeit Nazi plates, defusing bombs, and dealing with jewel smugglers, just like an undercover Nick and Nora Charles. Diving into adventure wherever they go, the Bakers are lighthearted and compatible, happy to work secretly for the good ol' U.S. of A.

The Bionic Woman (1976–1978, 58 episodes, USA)

Based on: The novel *Cyborg* by Martin Caidin
Created by: Kenneth Johnson
Production Co.: Universal TV, Harve Bennett Productions
Originally Aired: ABC (1976–1977), NBC (1977–1978)
Main Cast: Lindsay Wagner, Richard Anderson, Martin E. Brooks

The story of the bionic woman begins on *The Six Million Dollar Man*, when **Jaime Sommers** (Lindsay Wagner), a tennis star, is injured while parachuting with her bionic fiancé, Col. Steve Austin (Lee Majors). With Steve's intercession, Oscar Goldman (Richard Anderson) of the Office of Scientific Investigations agrees to allow an operation that will save Jaime by fitting her with bionic replacement parts. As *The Bionic Woman* opens, a now-recovered Jaime is working as a schoolteacher in Ojai, California, while undertaking missions as an agent for the OSI. Jaime's super-hearing, lightning speed, massive strength and other abilities make her a special, special agent, although the special effects used to demonstrate her powers are sometimes not so special, such as using slow motion whenever she's running or a close-up of her ear to demonstrate her profound

Jaime Sommers (Lindsay Wagner) uses enhanced abilities, such as super-speed, on secret missions in *The Bionic Woman* (ABC/Photofest).

hearing. Lindsay Wagner's sweet sincerity as Jaime, however, adds conviction to this SF/adventure series.

See also: **Sommers, Jaime** (*The Bionic Woman*)

Bionic Woman (2007, 8 episodes, USA)

Created by: David Eick
Production Co.: GEP Productions, David Eick Productions, Universal Media Studios
Originally Aired: NBC
Main Cast: Michelle Ryan, Miguel Ferrer, Molly Price, Lucy Hale, Will Yun Lee, Chris Bowers

A reimagining of the classic Lindsay Wagner series from the 70s, this short-lived SF drama stars Michelle Ryan as the retooled bionic woman. In the modern telling, Jaime Sommers is a bartender who must juggle work, home life with rebellious younger sister Becca (Lucy Hale), and romance with boyfriend Will Anthros (Chris Bowers). Jaime's life changes forever when she is almost killed in a car accident, but is saved by a miraculous operation, performed by boyfriend Will, which replaces her damaged body parts with bionic prosthetics and implants. Now with enhanced strength, speed, hearing, and eyesight, Jaime begins working for the Berkut Group, a private intelligence outfit responsible for her bionics surgery. Jaime undertakes missions for the organization, investigating terrorist threats, rescuing Americans in distress, and thwarting assassination plots. Viewers may not have been ready for the darker tone of the rebooted series, and a strike by the Writers Guild of America which halted production may not have helped, but, whatever the case, there was no resuscitation for this one after its eight-episode run.

Birds of Prey (2002–2003, 13 episodes, USA)

Based on: The comic book series created by Chuck Dixon, Jordan B. Gorfinkel, Gary Frank
Created by: Laeta Kalogridis
Production Co.: Warner Bros. Television, DC Entertainment, Tollin/Robbins Productions
Originally Aired: WB
Main Cast: Ashley Scott, Dina Meyer, Rachel Skarsten, Shemar Moore, Ian Abercrombie, Mia Sara

What is Gotham City to do once Batman leaves town? Enter Helena Kyle (Ashley Scott), also known as Huntress, the daughter of Batman and Catwoman, who possesses "metahuman" abilities, such as super-strength, enhanced agility, and a sixth sense for danger. Helena accepts the caped crusader's crime-fighting mantle with the help of Barbara Gordon (Dina Meyer), who used to be Batgirl, but had to leave the bat-life behind due to a paralyzing gunshot wound from the Joker. Barbara has rechristened herself as Oracle, and uses computers to battle baddies, while Huntress takes the non-virtual approach to confronting super-villains. Assisting Huntress and Oracle is teenager Dinah Lance (Rachel Skarsten), another metahuman, who has telepathic and telekinetic abilities (but who apparently was absent the day they handed out the cool superhero names). The Birds seek their prey in (now) New Gotham, assisted by Detective Jesse Reese (Shemar Moore), and thwarted at every turn by Harley Quinn (Mia Sara), the Joker's former lover, who masquerades as psychiatrist Dr. Harleen Quinzel, an expert on violent criminals. You needed a scorecard to keep track of all these characters and their alter-egos, but you didn't need it for long, because these birds were shot down after only 13 episodes.

Black Scorpion (2001, 22 episodes, USA)
Created by: Roger Corman, Craig J. Nevius
Originally Aired: Syfy
Main Cast: Michelle Lintel, Scott Valentine, B.T., Enya Flack, Steven Kravitz, Guy Boyd

The Black Scorpion is a vigilante superhero/crime-fighter in the Batman mold, but on the distaff side. By day, the Scorpion is Darcy Walker (Michelle Lintel), a police detective in Angel City, who never received justice for the murder of her father. By night, the Black Scorpion takes the law into her own hands, battling supervillains with clever names, such as Aerobicide, Clockwise, Flashpoint, Polutia, and Vox Populi. She has no superpowers per se, but relies on high-tech gadgets, such as her "Scorpionmobile," a super-car with the capability to disguise itself, and a ring which transforms her street clothing at an atomic level into the skimpy Black Scorpion costume. (Convenient!) Darcy/Scorpion is a martial arts expert and computer whiz, who somehow finds time for a relationship with Detective Steve Rafferty (Scott Valentine), but manages to keep the identity of her alter-ego a secret from him. In an otherworldly twist, Darcy's father is resurrected from the dead in series finale "Zodiac—Part 2" (2001), and the two battle the combined power of four supervillains together.

The Blacklist (2013– , 22 episodes, USA)
Created by: Jon Bokenkamp
Production Co.: Davis Entertainment, Universal Television, Sony Pictures Television, Open 4 Business Productions
Originally Aired: NBC
Main Cast: James Spader, Megan Boone, Diego Klattenhoff, Ryan Eggold, Parminder Nagra, Amir Arison, Harry Lennix, Hisham Tawfiq

Raymond "Red" Reddington (James Spader) is a criminal mastermind on the "most wanted" lists of the FBI and other law-enforcement agencies. It's an odd turn of events, then, when Red walks into FBI headquarters and turns himself in to Assistant Director Harold Cooper (Harry Lennix). Reddington offers to help the FBI apprehend criminals on his personal "most wanted" list of baddies a.k.a. "the blacklist," but insists on two conditions for his cooperation: he must receive immunity from prosecution and he will work only with Elizabeth Keen (Megan Boone), a rookie profiler at the bureau. It's an offer the FBI and Keen cannot refuse, but Liz has no idea why Red is interested in her. In "Wujing" (2013), while Liz and Red work to capture a spy killer, Red reveals that he has a connection to Liz's adoptive father. Family secrets, in fact, snake their way throughout Liz's personal and professional lives, as in "The Pavlovich Brothers" (2014), when Liz learns that her husband, Tom Keen (Ryan Eggold), is a private operative, a revelation which forces Tom to flee because his cover is blown. More secrets are revealed, people are tortured, viruses are unleashed, people are tortured, bodies disappear, and more secrets are revealed. Elizabeth Keen has a complicated life.

Blake, Allison (*Eureka*)

Scientist who helps to solve technological mysteries in a town full of geniuses.

See: *Eureka* (2006–2012, 77 episodes, USA)

Blake, Chryseis "Cricket" (*Hawaiian Eye*)

Photographer and singer at a Honolulu hotel who helps out private detectives on the side.

See: *Hawaiian Eye* (1959–1963, 134 episodes, USA)

The Bletchley Circle (2012–2014, 7 episodes, UK)

Production Co.: World Productions
Originally Aired: Public Television
Main Cast: Anna Maxwell Martin, Rachael Stirling, Sophie Rundle, Julie Graham, Hattie Morahan

Fascinating, complex historical mystery about four women who worked as codebreakers during World War II at Bletchley Park in the UK. While their code-breaking skills helped to defeat the Nazis, these brilliant women are sworn to secrecy due to The Official Secrets Act. Susan Gray (Anna Maxwell Martin) is a housewife seven years after the war, whose husband knows nothing of her Bletchley work, but recognizes her yen for puzzle books. Susan is secretly tracking a story about the gruesome murders of several women and begins to recognize a pattern in the serial killer's carnage. When the police dismiss her theories, Susan calls upon three of her former Bletchley colleagues to collate and analyze information about the crimes in hopes of preventing future murders. Assisting

Susan in cracking the killer's code are Millie (Rachael Stirling), the most modern and independent of the foursome and an expert at languages, Lucy (Sophie Rundle), whose shyness masks a prodigious eidetic memory, and Jean (Julie Graham), a former administrator at Bletchley and now a librarian who still has a few friends in high places.

Together these women use all the tools at their disposal to track down the killer, placing their personal relationships and even their lives in jeopardy. Later cases involve clearing Bletchley alum Alice Merren (Hattie Morahan) of murder charges before she is executed and investigating a human trafficking ring after Millie is kidnapped.

With its fine performances, emphasis on women's history, and intricate plotting, *The Bletchley Circle* is a treasure. It's a puzzle only these women could solve that this show was canceled after just two seasons/series.

Blood Ties (2007–2008, 22 episodes, Canada)
Based on: The novels of Tanya Huff
Created by: Peter Mohan
Production Co.: Insight Film Studios, Chum Television
Originally Aired: Lifetime
Main Cast: Christina Cox, Kyle Schmid, Dylan Neal, Gina Holden

Christina Cox stars as Victoria "Vicki" Nelson, a former Toronto homicide detective who leaves the force because of failing eyesight and opens her own private investigation firm. In the course of a gruesome murder investigation, Vicki meets Henry Fitzroy (Kyle Schmid), a centuries-old vampire, the kind who likes to help out attractive mortal women in need, and the illegitimate son of Henry VIII to boot. Their partnership leads Vicki to pursue unusual cases with supernatural overtones, much to the consternation of Detective Mike Celluci (Dylan Neal), Vicki's former partner on the police force, and sometimes lover. While the trio tries to navigate the dimensions of this otherworldly love triangle, Vicki, with Henry's assistance, battles demons, ghosts, zombies, mummies, and even Medusa herself. Not your typical villains, not your typical P.I.

Bloom, Samantha (*Undercovers*)
Spy/caterer who partners with her husband on special missions for the CIA.
See: *Undercovers* (2010, 11 episodes, USA)

Bo (*Lost Girl*)
Succubus who opens a detective agency with a fast-talking thief, while investigating her strange origins.
See: *Lost Girl* (2010– , 61 episodes, Canada)

Boa Vista, Natalia (*CSI: Miami*)

Former FBI informant, now a DNA analyst at the Miami-Dade crime lab.
See: *CSI: Miami* (2002–2012, 232 episodes, USA/Canada)

Bonasera, Stella (*CSI: NY*)

Tenacious detective with the New York City Crime Lab, who views its team as her family.
See: *CSI: NY* (2004–2013, 197 episodes, USA)

Bones (2005– , 190 episodes, USA)

Based on: The real-life experiences of Kathy Reichs
Created by: Hart Hanson
Production Co.: Josephson Entertainment, Far Field Productions, 20th Century–Fox Television
Originally Aired: Fox
Main Cast: Emily Deschanel, David Boreanaz, Michaela Conlin, Eric Millegan, T. J. Thyne, Jonathan Adams, Tamara Taylor, John Francis Daley

Dr. **Temperance Brennan** (Emily Deschanel) is a forensic anthropologist at the Jeffersonian Institute in Washington, D.C. Although it sounds like the past would be the paramount focus of such an occupation, Brennan stays rooted in the present by solving murders through the identification of human remains too far decomposed for investigation by conventional techniques. Brennan works with FBI Special Agent Seeley Booth (David Boreanaz), who calls her "Bones" in reference to the usual objects of her forensic attention. Booth, a tough guy with a heart who relies on instinct and faith, provides a counterpoint to Brennan's empirical, and sometimes literal, approach to the world. Assisting Brennan in the lab is a talented and colorful team of scientists and technicians, or "squints" as Booth calls them. Angela Montenegro (Michaela Conlin) is a forensic artist specializing in craniofacial reconstruction and is also Brennan's best friend, a caring soul who provides support to everyone on the team. Dr. Jack Hodgins (T. J. Thyne), an entomologist, deals with the yucky stuff, like bugs, slime, and spores, to help determine how long a body has been dead. Dr. Camille Saroyan (Tamara Taylor), a pathologist, is head of the Institute's Forensic Division, and once had a romantic relationship with Booth. Romances, in fact, somehow seem to flourish amidst the decaying corpses and specimen cases, even leading to marriage between Hodgins and Montenegro, and later Brennan and Booth. The couples have babies, as couples do, rounding out the circle of life in this long-running crime procedural.

See also: **Brennan, Temperance (*Bones*)**

Borrego, Carla (*Jonathan Creek*)
Crime-show host who works with an illusionist to solve elaborate mysteries.
See: *Jonathan Creek* (1997– , 31 episodes, UK)

Boston Blackie (1951–1953, 58 episodes, USA)
Based on: The short stories of Jack Boyle
Production Co.: ZIV Television Programs
Originally Aired: In Syndication
Main Cast: Kent Taylor, Lois Collier, Frank Orth

Horatio Black a.k.a. Boston Blackie (Kent Taylor) is a reformed criminal turned private detective, who cruises the streets of L.A. in sharp sports cars, while solving crimes. Helping this "friend of those who have no friends" are his girlfriend and assistant Mary Wesley (Lois Collier) and his precocious pooch Whitey. This threesome cracks cases one step ahead of the police, led by long-suffering Inspector Faraday (Frank Orth). While investigating murders, searching for missing persons, and chasing thieves, Blackie and Mary trade wisecracks and have fun à la *The Thin Man*, but with more noir and grit.

Boxer, Lindsay (*Women's Murder Club*)
San Francisco homicide detective obsessed with the "Kiss Me Not" killer case.
See: *Women's Murder Club* (2007–2008, 13 episodes, USA)

Boxer, Rosemary (*Rosemary & Thyme*)
Former botany professor who stumbles upon murder in the undergrowth.
See: *Rosemary & Thyme* (2003–2007, 22 episodes, UK)

Bradley, Adela (*The Mrs. Bradley Mysteries*)
Jazz Age amateur sleuth who solves crimes with her chauffeur.
See: *The Mrs. Bradley Mysteries* (1998–2000, 5 episodes, UK)

Branca, Susan (*Touching Evil*)
FBI agent who works on the darkest crimes with her eccentric partner.
See: *Touching Evil* (2004, 13 episodes, USA)

Brennan, Temperance (*Bones*)
Emily Deschanel portrays Temperance Brennan, a forensic anthropologist at the (fictional) Jeffersonian Institute in Washington, D.C. Brennan and her

team work to identify skeletal and other highly decomposed remains on their way to solving mysteries, usually involving murder. Dr. Brennan is a brilliant scientist, but has some deficiencies in the social skills department (not surprising for a TV scientist), especially when it comes to reading people or understanding sarcasm. She often draws a blank when someone makes a popular culture reference, using her standard, "I don't know what that means," in a flat voice. She works with FBI Agent Seeley Booth (David Boreanaz), and the two are like oil and water. "Bones," as Booth calls her, is an atheist, guided by rationality and science, while Booth is a Catholic who goes with his gut when evidence is lacking. Although their partnership gets off to an awkward and contentious start, Brennan and Booth begin to trust each other and recognize they work well as a team. A romance blooms very slowly, and in "The Change in the Game" (2011), Brennan reveals that Booth is the father of her unborn child. Bones and Booth later marry in "The Woman in White" (2013), but not before dealing with the usual unrecognizable remains at the lab and the transfer of the wedding to the Jeffersonian Rose Garden because their church burned down. Temperance writes crime novels about a forensic anthropologist named Kathy Reichs (the name of the real-life inspiration for the series), although where she finds the time with such a full life remains a mystery.

See also: *Bones* (2005– , 190 episodes, USA)

Bring 'Em Back Alive (1982–1983, 17 episodes, USA)

Based on: The book by Frank Buck, Edward Anthony
Created by: Frank Cardea, George Schenck
Production Co.: Schenck/Cardea Productions, Thompson/Bernstein/Boxleitner Productions, Columbia Pictures Television
Originally Aired: CBS
Main Cast: Bruce Boxleitner, Clyde Kusatsu, Cindy Morgan, Ron O'Neal

Bring 'Em Back Alive is loosely based on the adventures of real-life game-trapper Frank Buck, who wrote a book of the same title in 1930. Bruce Boxleitner portrays Buck here, a trapper and collector of wild animals, yes, but one who manages to pursue smugglers, spies, and Nazis à la Indiana Jones. Sometimes prompting these pursuits is the young U.S. vice consul in 1939 Singapore, Gloria Marlowe (Cindy Morgan), who wants to prove she can do her job as well as a man. In "Bring 'Em Back Alive" (1982 pilot), Gloria hires Frank to guide her to the Kuala Highlands, where the plane of an American agent bearing important documents about Japanese war plans has gone down in a storm. After the perilous rescue of the American agent, more intrigue and adventures ensue for Frank and Gloria, including "There's One Born Every Minute" (1982), wherein Frank competes to see who can capture a black leopard, while Gloria tries to recover the stolen jewelry of an American citizen. Assisting the gorgeous duo are Buck's pals Ali (Clyde Kusatsu) and H.H., a.k.a. His Royal Highness, the Sultan of Johore (Ron O'Neal).

Although this action series lasted only 17 episodes, Boxleitner made a comeback just a few months later with the hit series about a housewife-turned-spy and her dashing partner, *Scarecrow and Mrs. King*.

Bristow, Sydney (*Alias*)

Sydney Bristow is having a happy engagement until she tells her fiancé she is an intelligence operative, a revelation which brings about his murder and sets Sydney off on the precarious path of becoming a double agent. As portrayed by Jennifer Garner, Sydney has spying in her blood, with both of her parents agents, and not necessarily on the same side(s). She often confronts the fact that knowing her is dangerous to her loved ones. In "The Telling" (2003), she realizes her friend Francie Calfo (Merrin Dungey) has been killed and replaced by a doppelgänger, whom Sydney must battle. She must also navigate an ocean of continually shifting alliances, as in "Authorized Personnel Only—Part 2" (2005), when she finds that her new CIA boss is Arvin Sloane (Ron Rifkin), her former nemesis at enemy organization SD-6. Her on-again, off-again romance with fellow agent Michael Vaughn (Michael Vartan) survives attempted assassinations, kidnappings, and betrayals, ultimately achieving domestic bliss in series finale "All the Time in the World" (2006).

See also: *Alias* (2001–2006, 105 episodes, USA)

Bryan, Maggie (*Codename: Foxfire*)

Cat burglar and spy who saves the world while looking beautiful.
See: *Codename: Foxfire* (1985, 8 episodes, USA)

Burn Notice (2007–2013, 111 episodes, USA)

Created by: Matt Nix
Production Co.: Fox Television Studios, Fuse Entertainment, Flying Glass of Milk Productions
Originally Aired: USA Network
Main Cast: Jeffrey Donovan, Gabrielle Anwar, Bruce Campbell, Sharon Gless, Coby Bell

"When you're burned, you've got nothing: no cash, no credit, no job history."

Action/espionage series starring Jeffrey Donovan as Michael Westen, a CIA contractor who has been "burned" by the agency—dismissed, discredited, and dumped in Miami, where he must now try to make a new life, while investigating the circumstances surrounding his burn notice. Although Michael has no financial assets, he has his a unique skill set, which he puts to use helping people who can't go to the police—people in trouble with the mob, or blackmailers, or drug traffickers, or con artists—desperate people in need of a miracle worker. Assisting Michael in his new role as investigator/fixer are his ex-girlfriend, **Fiona Glenanne** (Gabrielle Anwar), an explosives enthusiast and former IRA member, and Sam Axe (Bruce Campbell), Michael's wisecracking old buddy, a freelance operative and FBI informant. Sometimes helping Michael (and sometimes getting in his way) is Madeline Westen (Sharon Gless), Michael's chain-smoking, retired mother, whose house often serves as a base camp for the group. The team works on two fronts, running stings and other operations to get Michael's clients out of trouble, and searching for contacts and clues to clear Michael's name. Along the way, they meet more than their share of psychotic, violent, and double-dealing villains, but they take them in stride with grace, style, and plenty of Mojitos.

See also: **Glenanne, Fiona** (*Burn Notice*)

Busiek, Zoe (*Wild Card*)

Blackjack dealer turned insurance fraud investigator and sudden mom.
See: *Wild Card* (2003–2005, 36 episodes, USA)

Cagney & Lacey (1982–1988, 125 episodes, USA)

Created by: Barbara Avedon, Barbara Corday
Production Co.: Columbia Broadcasting System, Filmways Pictures, Orion Television
Originally Aired: CBS
Main Cast: Tyne Daly, Sharon Gless, Al Waxman, John Karlen, Carl Lumbly, Martin Kove, Meg Foster

Groundbreaking police procedural about two female NYPD detectives who must navigate a male-dominated work environment while balancing their home and personal lives. Tyne Daly stars as working-class **Mary Beth Lacey**, a wife and mother of two boys, and Sharon Gless costars as **Christine Cagney**, Mary Beth's single and more worldly partner. The women hold their own in a squad room full of men, including their boss, Lt. Samuels (Al Waxman), and solve crimes while confronting social issues, such as homelessness, drug abuse, affirmative action, and race relations. Mary Beth is backed up at home by husband Harve Lacey (John Karlen), and Christine draws inspiration from her retired cop father, Charlie Cagney (Dick O'Neill). In the meantime, problems intrude for both women, such as Harvey's unemployment and Christine's alcoholism, but these are strong women, who always manage to find their way into the light.

See also: **Cagney, Christine** (*Cagney & Lacey*); **Lacey, Mary Beth** (*Cagney & Lacey*)

Tyne Daly (left, as Lacey) and Sharon Gless locked up Emmy Awards for six years with their portrayals of NYPD detectives *Cagney & Lacey* (CBS/Photofest).

Cagney, Christine (*Cagney & Lacey*)

Sharon Gless portrays New York City police detective Christine Cagney, a sophisticated, but tough urbanite who partners with **Mary Beth Lacey** (Tyne Daly) to solve crimes and blaze a trail for women in the NYPD. In "Jane Doe #37" (1983), Chris and Mary Beth are selected to shoot a recruiting commercial for the department, but playing themselves proves to be more of a challenge than they anticipated. In the meantime, Chris fights to determine the identity of a murdered homeless woman close to her own age, so that the woman can receive a proper burial. Chris struggles at times to find her place in a male-dominated profession, and in "Date Rape" (1983), she feels like one of the boys to be included in the men's practical jokes, while arguing with Lacey over whether a date rape victim brought the crime upon herself. Cagney battles alcoholism and navigates the singles scene, but remains a good cop and a steadfast partner to her friend Mary Beth.

Although Sharon Gless was a replacement in the role of Christine Cagney, stepping in for Meg Foster, whom network executives thought came across as too masculine, the allegedly more frilly Gless went on to earn two Emmy Awards and one Golden Globe for a part that is now indelibly hers.

See also: *Cagney & Lacey* (1982–1988, 125 episodes, USA)

Calabrese, Gina Navarro (*Miami Vice*)

Miami vice cop specializing in undercover assignments, especially posing as a prostitute. See: *Miami Vice* (1984–1989, 111 episodes, USA)

Cameron, Kiera (*Continuum*)

Police officer in the year 2077 who is pulled to 2012 and must work to preserve the future she knows.

See: *Continuum* (2012– , 36 episodes, Canada)

Campbell, Joan (*Covert Affairs*)

Head of the CIA's Domestic Protection Division, who is married to another CIA honcho.

See: *Covert Affairs* (2010– , 69 episodes, USA)

Carson, Fay (*Chaos*)

CIA officer who runs bureaucratic interference for some agency bad boys.
See: *Chaos* (2011, 13 episodes, USA)

Carter, Cinnamon (*Mission: Impossible*)

Cinnamon Carter (Barbara Bain) is an elite operative with the Impossible Missions Force (IMF), a team of secret agents specializing in assignments which involve intricate planning and large-scale deceptions. Under the leadership of Jim Phelps (Peter Graves), Cinnamon works with master of disguise Rollin Hand (Martin Landau) et al. to effect coups, rescue prisoners, and foil assassination plots. As a former top model, Cinnamon uses her physical attractiveness to advantage, luring powerful men to work against their own evil interests.

Carter, though, is not just window-dressing for the squad—she is intelligent and forceful, never breaking under psychological torture in "The Exchange" (1969), never giving up her colleagues to their adversaries. She is also adept at role-playing, posing as a psychic, a photographer, or a lost princess. Missions are possible with Cinnamon Carter on the team.

See also: *Mission: Impossible* (1966–1973, 171 episodes, USA)

Carter, Jocelyn "Joss" (*Person of Interest*)

Jocelyn "Joss" Carter (Taraji P. Henson), a homicide detective for the NYPD, runs into a mysterious vigilante in a suit and her life changes forever. Carter slowly gets pulled into the private operations conducted by the vigilante, John Reese (Jim Caviezel), and his employer Harold Finch (Michael Emerson), who developed a machine for the government which can predict acts of terror, but which Harold now uses secretly because it can also predict less massive crimes. While originally John's pursuer, Carter begins to see that Reese and Finch are actually helping people, and her loyalty is forever secured when Reese saves her son from a mob kidnapping in "Flesh and Blood" (2012). Fiercely honest Joss gets embroiled in a battle of wills with HR, a corrupt group within the NYPD with ties to organized crime, and, with Reese's help, she manages to capture the secret head of HR, Alonzo Quinn (Clarke Peters), the mayor's Chief of Staff. Carter's actions break the back of the organization, but she pays the ultimate price when one of HR's escaped members shoots her through the heart in "The Crossing" (2013).

Joss Carter's tragic demise was completely in character for a woman

Taraji P. Henson as doomed NYPD Detective Joss Carter in *Person of Interest* (CBS/Photofest).

willing to sacrifice everything for what she believed in, and, yet, her death left a major void in this series, which needed a pure role model, had one, and then gave her up in a hail of bullets.

See also: *Person of Interest* (2011– , 68 episodes, USA)

Carter, Theresa "Terry" (*Two*)

FBI agent obsessed with the capture of an alleged wife-killer.
See: *Two* (1996–1997, 22 episodes, Canada)

Casey, Lisa (*Mission: Impossible*)

Disguise expert working with a team of secret agents on elaborate cons/assignments.
See: *Mission: Impossible* (1966–1973, 171 episodes, USA)

Cassie & Co. (1982, 13 episodes, USA)

Production Co.: Carson Productions
Originally Aired: NBC
Main Cast: Angie Dickinson, Alex Cord, Dori Brenner, A Martinez, John Ireland

Angie Dickinson stars as Cassie Holland, a former Los Angeles cop turned private investigator, in a sort of "Pepper Anderson Returns" updating of her character from *Police Woman*. Sassy Cassie takes over a detective agency from retiring PI Lyman "Shack" Shackelford (John Ireland), who still hangs around to offer advice when needed. Cassie uses her finely honed analytical skills to solve cases, but isn't averse to trading on her looks if it will help, a fact emphasized in the "leggy" opening credits of the series. Mike Holland (Alex Cord), Cassie's ex-husband, feeds her inside information from his post at the District Attorney's office, and her former cop buddies lend a hand as well.

Unfortunately for Dickinson, a new *Police Woman* it wasn't, and this midseason replacement quickly disappeared from the TV landscape.

Castle (2009– , 128 episodes, USA)

Created by: Andrew W. Marlowe
Production Co.: ABC Studios, Beacon Pictures, Experimental Pictures, Milmar Pictures
Originally Aired: ABC
Main Cast: Nathan Fillion, Stana Katic, Susan Sullivan, Molly Quinn, Jon Huertas, Tamala Jones, Seamus Dever, Ruben Santiago-Hudson, Penny Johnson Jerald

The Castle of the title is Richard Castle (Nathan Fillion), a best-selling mystery author who is granted permission to shadow an NYPD homicide detective in hopes of gaining inspiration for a new series of novels. The unwilling object of Castle's attention is Detective **Kate Beckett** (Stana Katic), a top-notch investigator who comes to realize that Castle's imagination and plotting skills help to solve cases, even if she has to abide an outlandish theory or two (or seven). Castle becomes a private consultant to Beckett's homicide team, which includes Detectives Javier Esposito (Jon Huertas) and Kevin Ryan (Seamus Dever), who like to bicker almost as much as they like to close cases. They watch as the relationship between immature Castle and driven Beckett continues to blossom, and Captain Victoria Gates (Penny Johnson Jerald), no fan of Castle, keeps an eye out as well.

Rooting for the Castle-Beckett relationship at home is Richard's live-in mother, Martha Rodgers (Susan Sullivan), a stage actress, who helps out with Castle's daughter, Alexis (Molly Quinn), a student and responsible role model for her father. Events and people from the past, such as the murder of Beckett's mother and the appearance of Castle's long-lost father (James Brolin), an undercover operative for the United States, complicate their lives, but hope springs eternal that love will conquer all.

See also: **Beckett, Kate (*Castle*)**

Castle, Jane (*Space Precinct*)

Police officer in Demeter City, "the crime capital of the galaxy," on the planet Altor.

See: *Space Precinct* **(1994–1995, 24 episodes, UK)**

Cavanaugh, Jordan (*Crossing Jordan*)

Crusading coroner who crosses people at every turn to bring justice to murder victims.

See: *Crossing Jordan* **(2001–2007, 117 episodes, USA)**

Chambers, Wilhelmina "Billie" (*Fastlane*)

Head of a unit which uses confiscated loot to bring down bad guys.
See: *Fastlane* **(2002–2003, 22 episodes, USA)**

The Champions **(1968–1969, 30 episodes, UK)**

Created by: Dennis Spooner, Monty Berman
Production Co.: ITC Entertainment
Originally Aired: NBC
Main Cast: Stuart Damon, Alexandra Bastedo, William Gaunt, Anthony Nicholls

"Their mental and physical capacities fused to computer efficiency; their sight, sense and hearing raised to their highest, futuristic stage of mental and physical growth."

SF/espionage hybrid chronicling the adventures of three secret agents who work for Nemesis, an international law-enforcement agency based in Geneva. During the course of a mission, the operatives crash-land in the remote mountains of Tibet, and are rescued by an advanced civilization which bestows enhanced powers, such as telepathy, precognition, and superior strength. The team, consisting of Craig Stirling (Stuart Damon), Sharron Macready (Alexandra Bastedo), and Richard Barrett (William Gaunt), attempts to keep their new abilities secret, while continuing their work for Nemesis, where said hidden talents often come in handy. The Champions battle Nazis, prevent foreign assassinations, investigate mysterious phenomena, such as ghost planes and cryogenic storage, and generally bring light to the world. Sixties-supermodel good looks accompany the amazing superpowers of Macready and Stirling, in particular.

Chandler, Catherine "Cat" (*Beauty & the Beast*)
New York homicide detective in love with a mutated man/beast.
See: *Beauty & the Beast* (2012– , 44 episodes, USA/Canada)

Chaos (2011, 13 episodes, USA)
Created by: Tom Spezianly
Production Co.: 20th Century–Fox Television, Rat TV, Certified Pulp, Chaos Series Productions
Originally Aired: CBS
Main Cast: Eric Close, Christina Cole, Carmen Ejogo, James Murray, Tim Blake Nelson, Freddy Rodriguez, Kurtwood Smith

Guys just wanna have fun in this series about rogue CIA operatives who get the job done when their by-the-book counterparts can't. Freddy Rodriguez stars as squeaky clean agent Rick Martinez, who is assigned to the ODS (Office of Disruptive Services) to spy on the spies, but finds the lure of being just one of the boys too appealing. The men travel the globe, dealing with terrorists, defections, and arms dealers, while their female coworkers are office-bound, notably Deputy Director Adele Ferrer (Christina Cole) and officer Fay Carson (Carmen Ejogo), Rick's new love interest. Fay, in particular, helps the boys in their long-running bureaucratic battle with Director H.J. Higgins (Kurtwood Smith).

Charles, Charlotte "Chuck" (*Pushing Daisies*)
Former "dead girl" who now serves pie and solves murders with her glum boyfriend.
See: *Pushing Daisies* (2007–2009, 22 episodes, USA)

Charles, Nora (*The Thin Man*)
A beautiful socialite who stumbles upon crimes with her husband and pooch.
See: *The Thin Man* (1957–1959, 72 episodes, USA)

Charlie's Angels (1976–1981, 110 episodes, USA)
Created by: Ivan Goff, Ben Roberts
Production Co.: Spelling-Goldberg Productions
Originally Aired: ABC
Main Cast: Farrah Fawcett, Kate Jackson, Jaclyn Smith, Cheryl Ladd, Shelley Hack, Tanya Roberts, David Doyle, John Forsythe (uncredited voice)

(Left to right) Kelly Garrett (Jaclyn Smith), Sabrina Duncan (Kate Jackson) and Jill Munroe (Farrah Fawcett) are the original, iconic *Charlie's Angels* (ABC/Photofest).

"Once upon a time, there were three little girls who went to the Police Academy, and they were each assigned very hazardous duties. But I took them away from all that, and now they work for me. My name is Charlie."

Iconic 70s detective series about three beautiful women who work as private investigators for a wealthy, unseen boss, after quitting their jobs as policewomen because of menial assignments. Charlie's original Angels are Kate Jackson as intelligent and self-sufficient **Sabrina Duncan**; Farrah Fawcett as athletic (and usually scantily clad) **Jill Munroe**; and Jaclyn Smith as sensitive and photogenic **Kelly Garrett**. The Angels receive their cases via speakerphone from the agency's owner, Charles Townsend, a.k.a. "Charlie," voiced by an uncredited John Forsythe. John Bosley (David Doyle) is the glue holding this arrangement together, feeding Charlie updates when the Angels are in the field and going undercover himself when needed. Driving their Ford Mustangs around Los Angeles, the Angels pose as masseuses, roller derby queens, prostitutes, heiresses, cops, dancers, jockeys ... whatever role is required to catch the bad guys.

Despite their sweet setup with Charlie, the Angels fly away, as angels do. In season two, Kris Munroe (Cheryl Ladd) replaces her sister Jill, and later Tiffany Welles (Shelley Hack) stands in for departed Sabrina, only to be replaced herself by Julie Rogers (Tanya Roberts).

Charlie's Angels breaks ground by placing women in the traditionally male role of private investigator, but then loses ground by focusing on the Angels' anatomical features, giving rise to the term "jiggle TV."

See also: **Duncan, Sabrina** (*Charlie's Angels*); **Garrett, Kelly** (*Charlie's Angels*); **Munroe, Jill** (*Charlie's Angels*)

Charlie's Angels (2011, 8 episodes, USA)

Created by: Ivan Goff, Ben Roberts
Production Co.: Millar Gough Ink, Panda Productions, Flower Films, Sony Pictures Television
Originally Aired: ABC
Main Cast: Annie Ilonzeh, Minka Kelly, Rachael Taylor, Ramon Rodriguez, Victor Garber (voice), John Terry

Gone-in-a-flash remake of the classic 70s series about three gorgeous women who work as detectives for reclusive rich man Charles Townsend. The rebooted Angels are Kate Prince (Annie Ilonzeh), a former Miami cop; Eve French (Minka Kelly), a street racer; and Abby Sampson (Rachael Taylor), a thief. Unlike the 70s Angels who accepted work with Charlie because they were underutilized as policewomen, the 21st century Angels all have criminal pasts, and find redemption and a second chance with Charlie (voiced by Victor Garber). Rounding out the Townsend Agency's personnel list is John Bosley (Ramon

Rodriguez), a hacker in the new age incarnation. "Angels in Chains" (2011) reimagines the titillating episode of the same title from 1976, where the women go undercover in prison, and the throwback is apt, as these Angels remain captives of the past.

Chase (2010–2011, 18 episodes, USA)

Created by: Jennifer Johnson
Production Co.: Warner Bros. Television, Jerry Bruckheimer Television, Bonanza Productions
Originally Aired: NBC
Main Cast: Kelli Giddish, Cole Hauser, Amaury Nolasco, Rose Rollins, Jesse Metcalfe

Kelli Giddish stars as U.S. Deputy Marshal Annie Frost, part of a crack fugitive apprehension team based in Houston, Texas. Assisted by other Marshals, such as Jimmy Godfrey (Cole Hauser) and Daisy Ogbaa (Rose Rollins), Annie hunts down desperate and dangerous criminals, frequently placing her own life in jeopardy. In "Narco" (parts one and two, 2011), Annie is kidnapped by a drug cartel, taken to Mexico, and must be rescued by the team. The past comes back to haunt her in the eponymous "Annie" (2011), when her estranged father, a suspected bank robber, is next on the hit list of his murderous ex-partner. Annie and her father reconcile, bringing some closure in this unintentional series finale.

Chuck (2007–2012, 91 episodes, USA)

Created by: Josh Schwartz, Chris Fedak
Production Co.: College Hill Pictures, Fake Empire Productions, Wonderland Sound and Vision, Warner Bros. Television
Originally Aired: NBC
Main Cast: Zachary Levi, Yvonne Strahovski, Adam Baldwin, Joshua Gomez, Sarah Lancaster, Ryan McPartlin, Mark Christopher Lawrence, Vik Sahay, Scott Krinsky, Bonita Friedericy

Chuck Bartkowski is all nerd. He works at the local Buy More (read: Best Buy) as part of its "Nerd Herd" of computer repair experts, and is happily underachieving after his expulsion from Stanford University. One day Chuck (Zachary Levi) opens an e-mail and downloads "The Intersect," the entire CIA/NSA database, into his BRAIN, and his life changes forever. The Intersect needs government babysitting, of course, so operatives are dispatched, CIA Agent **Sarah Walker** (Yvonne Strahovski) and Major John Casey (Adam Baldwin) of the NSA. Sarah takes the cover identity of Chuck's girlfriend, working at a yogurt shop near the Buy More, while Casey must suffer the indignity of becoming a sales associate at the electronics superstore. The trio must fight off repeated attempts by enemy spy organizations, large and small, to steal/kidnap the Intersect for the valuable information it/he contains. In the meantime, faux couple Sarah and Chuck start to develop genuine feelings for each other, complicating missions, especially at the times when Chuck is considered expendable. But as *Scarecrow and Mrs. King* showed us, spies and civilians make strange, but lasting bedfellows, so a little thing like having every coveted piece of spy information in your brain isn't going to get in their way.

See also: **Walker, Sarah (*Chuck*)**

Clare, Veronica (*Veronica Clare*)

Jazz club owner and private investigator in Los Angeles.
See: *Veronica Clare* **(1991, 9 episodes, USA)**

The Closer (2005–2012, 109 episodes, USA)

Created by: James Duff, Michael M. Robin, Greer Shephard
Production Co.: The Shephard/Robin Company, Walking Entropy, Warner Bros. Television
Originally Aired: TNT
Main Cast: Kyra Sedgwick, J. K. Simmons, Corey Reynolds, Robert Gossett, G. W. Bailey, Tony Denison, Michael Paul Chan, Raymond Cruz, Phillip P. Keene, Jon Tenney

Brenda Leigh Johnson (Kyra Sedgwick) is Deputy Chief of the LAPD's Priority Homicide Division (later the Major Crimes Division). A CIA-trained interrogator, Johnson is recruited for the job by her former lover, Assistant Chief for Operations, Will Pope (J.K. Simmons), because of her ability to elicit confessions from suspects, making her a "closer" of cases. Her honeyed southern tones can't hide her blunt talk and no-nonsense attitude, and before long this outsider is facing a full revolt from her squad, instigated by Robbery-Homicide Captain Russell Taylor (Robert Gossett), whom Johnson has replaced. Much like Jane Tennison (Helen Mirren) in *Prime Suspect*, Johnson shows that a little sabotage isn't going to get in her way, and she begins to win the respect of her team members one by one, starting with her assistant, Sergeant David Gabriel (Corey Reynolds). Johnson and her (at first) grudging crew solve high-profile murders in the City of Angels, with victims of all stripes, from reclusive mathematician to Russian call girl, from college student to retirement home resident. In the little spare time workaholic Johnson manages to find, she navigates a relationship with her patient boyfriend (later husband), FBI Special Agent Fritz Howard (Jon Tenney), who sometimes helps her out by using Bureau resources.

Kyra Sedgwick won a 2010 Emmy Award and a 2007 Golden Globe for her portrayal of this junk food–loving Scarlett O'Hara. While *The Closer* has received many accolades, it does rely heavily on documentary-style filming techniques, so it may not be suitable for viewers sensitive to "shaky-cam."

Codename: Foxfire (1985, 8 episodes, USA)
Created by: Richard Chapman, Joel Schumacher, Bill Dial
Production Co.: Universal TV
Originally Aired: NBC
Main Cast: Joanna Cassidy, Sheryl Lee Ralph, Robin Johnson, John McCook, Henry Jones

A *Charlie's Angels* wannabe (by way of *Mission: Impossible*), this action/adventure series stars Joanna Cassidy as Elizabeth "Foxfire" Towne, a former CIA operative framed for a crime she didn't commit. Liz is recruited by Larry Hutchins (John McCook), the President's brother, to thwart her former fiancé's plan to detonate a Soviet spy satellite over the U.S. She'll need help, of course, in the form of sexy fellow agents/Angels (are there any other kind?), so two women with the requisite looks and skills join the cause: stunt car driver Danny O'Toole (Robin Johnson) and con artist/cat burglar Maggie Bryan (Sheryl Lee Ralph). After saving the world from nuclear annihilation, the ladies take on further dangerous assignments, but for all their good (and good-looking) work, the team is decommissioned after eight missions. After all, they're no Angels.

Cohen, Lisa (*Line of Fire*)
FBI Special Agent who knocks heads with a crime boss in Virginia.
See: *Line of Fire* (2003–2004, 13 episodes, USA)

Cold Case (2003–2010, 156 episodes, USA)
Created by: Meredith Stiehm
Production Co.: Jerry Bruckheimer Television, CBS Television Studios, Warner Bros. Television
Originally Aired: CBS
Main Cast: Kathryn Morris, John Finn, Jeremy Ratchford, Thom Barry, Danny Pino, Tracie Thoms

Lilly Rush (Kathryn Morris) is a homicide detective in Philadelphia who specializes in "cold cases," unsolved crimes which receive renewed attention when a fresh lead is uncovered. Lilly's cases can be 50 or even 100 years old, frequently revealing the issues of their day, such as women's rights, race relations, and homophobia. As aging suspects and witnesses recount their tales to Lilly and her colleagues, flashbacks take over the storytelling, documenting history with period music, fashions, artifacts and customs. Each case is closed by the end of the episode, when the perpetrator is handcuffed and escorted through the police station, as the detectives look on, including Kat Miller (Tracie Thoms), Nick Vera (Jeremy Ratchford), and Lieutenant John Stillman (John Finn). A final, evocative scene features an evanescent murder victim, who offers a seeming acknowledgment to Lilly, the detectives, a friend or family member.

Sometimes *Cold Case* is confused with *Cold Squad*, which has a similar focus and a blonde female lead. *Cold Case* was accused more than once of ripping off the earlier offering, but was forgiven its alleged trespasses by establishing a high standard of quality.

See also: **Rush, Lilly (*Cold Case*)**

Cold Squad (1998–2005, 98 episodes, Canada)

Created by: Julia Keatley, Matt MacLeod, Philip Keatley
Production Co.: Alliance Atlantis Communications, CTV, Cold Squad VII Productions
Originally Aired: In Syndication
Main Cast: Julie Stewart, Garry Chalk, Tamara Marie Watson, Gregory Calpakis, Joely Collins, Michael Hogan, Joy Tanner, Stephen McHattie

Long-running Canadian police procedural which hit U.S. television sets in 2006 via syndication. *Cold Squad* stars Julie Stewart as Ali McCormick, a detective with a homicide unit in Vancouver which specializes in "cold cases," unsolved crimes in need of a fresh look as new technologies have appeared. The series went through a major overhaul after the second season, booting out most of the cast except for Stewart, disbanding the Cold Squad (while retaining the term for the series title), and changing McCormick's hair color from red/auburn to blonde. Newly coiffed, Sgt. McCormick soldiers on, now working on "hot" cases with or without the help of her uncooperative partner Frank Coscarella (Stephen McHattie). Further personnel changes ensue, but McCormick weathers all storms, like the consummate law-enforcement professional she is.

Actress Julie Stewart was no slouch in the professionalism department either, receiving a Gemini Award for her performance as Ali McCormick in 2002.

Cole, Amelia (*The Silent Force*)

Undercover government agent who works to bring down organized crime.
See: ***The Silent Force*** **(1970–1971, 15 episodes, USA)**

Collins, Helen "Amanda" (*Nikita*)

Interrogator and master manipulator at a rogue espionage organization.
See: ***Nikita*** **(2010–2013, 73 episodes, USA)**

Columbo, Kate (*Mrs. Columbo*)

Part-time reporter who solves crimes while avoiding her famous husband.
See: ***Mrs. Columbo*** **(1979–1980, 13 episodes, USA)**

Continuum (2012– , 36 episodes, Canada)

Created by: Simon Barry
Production Co.: Reunion Pictures, Boy Meets Girl Film Company, Shaw Media

Originally Aired: Syfy
Main Cast: Rachel Nichols, Victor Webster, Erik Knudsen, Stephen Lobo, Roger Cross, Lexa Doig, Omari Newton, Luvia Petersen, Jennifer Spence, Brian Markinson

Kiera Cameron (Rachel Nichols) is a police officer with the Vancouver City Protective Services in the year 2077. When a group of rebels known as Liber8 travels to the past, Kiera is unexpectedly pulled with them to the year 2012, where she works to thwart their plans, which involve changing the past to affect the future. Kiera must keep her origins secret, although her "new" partner in the 2012 Vancouver Police Department, Detective Carlos Fonnegra (Victor Webster), eventually learns the truth, and is further shocked when two Kieras appear after more time-travel mishaps. The Kiera from the original timeline survives, while the one they call "Green Kiera" dies, and Fonnegra agrees to conceal the body. While the death of Green Kiera keeps things (relatively) simple for "Red Kiera," two Alec Sadlers (Erik Knudsen), also referred to as Green and Red, create further complications, especially since Alec is a computer genius who will go on to found one of the mega-corporations ruling the world in 2077. (Scorecard, anyone?) Will Kiera unify the timeline so she can get back to the future where her husband and son are waiting? Stay tuned....

Contour, Charlie (*Mystery Girls*)

Former television detective turned housewife turned real-life private eye.
See: *Mystery Girls* (2014, 10 episodes, USA)

Conway, Connie (*Detective's Wife*)

Private investigator's wife who manages to get involved in his cases.
See: *Detective's Wife* (1950, 14 episodes, USA)

Cooper, Virginia (*New York Undercover*)

Police Lieutenant commanding the Fourth Precinct's detective squad in New York City.
See: *New York Undercover* (1994–1998, 89 episodes, USA)

Counterstrike (1990–1993, 66 episodes, Canada/France/USA)

Production Co.: Alliance Communications Corp., Grosso-Jacobson Productions, Atlantique Productions, et al.
Originally Aired: USA Network
Main Cast: Simon MacCorkindale, Christopher Plummer, Tom Kneebone, Sophie Michaud, Andre Mayers, Cyrielle Clair, Stephen Shellen

International industrialist Alexander Addington (Christopher Plummer), haunted by the kidnapping and death of his wife, assembles a crack team of private operatives to fight crime and terrorism around the world. Addington selects Peter Sinclair (Simon MacCorkindale), a former Scotland Yard inspector, to lead the unit, and they recruit Nicole "Nikki" Beaumont (Cyrielle Clair), a French con artist and thief, and Luke Brenner (Stephen Shellen), an American mercenary, to join them. But apparently private crime-fighting is a high turnover business, and after a year (season), Gabrielle Germont (Sophie Michaud), a French investigative reporter, replaces soon-to-be-married Nikki, while Hector Stone (James Purcell), a former Navy SEAL, stands in for soon-to-be-deceased Luke. The team soldiers on, dealing with murders, bombings, and kidnappings, but takes consolation from the fact that they get to jet around the world in a billionaire's high-tech airplane.

Cover Me: Based on the True Life of an FBI Family (2000–2001, 25 episodes, USA)

Created by: Shaun Cassidy
Production Co.: Shaun Cassidy Productions, Panomore Productions, USA Network
Originally Aired: USA Network
Main Cast: Peter Dobson, Melora Hardin, Cameron Richardson, Antoinette Picatto, Michael Angarano

Based on a true story, *Cover Me* follows the adventures of Danny Arno (Peter Dobson), an undercover operative who freelances for the FBI, DEA, DOJ, and Interpol. When Danny's partner is killed and the partner's family is executed, Danny decides his own family will be safer if he brings them in on his secret, trains them, and even uses them in his work. Danny's wife Barbara (Melora Hardin) tries to provide a normal home environment for their kids, dishing out healthy meals and instructing them in appropriate weapons protocols, while relishing her undercover assignments, such as posing as the intended murder victim of a hitman. Daughters Celeste (Cameron Richardson) and Ruby (Antoinette Picatto) flirt with the sons of mobsters to obtain information or go undercover as babysitters in the homes of corrupt officials. Underage son Chance (Michael Angarano) can be called upon as a wheelman when needed and is the narrator for the series. The Arnos bring a crime-fighting twist to the saying, "it's a family affair."

Cover Up (1984–1985, 22 episodes, USA)

Created by: Glen A. Larson
Production Co.: 20th Century–Fox Television, Glen A. Larson Productions
Originally Aired: CBS
Main Cast: Jennifer O'Neill, Jon-Erik Hexum, Richard Anderson, Antony Hamilton

Action-adventure series best known for the tragic accidental death on set of actor Jon-Erik Hexum, who shot himself in the head with a pistol loaded with blanks, unaware of the danger. Hexum plays Mac Harper, ostensibly a male model, but in reality a secret agent for the U.S. government. Jennifer O'Neill is Dani Reynolds, a fashion photographer/covert operative who travels with Mac to trouble spots around the world, helping Americans in need or bringing down bad guys. Dani was drawn into intelligence when she learned her murdered husband was an agent, seeking out his killers and ultimately taking his job, under the watchful eye of Henry Towler (Richard Anderson). Jack Striker (Antony Hamilton) replaces Harper as Dani's partner in espionage and favorite male model, as they solve a murder in Malibu, recover stolen money in Paris, and follow an American scientist to Turkey.

TV spies tend to be a fashionable lot, but *Cover Up* definitely raises the glamour ante.

Covert Affairs (2010– , 69 episodes, USA)

Created by: Matt Corman, Chris Ord
Production Co.: Universal Cable Productions, Hypnotic Films & Television, Open 4 Business Productions, Corman & Ord
Originally Aired: USA Network
Main Cast: Piper Perabo, Christopher Gorham, Kari Matchett, Anne Dudek, Sendhil Ramamurthy, Peter Gallagher, Hill Harper, Nic Bishop

Annie Walker (Piper Perabo) is a rookie field agent in the CIA's Domestic Protection Division (DPD). Walker speaks seven languages fluently, including Russian, German, and Persian, and can fake it in several others, such as Chinese and Turkish, a talent which comes in handy in her line of work. Her initial cover story is that she works in Acquisitions at the Smithsonian Institution, a job that requires a lot of travel, allowing Annie to carry out her secret missions abroad without worrying her sister, Danielle Brooks (Anne Dudek), in whose guest house she resides. Since Annie's occupation is dangerous and stressful, she needs someone to confide in, and tech operative Auggie Anderson (Christopher Gorham), blinded on an Army mission in Iraq, gives her both professional and personal advice, when he's not feeding her intelligence during operations. Annie and Auggie develop a close bond of friendship, which veers into romantic territory, but love is complicated when you're in the spy business, as Annie has learned from her boss, Joan Campbell (Kari Matchett), head of the DPD. Joan is married to Arthur Campbell (Peter Gallagher), Director of the CIA's National Clandestine Service, and a scandal which forces his resignation from the agency haunts her professional and personal life. Despite their complicated existences, Annie and her colleagues soldier on in the espionage wars, and look good while they're doing it, an important trait for secret agents, or so the spy shows tell us. It also helps to have cool titles for your adventures, or, in this case, to borrow them from the songs of one recording artist per season, such as Led Zeppelin in season one and David Bowie in season three. There must be a special spy rate in "Suffragette City."

Crime with Father (1951–1952, 16 episodes, USA)
Originally Aired: ABC
Main Cast: Rusty Lane, Peggy Lobbin

The fictional premise of private consultants, whether paid or unpaid, who assist the police with cases, goes all the way back to Sherlock Holmes, and has often found its way into TV shows, including *McMillan and Wife*, *Monk*, and *Castle*. The earliest example may well be the short-lived series *Crime with Father*, starring Rusty Lane as Captain Jim Riland of the homicide squad. When Jim's officers are stumped on a case, Jim turns to an unlikely source, his teenage daughter Chris Riland (Peggy Lobbin), who has a knack for crime-solving. Sounds like she deserves an increase in her allowance.

Criminal Minds (2005– , 209 episodes, USA)
Created by: Jeff Davis
Production Co.: The Mark Gordon Company, ABC Studios, CBS Television Studios, et al.
Originally Aired: CBS
Main Cast: Mandy Patinkin, Thomas Gibson, Lola Glaudini, Shemar Moore, Matthew Gray Gubler, A.J. Cook, Kirsten Vangsness, Paget Brewster, Joe Mantegna, Rachel Nichols, Jeanne Tripplehorn, Jennifer Love Hewitt

Long-running police procedural with a large and oft-changing cast of characters. Thomas Gibson is a mainstay as Aaron Hotchner, leader of a team from the FBI's Behavioral Analysis Unit (BAU) based in Quantico, Virginia. The team focuses on serial crimes, especially murders, creating a profile of the perpetrator or "unsub" (unknown subject) with an eye to a quick identification in order to prevent further carnage. When Hotchner says, "Wheels up in 30," others flying with him via private jet to crime scenes include Supervisory Special Agents Derek Morgan (Shemar Moore), Dr. Spencer Reid (Matthew Gray Gubler), and Jennifer "JJ" Jareau (A.J. Cook), who initially serves as the Communications Liaison with local police agencies, but later becomes a full-fledged profiler. Staying behind in Quantico is Technical Analyst and self-proclaimed "goddess of information" Penelope Garcia (Kirsten Vangsness), who searches databases at lightning speed to feed the team info about suspects and locations. Garcia wears colorful eyeglasses, clothing, and hair accessories, trying to keep the mood light amidst the darkness of the BAU's work. Other agents come and go (and sometimes come back again), including Emily Prentiss (Paget Brewster) and Jason Gideon (Mandy Patinkin), and even appear in a short-lived spinoff series

Criminal Minds: Suspect Behavior, but the warhorse parent series soldiers on, having profiled the formula for ensemble drama success.

Crossing Jordan (2001–2007, 117 episodes, USA)
Created by: Tim Kring
Production Co.: Tailwind Productions, Kaledo Dritte Productions, NBC Universal Television
Originally Aired: NBC
Main Cast: Jill Hennessy, Miguel Ferrer, Ravi Kapoor, Kathryn Hahn, Steve Valentine, Jerry O'Connell, Ken Howard

Jill Hennessy stars as Dr. Jordan Cavanaugh, a crusading forensic pathologist in the *Quincy M.E.* mold. Jordan believes that it's her job not only to ascertain causes of death, but also to solve murders, whether the police want her help or not. Her buttinsky tendencies coupled with anger management issues have led to a checkered employment history, but Chief Medical Examiner Dr. Garret Macy (Miguel Ferrer) rehires her for a job in his Boston office, because he knows she is brilliant, even if she "crosses" people a lot. Her enabler on the crime-solving front is her father, Max Cavanaugh (Ken Howard), a former police detective, who role-plays murders with Jordan in a bizarre version of family game night. Both daughter and father are haunted by a tragedy which occurred during Jordan's childhood, the unsolved murder of her mother, and they continue to search for clues to solve the mystery. Jordan sometimes works on cases with Woody Hoyt (Jerry O'Connell), an eager-to-please detective originally from Wisconsin, and sparks fly in an "opposites attract" kind of way, but Jordan has intimacy issues that keep them mostly apart. When they are stranded on a mountaintop with little hope for survival in series finale "Crash" (2007), Jordan professes her love to Woody before it's too late, and they kiss. The sound of a helicopter overhead signals salvation and possibly more in an episode that was promoted as a cliffhanger but was changed to a happy ending due to cancellation of the series.

CSI: Crime Scene Investigation (2000– , 318 episodes, USA/Canada)
Created by: Anthony E. Zuiker
Production Co.: Jerry Bruckheimer Television, CBS Television Studios, Alliance Atlantis Communications, et al.
Originally Aired: CBS
Main Cast: William Petersen, Marg Helgenberger, Gary Dourdan, George Eads, Paul Guilfoyle, Jorja Fox, Eric Szmanda, Robert David Hall, Louise Lombard, Wallace Langham, David Berman, Liz Vassey, Ted Danson, Elisabeth Shue

An internationally popular and amazingly durable procedural that continues to spawn spinoffs, *CSI: Crime Scene Investigation* examines the work of crime scene investigators, forensic analysts who solve murders through physical examination of often grisly evidence. The setting for the original is Las Vegas, where the first night-shift supervisor for the Clark County CSI team is Dr. Gil Grissom (William Petersen), a forensic entomologist and brilliant investigator, who has problems making human connections, preferring to gaze through the lens of his microscope. Grissom's second-in-command is Catherine Willows (Marg Helgenberger), a one-time exotic dancer in Vegas, who puts herself through school and becomes a blood-spatter analyst. (Talk about a career change!) Although plagued by personal problems, including the murder of her ex-husband, Catherine is dedicated to her work, and later replaces Grissom as the head of the team.

Another long-tenured member of the cast is Jorja Fox as Sara Sidle, a materials and element analyst for the team, who suffered a traumatic childhood, which included the murder of her abusive father by her schizophrenic mother. Sara's past leaves her with anger management and depression issues in the present, which she tries to resolve with Grissom's help via a late-blooming romantic relationship.

Cast changes ensue (they would almost have to over the course of 15 years), but viewers don't seem to mind. Neither are they concerned that the unchanging concept for the CSI franchise isn't terribly realistic ... that the same people are collecting evidence, analyzing it, questioning suspects, and solving crimes. (Detectives? Who needs detectives?) But it makes for good TV and a great, if unintentional, recruitment program for potential forensic analysts, who may find themselves disappointed when they actually get on the job.

CSI: Miami (2002–2012, 232 episodes, USA/Canada)
Created by: Anthony E. Zuiker, Carol Mendelsohn, Ann Donahue
Production Co.: Jerry Bruckheimer Television, CBS Television Studios, Alliance Atlantis Communications, et al.
Originally Aired: CBS
Main Cast: David Caruso, Emily Procter, Adam Rodríguez, Khandi Alexander, Rory Cochrane, Kim Delaney, Sofia Milos, Jonathan Togo, Rex Linn, Eva LaRue, Megalyn Echikunwoke

The scene shifts from Las Vegas to Miami for this first spinoff from *CSI: Crime Scene Investigation*. Lieutenant Horatio Caine (David Caruso), an expert in explosives, leads the Miami-Dade crime lab through its grisly paces, as members study physical evidence to solve murders. "H's" second-in-command is Detective Calleigh Duquesne (Emily Procter), a ballistics specialist with a Louisiana drawl, who likes to follow the rules. Everything about Calleigh is sunny, from her blonde hair to her bright smile to her happy disposition, but she sees her share of darkness in this work, especially when she is kidnapped to clean up a murder scene in "All In" (2008).

Latter-day procedurals are known to have revolving doors for their casts, but in addition to Caruso and Procter, Adam Rodríguez stuck it out for all 10 seasons (minus a brief departure in season eight) as Detective Eric Delko, who later becomes a love interest for Calleigh. Eva LaRue had a shorter stay, joining the cast in season four as Natalia Boa Vista, a DNA analyst assigned to cold cases, who turns out to be an informant for the FBI. Natalia later resigns from the FBI, joining the Miami-Dade crime lab as a Crime Scene Investigator, where she remains for the rest of the series.

Cast changes sometimes brought about dramatic fates for characters, as when Detective Tim Speedle (Rory Cochrane) is killed in the line of duty, and Medical Examiner Tara Price (Megalyn Echikunwoke) is arrested for stealing prescriptions from corpses and leaves in disgrace.

But the work goes on, because new cast members replace old, and when one CSI dies, another arises Hydra-like to take its place.

CSI: NY (2004–2013, 197 episodes, USA/Canada)

Created by: Anthony E. Zuiker, Carol Mendelsohn, Ann Donahue
Production Co.: Jerry Bruckheimer Television, CBS Television Studios, Alliance Atlantis Productions, Clayton Entertainment, et al.
Originally Aired: CBS
Main Cast: Gary Sinise, Melina Kanakaredes, Carmine Giovinazzo, Vanessa Ferlito, Hill Harper, Eddie Cahill, Anna Belknap, Robert Joy, A. J. Buckley, Sela Ward

The third entry in CBS's large *CSI* franchise, and a direct spinoff from *CSI: Miami*, *CSI: NY* stars Gary Sinise as Detective Mac Taylor, head of the New York City Crime Lab and its team of forensic investigators. Par for the course with long-running procedurals such as this, the cast is large and oft-changing, but Sinise's Taylor is a mainstay throughout the nine seasons, along with Carmine Giovinazzo as Detective Danny Messer and Eddie Cahill as Detective Don Flack.

The women tended to be of shorter tenure, although Anna Belknap stayed for the duration after joining the series in season two, portraying Detective Lindsay Monroe. Lindsay, a Montana native, contributes her amazing head for detail to the team's work, and even finds love in its midst, later marrying Detective Messer.

Melina Kanakaredes remained with the show for six seasons before declining to renew her contract as Detective Stella Bonasera. Stella, a tough and tenacious cop, was orphaned as a child, and so views the team as her family, serving as a maternal figure for them. Stella is replaced by Detective Jo Danville (Sela Ward), a DNA analyst from Virginia, who has expertise in criminal psychology as well, useful during interrogations.

The faces change, but the work remains the same ... sifting through physical evidence, most of it not pretty, and bringing murderers to justice.

Cummings, D.D. (*She Spies*)

Hacker released from jail to assist with U.S. undercover ops.
See: *She Spies* (2002–2004, 40 episodes, USA)

Dancer, April (*The Girl from U.N.C.L.E.*)

Secret agent who battles the enemies of good while wearing the latest mod fashions.
See: *The Girl from U.N.C.L.E.* (1966–1967, 29 episodes, USA)

Danger Man (1960–1962, 39 episodes; 1964–1966, 47 episodes, UK)

Created by: Ralph Smart
Production Co.: Incorporated Television Company
Originally Aired: CBS
Main Cast: Patrick McGoohan

Debonair secret agent John Drake undertakes international missions for NATO and later "M9" in a retooled, one-hour version of this series, which was broadcast in the U.S. as *Secret Agent*. Drake never carries a gun or kisses a girl, and actor Patrick McGoohan imbues the character with a quiet intensity and an appealing quirkiness. Although there were no female co-stars in this series, a number of guests made indelible impressions in their roles as female spies, most notably Susan Hampshire in "Are You Going to Be More Permanent?" (1965), Joan Greenwood in "The Paper Chase" (1966), and Jane Merrow in "A Date with Doris" (1964).

Dangerous Curves (1992–1993, 34 episodes, USA/Spain)

Created by: Leonard Katzman, David Paulsen
Production Co.: Hemisphere Group, Tesauro, Telecinco
Originally Aired: CBS
Main Cast: Lise Cutter, Michael Michele, Gregory McKinney

Gina McKay (Lise Cutter) and Holly Williams (Michael Michele) work as operatives for Personal Touch, a private security and investigation firm based in Dallas. The two former policewomen use their crime-fighting skills to track down jewel thieves and protect the glitterati from assassination, going undercover as models when needed (like all the pretty lady detectives do). Assisting the glamorous duo is the requisite police contact, Lt. Ozzie Bird (Gregory McKinney), who feeds them information and is also Gina's boyfriend. As the title suggests, sex is one of the lures here, with the ladies clad in tight miniskirts and spike heels as they chase down the bad guys, their potentially injury-inducing attire giving new meaning to the term "dangerous curves."

Danton, Toni "Feather" (*The Feather and Father Gang*)

Los Angeles attorney who solves crimes by running cons with her father.
See: *The Feather and Father Gang* (1976–1977, 14 episodes, USA)

Danville, Jo (*CSI: NY*)

Virginia native and DNA analyst with the New York City Crime Lab.
See: *CSI: NY* (2004–2013, 197 episodes, USA)

Dark Blue (2009–2010, 20 episodes, USA)

Created by: Danny Cannon, Doug Jung
Production Co.: Water Chopping Entertainment, Warner Horizon Television, TNT Originals
Originally Aired: TNT
Main Cast: Dylan McDermott, Omari Hardwick, Logan Marshall-Green, Nicki Aycox

Lieutenant Carter Shaw (Dylan McDermott) heads an undercover unit within the Los Angeles Police Department which prides itself on secrecy. Shaw's team includes newlywed Ty Curtis (Omari Hardwick), loose cannon Dean Bendis (Logan Marshall-Green), and rookie Jaimie Allen (Nicki Aycox), whose shady past and proficiency at deception seem tailor-made for the deep-cover outfit. The members of this brave if troubled crew put their lives on the line, posing as gang members, junkies, and assorted hoodlums to take the worst of the worst off the street. Their double-lives strain personal relationships, as they miss holidays and dodge communications, but it's the price they pay for wearing dark blue.

Dateline Europe

See: *Foreign Intrigue* (1951–1955, 156 episodes, USA)

David, Ziva (*NCIS*)

Former Mossad liaison, now an agent investigating crimes related to Navy and Marine Corps personnel.
See: *NCIS* (2003– , 258 episodes, USA)

Davis, Cathy (*Jane Doe*)

Suburban housewife who solves intricate puzzles for the CIA.
See: *Jane Doe* (2005–2008, 9 episodes, USA)

Davis, Helen (*Foreign Intrigue*)
European correspondent for *Consolidated News*, who specializes in busting spy rings.
See: *Foreign Intrigue* (1951–1955, 156 episodes, USA)

Dear Detective (1979, 4 episodes, USA)
Production Co.: Kibbee/Hargrove Productions, Viacom Productions
Originally Aired: CBS
Main Cast: Brenda Vaccaro, Arlen Dean Snyder, Ron Silver

Brenda Vaccaro stars as Kate Hudson, head of a police homicide unit years before Jane Tennison tackles a similar position in *Prime Suspect*. Kate juggles three roles. She is a brilliant detective, always one step ahead of her male counterparts, solving murders such as the stabbing deaths of City Councilmen by a serial killer in Los Angeles. She's a loving single-mother, sending a daughter to Catholic school, while negotiating a new relationship with her ex-husband. Her toughest role, however, may be the newest, as a single woman back on the dating scene. Here she is helped by the accidental meeting of Prof. Richard Weyland (Arlen Dean Snyder), who becomes her love interest, after she almost runs him down on his moped.

Alas, this groundbreaking series was not allowed to bloom beyond four episodes.

Deception (2013, 11 episodes, USA)
Created by: Liz Heldens
Production Co.: Universal Television, BermanBraun
Originally Aired: NBC
Main Cast: Meagan Good, Laz Alonso, Tate Donovan, Wes Brown, Katherine LaNasa, Ella Rae Peck, Victor Garber, Marin Hinkle

Primetime soap opera starring Meagan Good as Joanna Locasto, a detective for the SFPD, who agrees to work undercover for the FBI in the investigation of a socialite's death. The deceased, one Vivian Bowers (Bree Williamson), was Joanna's childhood friend, and Joanna must now infiltrate Vivian's wealthy and powerful family, one of whom may be a murderer. During the course of Joanna's investigation, dark secrets are revealed, such as the true parentage of Mia Bowers (Ella Rae Peck), Vivian's "sister." Joanna discovers the killer's identity in "I'll Start with the Hillbilly," but the motive for Vivian's murder is not revealed before the demise of this short-lived series.

Decoy: Police Woman (1957–1958, 39 episodes, USA)
Production Co.: Official Films

Originally Aired: In Syndication
Main Cast: Beverly Garland

Trailblazing police procedural starring Beverly Garland as Casey Jones, an undercover policewoman with the New York City Police Department. Casey's assignments require versatility and bravery, whether she's posing as an exotic dancer, a blackmailer, a nurse or a gun moll. Her cases take her all over New York, to basketball games, racetracks, society parties, and, when she needs to smoke out a "Ladies' Man" (1958), the Catskills. Casey is married to the job, and in "The Sound of Tears" (1958), she reveals that her former fiancé, a police officer, was killed in the line of duty. Like David Janssen's Richard Kimble in *The Fugitive*, Casey is the only main character in the series, but a bevy of up-and-coming actors lend guest-star support, such as Ed Asner, Larry Hagman, Suzanne Pleshette, and Peter Falk.

The history of policewomen as TV lead characters doesn't begin with *Cagney & Lacey* or *Police Woman*, it begins with *Decoy: Police Woman*.

Del'Amico, Kate (*Under Cover*)

Covert operative, along with hubby, for the National Intelligence Agency. See: **Under Cover (1991, 13 episodes, USA)**

Delgado, Elena (*Without a Trace*)

Member of the FBI's Missing Persons Squad in New York City. See: **Without a Trace (2002–2009, 160 episodes, USA)**

The Delphi Bureau (1972–1973, 8 episodes, USA)

Created by: Sam Rolfe
Production Co.: Warner Bros. Television
Originally Aired: ABC
Main Cast: Laurence Luckenbill, Anne Jeffreys

The Delphi Bureau, as imagined in this short-lived series, is a highly secret government intelligence agency answerable directly to the President of the United States. The Bureau is so secret, in fact, that agent Glenn Garth Gregory (Laurence Luckenbill) is aware of only two employees—himself and his handler, Sybil Van Loween (Anne Jeffreys), a DC socialite. The reluctant Gregory, ostensibly a researcher, receives his assignments from Van Loween at various locations around Washington, and then fights the good fight, with a photographic memory as his main weapon instead of a gun.

Part of three revolving series known collectively as *The Men*, *The Delphi Bureau* wears its obscurity like a badge of spy–TV honor.

DeMarco, Catherine "Charlie" (*Graceland*)
FBI agent specializing in undercover work involving drugs and weapons.
See: *Graceland* (2013– , 25 episodes, USA)

Dempsey and Makepeace (1985–1986, 30 episodes, UK)
Created by: Ranald Graham
Production Co.: Golden Eagle Films, London Weekend Television
Originally Aired: In Syndication
Main Cast: Michael Brandon, Glynis Barber, Ray Smith, Tony Osoba

Buddy-cop premise with a twist. Lt. James Dempsey (Michael Brandon) is a tough, working-class, New York cop, who needs to get out of town fast because of an assassination threat, and joins the London police force after a few strings are pulled. Det. Sgt. Harriet "Harry" Makepeace (Glynis Barber) is a British noblewoman, daughter of a Lord, and member of the elite SI 10 police unit, forced to partner with the brash, violence-loving Yank. Although initially reluctant, Dempsey and Makepeace learn to work together, and, not surprisingly, their relationship begins to display a "will they or won't they" sexual tension. Under the watchful eye of Chief Supt. Gordon Spikings (Ray Smith), Dempsey and Makepeace pursue London's drug dealers, murderers, burglars, kidnappers, and gunrunners, while trying to sort out their complex feelings for each other.

Dennis, Micki (*Snoops*)
State Department protocol officer who sleuths with her criminologist hubby on the side.
See: *Snoops* (1989–1990, 13 episodes, USA)

Department S (1969–1970, 28 episodes, UK)
Created by: Dennis Spooner, Monty Berman
Production Co.: Incorporated Television Company, Scoton
Originally Aired: In Syndication
Main Cast: Peter Wyngarde, Joel Fabiani, Rosemary Nicols, Dennis Alaba Peters

Department S is a special branch of Interpol, whose members are called to assist with cases which have baffled other agents and authorities. Stewart Sullivan (Joel Fabiani), an American, is field leader of the department, and likes to apply the rules of logic to the section's peculiar investigations, such as the disappearance of an entire village. The hedonistic Jason King (Peter Wyngarde), a novelist, approaches crime-solving the way his fictional alter-ego Mark Caine would, working his way backward from outlandish scenarios. Annabelle Hurst (Rosemary Nicols), a computer expert, uses her machine, nicknamed "Auntie," to provide analysis, attempting to blow King's wild theories out of the water.

Hurst also works in the field, sometimes appearing in disguise, and seems to have a romantic link with Sullivan. The three agents, under the leadership of Department Director Sir Curtis Seretse (Dennis Alaba Peters), combine their unique perspectives on cases, such as "The Man from X" (1970), just your run-of-the-mill "death by spacesuit" affair.

Derevko, Irina (*Alias*)

Former Russian spy, presumed dead, and mother of an American spy.
See: *Alias* (2001–2006, 105 episodes, USA)

Desmond, Francine (*Scarecrow and Mrs. King*)

A clotheshorse spy who works for The Agency alongside fellow agent Lee "Scarecrow" Stetson (Bruce Boxleitner) and civilian/rookie agent **Amanda King** (Kate Jackson), Francine has as her main tasks: research, carrying folders, and taunting former housewife Mrs. King for her lack of sophistication, style, experience—her general LACK. Francine, portrayed by Martha Smith, spends most of her time in the office, but makes it into the field occasionally, most notably in the episode "Dead Ringer" (1984), where she must double for a Hungarian defector (Martha Smith in a dual role). Even when she makes it to Germany for a mission in "The Times They Are a Changin'" (1984), her main accomplishment is to loan Amanda eveningwear for a posh party with a baron. Somehow old pro Francine is always more dispensable to Agency operations than neophyte Amanda.
See also: *Scarecrow and Mrs. King* (1983–1987, 88 episodes, USA)

Detective School (1979, 13 episodes, USA)

Production Co.: Kukoff-Harris Partnership
Originally Aired: ABC
Main Cast: James Gregory, Douglas Fowley, Randolph Mantooth, Melinda Naud, Taylor Negron, LaWanda Page, Pat Proft

James Gregory stars as Nick Hannigan, a bumbling private investigator who opens a detective school on the theory that "those who can't, teach." Enrolling in Nick's school is a motley crew of P.I. wannabes, including Robert Redford (Douglas Fowley), an elderly gentleman with no relation to the famous actor; Charlene Jenkins (LaWanda Page), a housewife with an attitude; Maggie Ferguson (Melinda Naud), a lingerie model; and Silvio Galindez (Taylor Negron), a disco-dancing mailroom clerk. Evidence of actual criminal activity seems to seek out the novices and their mentor, so they get plenty of experience in the field, investigating a diamond-stealing ring in "Lucy in the Sky with Pizza" (1979) and searching for a blackmailer in "One Word Is Worth a Thousand Pictures."

Alas, this situation comedy, which had a brief run during the summer, didn't find an audience in the fall against stiffer competition.

Detective's Wife (1950, 14 episodes, USA)

Originally Aired: CBS
Main Cast: Donald Curtis, Lynn Bari

Lynn Bari portrays Connie Conway, the detective's wife, who manages to get involved in the cases of her P.I. spouse, whether she plans to or not. Donald Curtis plays her harried husband, Adam Conway, who hopes for an easy-going detective practice, but solving one newsworthy murder brings additional homicide cases his way. This comedy/mystery series was broadcast live from New York as a summer replacement for *Man against Crime*.

Dexter (2006–2013, 96 episodes, USA)

Based on: The novel *Darkly Dreaming Dexter* by Jeff Lindsay
Created by: James Manos, Jr.
Production Co.: John Goldwyn Productions, The Colleton Company, Clyde Phillips Productions, Devilina Productions, Showtime Networks
Originally Aired: Showtime
Main Cast: Michael C. Hall, Jennifer Carpenter, Desmond Harrington, Julie Benz, David Zayas, C.S. Lee, Aimee Garcia, Geoff Pierson, Lauren Vélez, James Remar, Christina Robinson

Dexter Morgan (Michael C. Hall) is a blood-spatter analyst for the Miami Metro Police Department. Dexter is a one-man, crime-stopping machine. By day, he visits crime scenes and helps the police figure out how things happened, leading to arrests and convictions. By night, he is a serial killer, tracking down those who have escaped justice, murdering them, and then using his technical skills to make sure he is never caught. This keeps him one step ahead of his adoptive sister, Debra Morgan (Jennifer Carpenter), a homicide detective, who initially knows nothing of Dexter's secret life and frequently consults him for advice on her work, especially "The Ice Truck Killer" case. When the man Debra is dating, Rudy Cooper (Christian Camargo), turns out to be the Ice Truck Killer, much of Dexter's early history is revealed, and it's not a pretty picture. The past, in fact, is inescapable for Dexter and Debra. Dexter's initial trauma, his subsequent bloodlust, and its later channeling into a "positive" direction by his adoptive father, Harry Morgan (James Remar), a cop who found him at his mother's murder site, are all part of the twisted man Dexter is today. Dexter's relationship with Harry, Debra's competition with Dexter for her father's attention, and her (rightful) sense that she was being excluded from something, have led to a lack of confidence, poor people skills, and, perhaps, her incessant use of foul language. Dexter's and Debra's journey continues for seven more years, but, needless to say it's not a happy ending.

Dexter is dark with a capital D.

Dexter, Tasha (*V.I.P.*)

Former model and spy, now part of a team of gorgeous bodyguards. See: *V.I.P.* (1998–2002, 88 episodes, USA/Germany)

Diamonds (1987–1989, 44 episodes, Canada)

Production Co.: Alliance Entertainment Corp., Atlantique Productions, Global Television Network, Grosso Jacobson, USA Television Network
Originally Aired: CBS
Main Cast: Nicholas Campbell, Peggy Smithhart, Tony Rosato, Roland Magdane

Moonlighting-esque series about a divorced couple who once starred together on a detective series called *Two of Diamonds*, but now decide to give the P.I. biz a chance in real life. Nicholas Campbell is Mike Devitt, the down-on-his-luck former actor, and Peggy Smithhart is Christina Towne, his still loyal former spouse, who agrees to join him in opening a fledgling detective agency in New York. Cases find them trying to distinguish between twin murder suspects in "Family Plot" (1988) and searching for the runaway son of a hockey star in "Life Is a Lot like Hockey" (1989). Their TV pasts sometimes catch up with them, as in "Sweetheart Deal" (1988), when their former Hollywood agent thinks someone is trying to kill him. The pair's mutual romantic past also threatens to intrude, but the ex-marrieds somehow manage to keep their minds on sleuthing.

Dick and the Duchess (1957–1958, 26 episodes, USA/UK)

Production Co.: Associated-Rediffusion Television, Sheldon Reynolds TV
Originally Aired: CBS
Main Cast: Patrick O'Neal, Hazel Court, Richard Wattis, Beatrice Varley

London-based comedy starring Patrick O'Neal as Dick Starrett, an American insurance investigator, who is married to Jane Starrett (Hazel Court), "Duchess," as he calls her. Jane, the daughter of a British peer, gets involved in Dick's cases, sometimes accidentally, sometimes on purpose, although she is frequently more of a hindrance than a help. When Dick comes down with a bad cold in "The Painting" (1957), Jane takes it upon herself to investigate the theft of a valuable piece of art with chaotic and comic results. In "The Kissing Bandit" (1957), Jane and one of Dick's insurance clients search for a jewel thief, who is suspected in a string of robberies, where he always kisses his female victims before absconding with the loot. Somehow the marriage between trouble-prone noblewoman Jane and long-suffering commoner Dick seems to prosper amid the mayhem.

di Contini, Caroline (*The Protectors*)

Italian investigator who works with two other jet-setting detectives to foil crimes in Europe.
See: *The Protectors* (1972–1974, 52 episodes, UK)

di Luzio, Marina (*Stone Undercover*)

Royal Canadian Mounted Police Corporal and specialist in commercial crime.
See: *Stone Undercover* (2002–2003, 26 episodes, Canada)

The District (2000–2004, 89 episodes, USA)

Created by: Terry George, Jack Maple
Production Co.: Cinemaline Productions, DiNovi Pictures, Universal Network Television
Originally Aired: CBS
Main Cast: Craig T. Nelson, Lynne Thigpen, Jayne Brook, Roger Aaron Brown, Sean Patrick Thomas, Justin Theroux, David O'Hara, Elizabeth Marvel

Craig T. Nelson stars as Washington, D.C. Police Chief Jack Mannion, who comes to the outlaw "District," promising to take a big bite out of crime. Mannion is a maverick, and doesn't mind using his two-toned Spectator shoes to step on some toes when the need arises. He draws together an inner circle of administrators and cops, including statistician **Ella Farmer** (Lynne Thigpen), Detective Temple Page (Sean Patrick Thomas), and patrol officer **Nancy Parras** (Elizabeth Marvel). In their personal lives, the chief and his crew are all too vulnerable, struggling with illnesses, relationship issues, drug addiction, and the death of loved ones. But on the job, they are pros, taking on drug dealers, serial killers, the Russian mob, and even the D.C. Mayor himself, because no one is above the law in Mannion's District.

See also: **Farmer, Ella** (*The District*); **Parras, Nancy** (*The District*)

The Division (2001–2004, 88 episodes, USA)

Created by: Deborah Joy LeVine
Production Co.: Kedzie Productions, Viacom Productions
Originally Aired: Lifetime
Main Cast: Bonnie Bedelia, Lela Rochon, Nancy McKeon, Tracey Needham, Lisa Vidal, Taraji P. Henson, Amy Jo Johnson, Jose Yenque, David Gianopoulos, Jon Hamm

The Division is an ensemble police procedural with a twist—all five of its main characters are female cops. Captain Kate McCafferty (Bonnie Bedelia) heads a team of police officers in the Felony Division of the San Francisco Police

Department. She and her charges attempt to balance their professional lives with their personal ones, which seem particularly trouble-prone. Inspector Jinny Exstead (Nancy McKeon), for example, battles alcohol and drug addiction, as well as concomitant promiscuity, while trying to hold onto her job. Magda Ramirez (Lisa Vidal), a single mother, deals with the amorous attentions of her married partner and a leukemia diagnosis for her son. Partners Angela Reid (Lela Rochon) and C.D. DeLorenzo (Tracey Needham) act like the Bickersons on the job, while C.D. must also contend with a cheating husband at home. McCafferty herself confronts partial paralysis from a stroke while bucking for the Chief of Police spot. As the world turns with new (and sometimes old) love interests, health issues, and staff changes, the inspectors do their work, investigating murders, kidnappings, bombings, and rapes, sometimes finding themselves or loved ones in the line of fire. But amidst the personal and professional chaos, there are opportunities for happiness, as when a now sober Jinny gets married in series finale "Somewhere in America" (2004).

Dog and Cat (1977, 6 episodes, USA)
Created by: Walter Hill
Production Co.: Largo Productions, Paramount Network Television
Originally Aired: ABC
Main Cast: Lou Antonio, Kim Basinger, Matt Clark

Short-lived buddy-cop show with a twist—the partnership is between male and female detectives, referred to as "dog and cat" in police slang. As the title suggests, this series is about opposites. Sgt. Jack Ramsey (Lou Antonio) is a veteran of the LAPD, who has conservative tastes and isn't exactly thrilled that his new partner is a woman. J.Z. Kane (Kim Basinger) is a rookie officer, young, hip, and beautiful to boot, tooling around town in a souped-up Volkswagen Beetle with a Porsche engine. Clearly these two have some work to do in the bridge-building department, but in between arguments, they have each other's backs, especially when danger threatens. No "will they or won't they" frisson here—the relationship remains platonic for its brief duration.

Donner, Lindsay (*Psi Factor: Chronicles of the Paranormal*)
Data analyst and agent for a covert organization investigating paranormal activity.
See: *Psi Factor: Chronicles of the Paranormal* (1996–2000, 88 episodes, Canada)

Donovan, Claudia (*Warehouse 13*)
Claudia Donovan (Allison Scagliotti) is a techie wunderkind at Warehouse 13, a repository for supernatural artifacts located in the Badlands of South

Dakota. Claudia's mechanical expertise and hacking skills come in handy at the warehouse, both in locating artifacts around the world and in designing devices to defeat them. After a period of apprenticeship and warehouse-bound duties, Claudia moves on to fieldwork, partnering with Steve Jinks (Aaron Ashmore), who becomes her BFF. In "An Evil Within" (2012), Claudia uses an artifact, Johann Maelzel's Metronome, to bring Steve back to life after a warehouse catastrophe, but experiences unintended consequences when she feels the pain of any injuries Steve receives. Teenaged Claudia is an orphan, but finds a substitute, albeit cranky, father in Warehouse 13's Agent in Charge, Artie Nielsen (Saul Rubinek). While Claudia grows into her role as field agent, she learns she is destined to become the future caretaker of the warehouse, replacing inimitably spooky Mrs. Frederic (CCH Pounder), a destiny that is fulfilled with Claudia's typical cool in series finale "Endless" (2014).

See also: *Warehouse 13* **(2009–2014, 64 episodes, USA)**

Doreau, Dori (*Sledge Hammer!*)

Intelligent cop saddled with a Neanderthal partner.
See: *Sledge Hammer!* **(1986–1988, 41 episodes, USA)**

The Dresden Files **(2007, 12 episodes, Canada/USA)**

Based on: The novels of Jim Butcher
Production Co.: Dresden Files Productions, Saturn Films, Lionsgate Television
Originally Aired: Syfy
Main Cast: Paul Blackthorne, Valerie Cruz, Terrence Mann, Conrad Coates, Raoul Bhaneja

Harry Dresden (Paul Blackthorne) is the only wizard listed in the Chicago Yellow Pages. Dresden won't perform at your party, but if you've lost something or think you're being haunted by a ghost, Harry's your man. Given his profession, Harry has a lot of unusual events swirling around him, which tend to draw the attention of the police, most of whom don't believe in magic. Lt. Connie Murphy (Valerie Cruz), however, is on the fence, disavowing magic, but turning to Harry for help on cases which might best be described as "hinky." In "Hair of the Dog" (2007), Murphy seeks Dresden's assistance in solving murders where the victims' hair and teeth are taken, and Harry realizes werewolves are involved—as victims. Not surprisingly, there is some romantic frisson between handsome Harry and comely Connie, but, like "Bob" (Terrence Mann), Harry's spirit-friend trapped for eternity in a skull, their unfulfilled romance is a specter, ensnared forever in the black box of premature series cancellation.

Drew, Nancy (*The Hardy Boys/Nancy Drew Mysteries*)

Teen sleuth with a propensity to run into spooky happenings.

See: *The Hardy Boys/Nancy Drew Mysteries* (1977–1979, 46 episodes, USA)

Drew, Nancy (*Nancy Drew*)

College student, temp worker, and amateur sleuth.
See: *Nancy Drew* (1995, 13 episodes, France/Canada)

DuBois, Allison (*Medium*)

Allison DuBois sees dead people—usually when she's asleep, but sometimes even when she's awake. She uses her psychic abilities to help murder victims find peace, and her job as a consultant in the Phoenix District Attorney's Office puts her in an ideal position to see that justice is done. But her visions, like the dreams that bring them, are often incoherent and sometimes surreal, making it difficult to make immediate sense of them. In "Being Mrs. O'Leary's Cow" (2005), Allison (Patricia Arquette) has confusing dreams about a pilot who may or may not save a plane from crashing, and who may or may not have murdered his wife. Allison and husband Joe (Jake Weber) must also raise three daughters, all of whom are beginning to display psychic abilities. In "Mother's Little Helper" (2007), Allison and eldest daughter Ariel (Sofia Vassilieva) have a series of interconnected dreams, and must work together to interpret their visions if they are to solve the double homicide of a mother and daughter.

Arquette's Allison is tenacious and strong, yet vulnerable and sympathetic, demonstrating that seeing dead people is a tough way to make a living.
See also: *Medium* (2005–2011, 130 episodes, USA)

Dulcett, Michelle (*The Protector*)

LAPD robbery-homicide detective specializing in high-profile crimes.
See: *The Protector* (2011, 13 episodes, USA)

Duncan, Sabrina (*Charlie's Angels*)

Kate Jackson stars as Sabrina Duncan, one of three female private investigators, a.k.a. "Angels," who work at a detective agency owned by the mysterious Charles Townsend (voiced by an uncredited John Forsythe). Sabrina is the brightest and most demurely dressed of the three, taking undercover roles such as reporter, racecar driver, flight attendant, jockey, and fashion designer—jobs which, in general, require her to keep her clothes on. In "The Blue Angels" (1977), Sabrina goes undercover as a vice cop, while Jill (Farrah Fawcett) is a suggestively clad masseuse and Kelly (Jaclyn Smith) poses as a prostitute. Sabrina is divorced from police detective Bill Duncan (Michael Bell), but enjoys an amicable split with her ex, even though he accidentally blows her vice-cop cover, endangering her life. After three years, Sabrina quits the agency and the Angels for marriage and motherhood, leaving behind some big and (classy) shoes to fill for Tiffany Welles (Shelley Hack).

See also: *Charlie's Angels* (1976–1981, 110 episodes, USA)

Dunham, Olivia (*Fringe*)

FBI agent with a federal task force investigating weird science and unexplained phenomena.

See: *Fringe* (2008–2013, 100 episodes, USA)

Duquesne, Calleigh (*CSI: Miami*)

Ballistics expert and second-in-command at the Miami-Dade crime lab.

See: *CSI: Miami* (2002–2012, 232 episodes, USA/Canada)

Dyna Girl (*Electra Woman and Dyna Girl*)

Magazine reporter who transforms into a caped alter-ego to fight crime.

See: *Electra Woman and Dyna Girl* (1976, 16 episodes, USA)

Eames, Alexandra (*Law & Order: Criminal Intent*)

Kathryn Erbe portrays Alexandra Eames, a no-nonsense detective with New York City's Major Case Squad, who partners with brilliant, but unpredictable Robert Goren (Vincent D'Onofrio) to solve the city's darkest crimes. Though their personalities and investigative techniques may clash at times, by complementing each other's weaknesses, Eames and Goren are a formidable team. Eames bleeds blue, following in the footsteps of her father, a police officer, and later marrying a cop, Joseph Dutton, who was killed in the line of duty. When the detectives investigate the murder of Dutton's former partner in "Amends" (2007), they find that the wrong man was convicted in Dutton's 1998 killing and reopen the case, dredging up painful memories for Eames. Although Eames focuses more attention on her career than her personal life, she does take time off in 2003 to serve as a surrogate mother for her sister's baby. Eames's complex, but professional relationship with Goren leads to her resignation in "Loyalty" (parts one and two, 2010), but the partners reunite to do what they do best—bring murderers to justice—in "Rispetto" (2011).

See also: *Law & Order: Criminal Intent* (2001–2011, 195 episodes, USA)

Edison, Eve (*Mann & Machine*)

Police officer who is actually a sophisticated robot under the skin.

See: *Mann & Machine* (1992, 9 episodes, USA)

Electra Woman and Dyna Girl (1976, 16 episodes, USA)
Created by: Joe Ruby, Ken Spears
Production Co.: Sid & Marty Krofft Television Productions
Originally Aired: ABC
Main Cast: Diedre Hall, Judy Strangis, Norman Alden

    A pastiche of the popular *Batman* TV series and comic books, *Electra Woman and Dyna Girl*, originally broadcast as part of *The Krofft Supershow*, brings us a pair of female caped crusaders who fight crime in spandex. Deidre Hall is Lori/Electra Woman and Judy Strangis portrays Judy/Dyna Girl, two magazine reporters who use their alter-egos and an array of gadgets (most with the prefix "Electra") to battle baddies, such as "Glitter Rock," "The Spider Lady," and "Empress of Evil." Professor Frank Heflin (Norman Alden) assists the Dyna duo at ElectraBase, manning the CrimeScope computer and feeding the superheroes information via their ElectraComs, amazing wrist-worn devices with a variety of functions, including a force field and tractor beam. Holy Electra-Change!

Elementary (2012– , 48 episodes, USA)
Based on: The novels and short stories of Sir Arthur Conan Doyle
Created by: Robert Doherty
Production Co.: CBS Television Studios, Timberman-Beverly Productions, Hill of Beans Productions
Originally Aired: CBS
Main Cast: Jonny Lee Miller, Lucy Liu, Aidan Quinn, Jon Michael Hill

    Jonny Lee Miller stars as Sherlock Holmes in this reimagining of Conan Doyle's brilliant consulting detective, now transplanted to New York City. Holmes is a recovering drug addict as the series opens, and his wealthy father has engaged the services of a "sober companion," Dr. **Joan Watson** (Lucy Liu), who will live with Sherlock to ensure he doesn't relapse. While continuing to work on his recovery, Holmes uses his prodigious skills of observation and deductive reasoning to assist the NYPD with major cases, working with Captain Thomas Gregson (Aidan Quinn) and Detective Marcus Bell (Jon Michael Hill) of the city's 11th precinct. Watson, a former surgeon, accompanies Holmes during these investigations, and her medical knowledge proves useful in solving crimes, while she displays superior analytical abilities in her own right. Once her stint as sober companion for Sherlock has ended, Watson becomes Holmes's apprentice, and the two continue their collaboration, fruitful in the professional realm, but also providing eccentric Holmes with a rare gift—an equal whom he respects and trusts.

    The series stays true to the spirit of Conan Doyle's famed character, while updating the canon for a modern audience. In addition to a female Watson and

78 ♦ **Elementary**

Lucy Liu as Joan Watson and Jonny Lee Miller as Sherlock Holmes on the streets of New York in *Elementary* **(CBS/Photofest).**

the extension of Holmes's drug use to include addiction and recovery, *Elementary* also features a female Moriarty (Natalie Dormer), Sherlock's former lover, and a transgender Ms. (Mrs.) Hudson (Candis Cayne), Sherlock's housekeeper. Despite these modern trappings, however, "the game is afoot" in *Elementary*.

See also: **Watson, Joan (*Elementary*)**

Ellerby, Mona (*Adderly*)

Secretary at International Security and Intelligence who yearns for and occasionally finds adventure.

See: *Adderly* (1986–1988, 44 episodes, Canada)

Eureka (2006–2012, 77 episodes, USA)

Created by: Andrew Cosby, Jaime Paglia
Production Co.: Universal Cable Productions, NBC Universal Television
Originally Aired: Syfy
Main Cast: Colin Ferguson, Salli Richardson-Whitfield, Joe Morton, Jordan Hinson, Ed Quinn, Erica Cerra, Neil Grayston, Niall Matter

Eureka is a fictional town in the Pacific Northwest, home to a cadre of brilliant scientists, most of whom work for Global Dynamics, a cutting-edge research facility under the aegis of the Department of Defense. While Eureka contributes technological advances to modern society, misuses of science, whether accidental or intentional, do occur (on almost a weekly basis), and someone must step in to ferret out the mysterious circumstances and clean up the mess. Town Sheriff Jack Carter (Colin Ferguson), though not a genius himself, has a knack for getting to the truth of the matter through intuition and common sense. Dr. Allison Blake (Salli Richardson-Whitfield), the liaison between GD and DOD, uses her intelligence and two PhDs to puzzle out the science of the matter. Among others assisting the sheriff and the doctor is Deputy Sheriff **Josefina "Jo" Lupo** (Erica Cerra), who goes by the book in keeping order among the eccentrics, not an easy job, especially when alternate timelines make things confusing. But this is Eureka, where thought is exalted, and problems made by the mind can be solved by the mind.

See also: **Lupo, Josefina "Jo"** (*Eureka*)

Evans, Erica (*V*)

FBI agent Erica Evans has a lot of secrets. While seemingly working to protect extraterrestrial "Visitors" from terrorist attacks in her day job, she conspires with resistance fighters and the Visitors' own Fifth Column by night to thwart the plans of evil alien leader Anna (Morena Baccarin). Erica, as portrayed by Elizabeth Mitchell, also hides the truth about the visitors' real intentions and reptilian undercarriage from everyone, including her impressionable teenage son Tyler (Logan Huffman), who is enamored with the aliens, especially Anna's pretty daughter Lisa (Laura Vandervoort). Somehow, though, Agent Evans manages to keep it all straight, juggling all her lies and lives, even going on to become the leader of the global Fifth Column in "Uneasy Lies the Head" (2011).

See also: **V** (2009–2011, 22 episodes, USA)

The Event (2010–2011, 22 episodes, USA)
Created by: Nick Wauters
Production Co.: Universal Media Studios, Steve Stark Productions
Originally Aired: NBC
Main Cast: Jason Ritter, Sarah Roemer, Laura Innes, Ian Anthony Dale, Scott Patterson, Taylor Cole, Lisa Vidal, Bill Smitrovich, Clifton Collins, Jr., Željko Ivanek, Blair Underwood

Complex SF thriller about the arrival of a small group of extraterrestrials on our planet at the end of World War II, and the political and worldwide ramifications of this secret, extending to the present day. Enter Sean Walker (Jason Ritter), an amiable everyman, who is thrust into the middle of the international conspiracy, when his girlfriend, Leila Buchanan (Sarah Roemer), is kidnapped during a Caribbean cruise. Leila's kidnapper is Vicky Roberts (Taylor Cole), a former CIA operative turned private security contractor/assassin, whose conscience leads her in unexpected directions. The small skirmishes fought by Sean and company are mirrored by big battles at the top between the extraterrestrials, led by Sophia (Laura Innes), and the U.S. government, fronted by President Elias Martinez (Blair Underwood). Sleeper extraterrestrials, double-crosses, assassination attempts, alien technology, and ever more secrets are just the tip of the iceberg for *The Event*.

Exstead, Jinny (*The Division*)
San Francisco police inspector with substance abuse issues.
See: *The Division* (2001–2004, 88 episodes, USA)

Fair, Peggy (*Mannix*)
Secretary and gal Friday for a hardboiled private detective in 60s Los Angeles.
See: *Mannix* (1967–1975, 194 episodes, USA)

Farmer, Ella (*The District*)
Washington, D.C. Police Chief Jack Mannion (Craig T. Nelson) pulls statistician Ella Farmer from her dungeon in the basement, bringing crime statistics out of the dark ages in the "District." Ella (Lynne Thigpen) isn't a detective per se, but helps track criminals and solve crimes using modern methods of computer and statistical analysis. She is also Chief Mannion's closest adviser and confidante, providing balance and perspective in a touching relationship of contrasts. Like all of the characters in the series, Ella must deal with multiple issues on the personal front—in her case, breast cancer, adoptive parenthood, and middle-aged romance.

Actress Lynne Thigpen died suddenly during filming of the third season, and Ella Farmer died with her. Ella receives full police honors at her funeral in the very moving "Ella Mae" (2003).

See also: *The District* (2000–2004, 89 episodes, USA)

Fastlane (2002–2003, 22 episodes, USA)

Created by: McG, John McNamara
Production Co.: Warner Bros. Television, 20th Century–Fox Television
Originally Aired: Fox
Main Cast: Peter Facinelli, Bill Bellamy, Tiffani Thiessen

"Everything we seize, we keep. Everything we keep, we use."

LAPD cops Van Ray (Peter Facinelli) and Deaq Hayes (Bill Bellamy) start living life in the "fastlane," when they are assigned to a special undercover unit headed by Wilhelmina "Billie" Chambers (Tiffani Thiessen). Billie runs the outfit from the "Candy Store," a secret warehouse chock-full of cool cars, glittery gadgets, and the best bling, all confiscated from bad guys and usable in future operations to bring down even more high-profile criminals. In "Ryde or Die" (2002), the boys open a hip Hollywood nightclub to lure an Ecstasy dealer, but Billie must take matters into her own hands to settle an old score dating back to her own days as a drug addict. The season-ending cliffhanger "Iced" (2003) was never resolved due to series cancellation, leaving Billie forever a kidnapped captive in a drug-induced haze.

The network needed its own Candy Store to keep this high-budget cross between *The Fast and the Furious* and *Miami Vice* going, since the flashy series never gained enough of a following to warrant the large expense.

Father Dowling Mysteries (1987–1991, 44 episodes, USA)

Based on: The novels of Ralph McInerny
Production Co.: Fred Silverman Company, Dean Hargrove Productions, Viacom Productions
Originally Aired: NBC (Season 1), ABC (Seasons 2–3)
Main Cast: Tom Bosley, Tracy Nelson, James Stephens, Mary Wickes

Father Frank Dowling (Tom Bosley) seems like a typical middle-aged parish priest in Chicago. But in between hearing confessions, saying Mass, and performing weddings, Father Frank has a startling propensity to stumble upon and solve crimes, especially murders. There is nothing typical about his partner in amateur sleuthing, Sister **Stephanie "Steve" Oskowski** (Tracy Nelson), a young nun who had a rough childhood in the neighborhood and thereby amassed an amazing array of skills, from lock-picking to mixology, from automotive repair to shooting pool. Together, Frank and Steve investigate the mysteries that fall into their laps (or pews), going wherever the clues take them,

from strip clubs to porno palaces, from dark alleys to City Hall. Long-suffering housekeeper Marie (Mary Wickes) is none too pleased with all the kerfuffle, while self-involved Father Philip Prestwick (James Stephens) manages to get in the way at every turn. But even Father Frank's evil twin brother Blaine (Tom Bosley in a dual role) is no match for these unlikely, albeit divine detectives.

See also: **Oskowski, Stephanie "Steve"** (*Father Dowling Mysteries*)

Two of TV's most unlikely amateur sleuths, Sister Steve (Tracy Nelson) and Father Dowling (Tom Bosley), in *Father Dowling Mysteries* (NBC/Photofest).

The Feather and Father Gang (1976–1977, 14 episodes, USA)

Production Co.: Columbia Pictures Television
Originally Aired: ABC
Main Cast: Stefanie Powers, Harold Gould, Lewis Charles, Frank Delfino, Monte Landis, Joan Shawlee, Edward Winter

Toni "Feather" Danton (Stefanie Powers) is a Los Angeles attorney who goes above and beyond the call of duty in defending her clients. Feather, with the help of her con-man father Harry (Harold Gould) and his band of fellow grifters, proves the guilt of the crime's true perpetrator by running an elaborate con, often obtaining an actual confession in the process. The cases/cons take Feather and Father from the arena of politics, when a senatorial candidate murders his wife, to the world of art, when a Picasso is stolen, from the realm of religion, when an evangelist kills one of his flock, to the spy game, when an operative frames his fellow spy for murder. Feather Danton has one interesting job description at the law firm of Huffaker, Danton and Binkwell.

Felsham, Jane (*Lovejoy*)

Upper-class interior designer who solves crimes with a roguish antiques dealer.

See: *Lovejoy* (1986–1994, 71 episodes, UK)

La Femme Nikita (1997–2001, 96 episodes, Canada)
Based on: The film *Nikita* directed by Luc Besson
Created by: Joel Surnow
Production Co.: Baton Broadcasting, LPN Productions, Inc., Fireworks Entertainment, Warner Bros. Television, CTV Television Network
Originally Aired: USA Network
Main Cast: Peta Wilson, Roy Dupuis, Matthew Ferguson, Don Francks, Eugene Robert Glazer, Alberta Watson

Fast-paced espionage thriller about the assignments and internal conflicts of female agent Nikita (Peta Wilson), who is recruited into antiterrorist organization Section One in exchange for freedom from a life sentence on a trumped-up murder charge. Learning that Section One is a kind of life sentence of its own, Nikita tries to retain a shred of humanity in the face of her heartless, bloody missions and the mind games of the power-hungry head of Section One, "Operations" (Eugene Robert Glazer), and his manipulative strategist Madeline (Alberta Watson). Complicating Nikita's status in section is her relationship with Michael (Roy Dupuis), her cold and taciturn handler, who later warms up to a romantic relationship with the beautiful operative. Double-crosses, murders, suicides, and sacrifices keep the plots twisting and turning until the end, when Nikita learns the secrets of her past and the promise of her future.

Ferguson, Maggie (*Detective School*)
Lingerie model studying to be a private eye.
See: *Detective School* (1979, 13 episodes, USA)

Ferrer, Adele (*Chaos*)
Deputy Director of the CIA Office of Disruptive Services.
See: *Chaos* (2011, 13 episodes, USA)

Fielding, Alex (*Wire in the Blood*)
Single mother and Detective Inspector who catches serial killers with a clinical psychologist.
See: *Wire in the Blood* (2002–2008, 31 episodes, UK)

Fisher, Phryne (*Miss Fisher's Murder Mysteries*)
Phryne Fisher (Essie Davis) is a wealthy, unconventional woman living in 1920s Melbourne, Australia, and a private detective to boot. Miss Fisher works with handsome police Inspector Jack Robinson (Nathan Page), whether Jack wants the help or not, although he grows to appreciate Phryne's unique skills, even if they aren't always legal. Phryne is usually accompanied by her shy maid/companion Dot Williams (Ashleigh Cummings), who is learning to spread her wings under the influence of her bohemian employer/friend. Dot

even tackles an undercover assignment for Miss Fisher, posing as a maid in a factory to investigate a gruesome murder in "Death by Miss Adventure" (2012). Miss Fisher does some undercover work of her own in "Murder Most Scandalous" (2013), posing as a fan dancer to discover the facts behind the death of a prostitute. The glamorous detective also solves a mystery close to home, one that has plagued her for most of her life, her little sister's childhood disappearance from a carnival. Placing her own life in jeopardy, Miss Fisher catches the culprit in "King Memses' Curse" (2012), but the outcome is a sad one, even if it does bring some closure. Still, Phryne soldiers on, sashaying through nightclubs, trafficking with communists, helping the helpless, and breathing new life into the private detective genre.

See also: *Miss Fisher's Murder Mysteries* (2012– , 26 episodes, Australia)

FlashForward (2009–2010, 22 episodes, USA)

Based on: The novel *Flashforward* by Robert J. Sawyer
Created by: Brannon Braga, David S. Goyer
Production Co.: HBO Entertainment, ABC Studios, Phantom Four Films
Originally Aired: ABC
Main Cast: Joseph Fiennes, John Cho, Jack Davenport, Zachary Knighton, Peyton List, Dominic Monaghan, Brían F. O'Byrne, Courtney B. Vance, Sonya Walger, Christine Woods

Complex, character-laden SF mystery about a brief worldwide loss of consciousness wherein (almost) everyone receives a glimpse of their lives six months into the future. The FBI is immediately on the case, trying to determine the who/what/why of the matter, with Assistant Director Stanford Wedeck (Courtney B. Vance) in charge, Mark Benford (Joseph Fiennes) as the lead agent in the field, and a bevy of associates, including Special Agent Janis Hawk (Christine Woods). Clues in the tangled scientific puzzle take the agents from their home base of Los Angeles to Somalia, where a smaller, but similar event had occurred years earlier. Janis, who becomes pregnant, has her hands full as a double (triple?) agent, infiltrating the blackout conspiracy at the behest of the CIA, while hiding that fact from the FBI in "Goodbye Yellow Brick Road" (2010). In the meantime, the team grapples with some of the personal revelations of their flashforwards, such as infidelity, alcoholism, and even death.

Fleming, Sharona (*Monk*)

Nurse and assistant to police consultant Adrian Monk, Sharona guides her boss through a world where simple things such as milk and dust can impede the detective from exercising his prodigious skills due to his long list of phobias. Bitty Schram's Sharona is not a detective per se, though she provides Monk

(Tony Shalhoub) with advice, and occasionally questions witnesses directly, as in "Mr. Monk and the Billionaire Mugger" (2002), when Monk shuts down after Sharona quits (temporarily). Sharona, unlike her successor **Natalie Teeger**, addresses Monk by his first name and practices a "tough love" approach in dealing with his neuroses. Sharona returns at the end of the series, beginning a romantic relationship with Lt. Disher (Jason Gray-Stanford) in "Mr. Monk and Sharona" (2009), with the implication in the series finale that the two will be living happily ever after together in New Jersey.

See also: *Monk* (2002–2009, 125 episodes, USA)

Fletcher, Jessica (*Murder, She Wrote*)

Maine's answer to Miss Marple, Mrs. Fletcher keenly observes the doings of her small town, which, for some unfathomable reason, involve murder on a weekly basis. A widowed mystery writer, Jessica (Angela Lansbury) uses the skills of analysis and deduction she writes about in her novels to help the Cabot Cove Sheriff's office solve cases, as in "Dead Man's Gold" (1986), when the arrival of her old beau and hints of treasure in the harbor lead to homicide. Murder magnet Jessica even manages to draw murder out of the phone when crossed wires lead to an overheard murder plot in "Crossed Up" (1987). When the scene switches to the more probable murder venue of New York in later episodes, accidental detective Jessica attracts murder from the innocent TV in "The Murder Channel" (1994), where the crossed wires this time are from a surveillance feed of a crime in the making.

While Jessica's propensity to run into homicide may seem unnatural, Angela Lansbury's genuineness and warmth in her portrayal of the character serve as a counterbalance in this long-running series and netted the actress four Golden Globe Awards.

See also: *Murder, She Wrote* (1984–1996, 264 episodes, USA)

Flores, Lina (*Against the Wall*)

Chicago Internal Affairs Detective whose partner leads a complicated life.
See: *Against the Wall* (2011, 13 episodes, USA)

Flynn, Angie (*Motive*)

Working-class homicide detective and single mother living in Vancouver.
See: *Motive* (2013– , 26 episodes, Canada)

Fogg, Rebecca (*The Secret Adventures of Jules Verne*)

British Secret Service operative during the Victorian Era.
See: *The Secret Adventures of Jules Verne* (2000, 22 episodes, UK/Canada)

Foreign Intrigue (1951–1955, 156 episodes, USA)

Production Co.: Official Films, Sheldon Reynolds TV
Originally Aired: In Syndication
Main Cast: Jerome Thor, Sydna Scott, James Daly, Anne Preville, Gerald Mohr

This syndicated series, filmed in Europe, had three different formats and casts over four seasons, and three additional titles in second-run syndication, providing an aura of mystery that the producers perhaps didn't intend. Jerome Thor and Sydna Scott star in the first two seasons, later syndicated under the title *Dateline Europe*, portraying Robert Cannon and Helen Davis, correspondents for *Consolidated News*, who specialize in busting spy rings. In "Language School" (1951), Helen tracks a group of terrorists with a biological weapon to Hamburg, when the German police refuse to take her story seriously. The gendarmerie of Lausanne, Switzerland, is more friendly to Helen, however, inviting her to expose war criminals in "Underground" (1952).

Helen and Robert depart after season two, and are replaced by two different reporters, who work for *Associated News*. In this third season, known in rerun syndication as *Overseas Adventure*, Michael Powers (James Daly) and Patricia Bennett (Anne Preville) have a penchant for running into saboteurs, who seem to be on every street corner in postwar Europe. In "Fire Bombs" (1954), Patricia searches for information to prove that seemingly unrelated fires are the work of subversive agents out to disrupt a Western aid program.

The Patricia/Michael version lasted only one season, to be followed by the final incarnation of *Foreign Intrigue*, starring Gerald Mohr and later syndicated as *Cross Current*. In this last season, Mohr portrays Christopher Storm, owner of the Hotel Frontier in Vienna, who assists hotel patrons in trouble with international criminals.

With so many operatives, saboteurs, and criminals, there must have been a European black market in trenchcoats.

Forever Knight (1992–1996, 70 episodes, Canada/West Germany)

Created by: Barney Cohen, James D. Parriott
Production Co.: Glen Warren Productions, Paragon Entertainment Corporation, Tele München Fernseh Produktionsgesellschaft, TriStar Television, USA Network
Originally Aired: CBS
Main Cast: Geraint Wyn Davies, Catherine Disher, Nigel Bennett, Ben Bass, Deborah Duchene, Blu Mankuma, Natsuko Ohama, John Kapelos, Lisa Ryder, Gary Farmer

"He was brought across in 1228, preyed on humans for their blood. Now he wants to be mortal again...."

Forever Knight is the story of vampire Nicholas Knight (Geraint Wyn Davies), an immortal full of remorse for centuries of bloodthirsty sins, who wants to make amends, and become human again. In his current incarnation, Nick is a detective for the Toronto police department, and uses his supernatural powers to solve crimes and bring evildoers to justice. He partners first with boorish Detective Don Schanke (John Kapelos), and later with police commissioner's daughter **Tracy Vetter** (Lisa Ryder), neither of whom know that Nick is a vampire. The revolving roster of precinct captains includes Amanda Cohen (Natsuko Ohama), who dies in a plane bombing along with Detective Schanke at the beginning of season three. Nick's love interest is medical examiner Dr. Natalie Lambert (Catherine Disher), constantly searching for a cure for Nick's vampirism, so their love can finally be consummated. The villain of the piece is Nick's sire Lucien LaCroix (Nigel Bennett), who tries to ensure that Nick remains in the vampire family, and urges him to embrace his animal nature. In an unusual twist, Nick's conflict appears to end tragically in series finale, "Last Knight" (1996).

See also: **Vetter, Tracy** *(Forever Knight)*

The 4400 (2004–2007, 44 episodes, USA)

Created by: René Echevarria, Scott Peters
Production Co.: American Zoetrope, Renegade 83, 4400 Productions, CBS Paramount Network Television
Originally Aired: USA Network
Main Cast: Joel Gretsch, Jacqueline McKenzie, Mahershalalhashbaz Ali, Laura Allen, Patrick Flueger, Megalyn Echikunwoke, Chad Faust, Kaj-Erik Eriksen, Samantha Ferris, Jenni Baird, Brooke Nevin, Conchita Campbell, Karina Lombard, Bill Campbell, Peter Coyote

SF thriller about the return to Earth of 4400 people who had disappeared inexplicably in the years since World War II. The returnees suddenly appear near Mount Rainier in Washington state, and The National Threat Assessment Command (NTAC) investigates the circumstances surrounding the abduction and reappearance of the 4400. Lead agents Tom Baldwin (Joel Gretsch) and **Diana Skouris** (Jacqueline McKenzie) interview and track returnees, but their task is made more difficult when members of the 4400 begin to manifest special abilities such as telekinesis, healing powers, enhanced strength and precognition. Work intersects with family for both agents, since Tom's son Kyle (Chad Faust) is a 4400, and Diana adopts Maia (Conchita Campbell), a returnee child with the ability to predict the future. Factions within the U.S. government and among the 4400 press their agendas, sometimes with violence, ensuring that Tom and Diana will have their loyalties tested within the new world order.

See also: **Skouris, Diana** *(The 4400)*

Franco, Nikki *(V.I.P.)*

Weapons and explosives expert working for a personal protection firm.
See: **V.I.P.** (1998–2002, 88 episodes, USA/Germany)

French, Eve (*Charlie's Angels*)

Former street racer turned private detective working for a reclusive millionaire.

See: *Charlie's Angels* (2011, 8 episodes, USA)

Fringe (2008–2013, 100 episodes, USA)

Created by: J.J. Abrams, Alex Kurtzman, Roberto Orci
Production Co.: Bad Robot Productions, Warner Bros. Television, Fringe Element Films
Originally Aired: Fox
Main Cast: Anna Torv, Joshua Jackson, John Noble, Jasika Nicole, Lance Reddick, Blair Brown, Kirk Acevedo, Seth Gabel, Mark Valley

Science fiction drama about a Joint Federal Task Force known as the Fringe Division, which investigates weird science and unexplained phenomena a là *The X-Files*. Leading the way for the government is Olivia Dunham (Anna Torv), an FBI agent who is well suited to her assignment, given that she has special abilities gained from an experimental chemical administered to her as a child. Among other powers, Olivia is able to discern when an object originates in a parallel universe, a handy talent when an alternate dimension causes problems (as often happens). Olivia works with Dr. Walter Bishop (John Noble), a researcher on the hinterlands of science, who was institutionalized for many years, making him the "mad scientist" of the piece. Olivia recruits Walter's estranged son, Peter Bishop (Joshua Jackson), to work with his father, although, like any family, they have their problems, such as the fact that Walter kidnapped Peter from the alternate universe, when his own Peter had died (as often happens). The principals do what they can to diminish the interdimensional confusion of alternate characters and storylines by giving clever names to their doppelgängers, such as "Fauxlivia" for Olivia and "Walternate" for Walter. It turns out that Olivia and the boys are fighting for nothing less than the world as we know it, in this intricate, mythology-rich series, where past is future is past.

Frost, Annie (*Chase*)

U.S. Deputy Marshal, part of a fugitive apprehension team based in Houston.

See: *Chase* (2010–2011, 18 episodes, USA)

Gale, Cathy (*The Avengers*)

Dr. Cathy Gale, anthropologist, finds herself in the unlikely role of amateur operative when she assists secret agent John Steed (Patrick Macnee) on a case in "Mr. Teddy Bear" (1962). As portrayed by Honor Blackman, Cathy is smart, independent, assertive, and adept at hand-to-hand combat, whether attired in street clothes or her signature black leather suit and boots. She and Steed handle some strange cases, such as the "Death of the Great Dane" (1962), wherein a dead millionaire turns up in a burial plot at a pet cemetery. Cathy distinguishes herself from a trio of talented amateurs, going on to become Steed's regular partner in "Brief for Murder" (1963). All good things must come to an end, however, and Cathy departs after "Lobster Quadrille" (1964), having blazed a trail that other female spies, including her successor, **Emma Peel**, will follow.

See also: *The Avengers* (1961–1969, 161 episodes, UK)

The Gallery of Madame Liu-Tsong (1951, 10 episodes, USA)

Production Co.: DuMont Television Network
Originally Aired: DuMont
Main Cast: Anna May Wong

Anna May Wong stars as Madame Liu-Tsong, owner of a gallery specializing in Chinese art. In the course of her business dealings, Liu-Tsong becomes involved in mystery and foreign intrigue.

Unfortunately for modern audiences, no episodes of this groundbreaking series, which was broadcast on the DuMont Television Network, are known to exist anywhere today. Titles include, "The House of Quiet Dignity," "Shadow of the Sun God," and "The Golden Women." A lost treasure of early television.

Garcia, Penelope (*Criminal Minds*)

Technical Analyst and expert on bright colors for the FBI's Behavioral Analysis Unit.

See: *Criminal Minds* (2005– , 209 episodes, USA)

Garrett, Kelly (*Charlie's Angels*)

Jaclyn Smith portrays Kelly Garrett, one of three beautiful private investigators who work for wealthy, but unseen Charles Townsend (voiced by John Forsythe) in a plush Los Angeles office. Like the other "Angels," Kelly goes undercover to help clients in need, posing as a dancer, motorcycle stunt rider, prostitute and even an extraterrestrial in "Unidentified Flying Angels" (1977). She overcomes her difficult childhood as an abused orphan to face the dangers of her job courageously, surviving explosions, gunshot wounds, kidnappings, and in "Avenging Angel" (1979), forced heroin addiction. Kelly is the Angel of longest tenure, outlasting Jill (Farrah Fawcett), Sabrina (Kate Jackson), and the others to remain with Charlie from start to finish. She is truly Charlie's Angel.

See also: *Charlie's Angels* (1976–1981, 110 episodes, USA)

Germont, Gabrielle (*Counterstrike*)

French investigative reporter working as a private operative to fight international crime.

See: *Counterstrike* (1990–1993, 66 episodes, Canada/France/USA)

Get Christie Love! (1974–1975, 22 episodes, USA)

Based on: The novel *The Ledger* by Dorothy Uhnak
Production Co.: Universal TV, Wolper Productions
Originally Aired: ABC
Main Cast: Teresa Graves, Charles Cioffi, Jack Kelly

Influenced by "blaxploitation" film heroines of the era, such as *Cleopatra Jones* (1973), Christie Love (Teresa Graves) is the first African American female undercover cop on the LAPD. Christie poses as a heroin dealer, jewel thief, counterfeiter, flight attendant—whatever it takes to bring down the bad guys. Although Lieutenant Matthew Reardon (Charles Cioffi) urges her to be cautious, Christie is not one to wait for backup, relying upon her prodigious karate skills, and, when all else fails, a hefty swing of her giant handbag.

Alas, the groundbreaking nature of this series was not enough to prompt its renewal for a second season, but Christie will always be remembered for her faux-sweet declaration to her collars, "You're under arrest, Sugah!"

Get Smart (1965–1970, 138 episodes, USA)

Created by: Mel Brooks, Buck Henry
Production Co.: Talent Associates, CBS Productions (1969–1970)
Originally Aired: NBC (1965–1969), CBS (1969–1970)
Main Cast: Don Adams, Barbara Feldon, Edward Platt, Robert Karvelas

Maxwell Smart, Agent 86, works for CONTROL, a secret U.S. counterintelligence agency based in our nation's capital. While 86 (Don Adams) is a top agent, his success is based mostly upon accident, coincidence, dumb luck, and the skill of his partner, **Agent 99** (Barbara Feldon). Supervising the bumbling Smart is the long-suffering "Chief" of CONTROL (Edward Platt), whose office "Cone of Silence" serves only to hinder his communications with Max, while broadcasting them to the outside world. As the enemy of control is chaos, so the nemesis of CONTROL is KAOS, an international organization of evil, frequently fronted by the German-accented Siegfried (Bernie Kopell). Smart and 99 thwart the aspirations of KAOS and other evildoers with the help of a motley crew of fellow agents, including Hymie, the robot, (Richard Gautier) and Fang, the dog. Just a few of the pleasures of this innovative comedy series include the classic opening-title sequence with the automated underground doors, Max's "shoe-phone," and the many catchphrases, especially, "Sorry about that, Chief."

A short-lived sequel of the same title appeared in 1995, with Adams and Feldon reprising their roles as Smart and 99, but it lasted only seven episodes. As Smart would say, "Missed it by *that* much."

See also: **Agent 99 (*Get Smart*)**

Girard, Sylvie (*Sweating Bullets*)

Travel agent turned private detective in a Florida resort town.

See: *Sweating Bullets* (1991–1993, 66 episodes, Canada)

The Girl from U.N.C.L.E. (1966–1967, 29 episodes, USA)

Created by: Norman Felton
Production Co.: Arena Productions, MGM Television
Originally Aired: NBC
Main Cast: Stefanie Powers, Noel Harrison, Leo G. Carroll

Spoofy spy spinoff from *The Man from U.N.C.L.E.*, starring Stefanie Powers as "The Girl," a.k.a. April Dancer, an agent for The United Network Command for Law and Enforcement. April, along with partner Mark Slate (Noel Harrison), travels the globe battling the evil organization THRUSH and other enemies of good. Under the command of chief Alexander Waverly (Leo G. Carroll), April carries a purse full of gadgets and wears the latest mod fashions, while never engaging in much gunplay or fisticuffs, although she can call upon martial arts skills when needed. The tone of the episodes is broad, occasionally hitting farcical high notes, as in "The Mother Muffin Affair" (1966), with an in-drag Boris Karloff as the villainous Mother Muffin, who moons over her enemy Napoleon Solo (guest star Robert Vaughn), while despising April for her youth and proximity to the man from U.N.C.L.E. "The Atlantis Affair" (1966) finds April and Mark searching for a gateway to the famed lost continent in an episode penned by legendary SF/horror writer Richard Matheson. But many of the episodes slide into sheer silliness, dissipating the obvious potential of this spy-fi series.

Glenanne, Fiona (*Burn Notice*)

"Should we shoot them?"

Sultry Fiona Glenanne (Gabrielle Anwar) likes to shoot first and ask questions later. A former operative for the Irish Republican Army, Fiona now resides in Miami, where she helps ex-boyfriend Michael Westen (Jeffrey Donovan) in his new job as a private investigator/fixer, while Michael searches for clues as to why he was "burned" (discredited) by his CIA employers. In addition to being proficient with guns, Fiona is a precision driver, a specialist in hand-to-hand combat, and an expert in explosives, skills which she practices with high style and verve. She also enjoys freelance work, engaging in arms dealing and bounty hunting when the spirit moves her (or the price is right). Fiona has a stormy "can't live with him, can't live without him" romantic relationship with Michael, but their fates appear to be intertwined in series finale "Reckoning" (2013).

See also: *Burn Notice* (2007–2013, 111 episodes, USA)

Glynis (1963, 13 episodes, USA)

Created by: Jess Oppenheimer
Production Co.: Desilu Productions
Originally Aired: CBS
Main Cast: Glynis Johns, Keith Andes, George Mathews

Comedy series starring Glynis Johns as Glynis Granville, a mystery writer with a penchant for solving real-life crimes. Assisting Glynis in amateur sleuthing is Chick Rogers (George Mathews), a retired police officer and the Granvilles' building superintendent, who, with Glynis, has an infallible nose for trouble. Together they stumble upon crimes or attempt to help in the cases of Glynis's criminal defense attorney husband, Keith Granville (Keith Andes), whether Keith wants the help or not. From posing as a socialite to snare a jewel thief in "Crime after a Fashion" (1963) to dealing with Keith's client, a cat who's inherited a fortune in "Catsa Nostra" (1963), Glynis and her active imagination are always on the case.

The Good Witch of Laurel Canyon

See: *Tucker's Witch* (1982–1983, 12 episodes, USA)

Gordon, Barbara (*Batman*)

A librarian who dons the cowl to help Batman and Robin fight crime.
See: *Batman* (1966–1968, 120 episodes, USA)

Gordon, Barbara (*Birds of Prey*)

Former caped crusader, now paralyzed, who still fights crime via computer.
See: *Birds of Prey* (2002–2003, 13 episodes, USA)

Graceland (2013– , 25 episodes, USA)

Created by: Jeff Eastin
Production Co.: Jeff Eastin & Warrior George Productions, Fox Television Studios
Originally Aired: USA Network
Main Cast: Daniel Sunjata, Aaron Tveit, Brandon Jay McLaren, Vanessa Ferlito, Manny Montana, Serinda Swan

A group of undercover agents from the FBI, DEA, and ICE share a confiscated Southern California beach house known as "Graceland" in this slick, summer series. Daniel Sunjata leads the way as FBI agent Paul Briggs, whose prior assignment included a different house full of agents, all of whom died in a mysterious fire. Briggs is the training officer for rookie FBI agent Mike Warren (Aaron Tveit), another Graceland resident, who is secretly investigating Briggs for his part, if any, in the deadly fire. Briggs has an on-again, off-again romantic relationship with FBI agent Catherine "Charlie" DeMarco (Vanessa Ferlito), the group's undercover ace, who can blend into any environment, from the Venice boardwalk to Rodeo Drive. The DEA's contribution to Graceland's agency alphabet soup is Paige Arkin (Serinda Swan), a tough, but sexy (what a surprise) agent, who is attracted to rookie Mike. Along with Dale Jakes (Brandon Jay McLaren) of ICE and Joe "Johnny" Tuturro (Manny Montana) of the FBI, the team chases drug dealers, crime bosses, and weapons suppliers, while trying to ensure that their make-believe personas don't slowly erode who they really are. It's not a day at the beach.

Granger, Hildy (*She's the Sheriff*)
Widow who replaces her late husband as a sheriff in Nevada.
See: *She's the Sheriff* (1987–1989, 44 episodes, USA)

Granville, Glynis (*Glynis*)
Mystery writer with a penchant for solving real-life crimes.
See: *Glynis* (1963, 13 episodes, USA)

Gray, Cordelia (*An Unsuitable Job for a Woman*)
Apprentice investigator who inherits a floundering detective agency from her boss.
See: *An Unsuitable Job for a Woman* (1997–2001, 9 episodes, UK/USA)

Gray, Susan (*The Bletchley Circle*)
Housewife and former Bletchley Park code-breaker drawn to the patterns in crimes.
See: *The Bletchley Circle* (2012–2014, 7 episodes, UK)

Greggs, Shakima "Kima" (*The Wire*)
Baltimore detective working a major drug investigation and trying to placate a worried girlfriend.
See: *The Wire* (2002–2008, 60 episodes, USA)

Hall, Glenn (*Snoops*)
Head of a Los Angeles detective agency known for its sexy operatives.
See: *Snoops* (1999, 13 episodes, USA)

Hamilton, Holly (*Mystery Girls*)

Former television detective turned real-life private investigator in Beverly Hills.

See: *Mystery Girls* (2014, 10 episodes, USA)

Hanadarko, Grace (*Saving Grace*)

Oklahoma City police detective whose bad behavior brings her in contact with an angel.

See: *Saving Grace* (2007–2010, 46 episodes, USA)

The Hardy Boys/Nancy Drew Mysteries (1977–1979, 46 episodes, USA)

Based on: The novels of Franklin W. Dixon (*The Hardy Boys*) and Carolyn Keene (*Nancy Drew Mystery Stories*)
Created by: Edward Stratemeyer
Production Co.: Glen A. Larson Productions, Universal TV
Originally Aired: ABC
Main Cast: Shaun Cassidy, Parker Stevenson, Pamela Sue Martin, William Schallert, Janet Louise Johnson

Teen mystery adventure which begins as two separate series sharing a title, later combines casts from both series for crossover episodes, and finally drops Nancy Drew altogether to become simply *The Hardy Boys*. Shaun Cassidy and Parker Stevenson star as amateur sleuths and well-coiffed brothers, Joe and Frank Hardy, while Pamela Sue Martin is Nancy Drew, part-time investigator and independent-minded daughter of attorney Carson Drew (William Schallert). All three are quintessential 70s kids except that they have a high aptitude for solving crimes and a propensity to run into spooky happenings. In "A Haunting We Will Go" (1977), Nancy and her friends revive a 20-year-old play but must contend with a theater that may be haunted. The boys join forces with Nancy in "The Mystery of the Hollywood Phantom" (parts one and two, 1977), when detectives begin to go missing during a Hollywood studio tour. Janet Louise Johnson replaces Pamela Sue Martin for the last four Nancy Drew episodes, appropriate for a series with identity issues from the start.

Hart, Jennifer (*Hart to Hart*)

Stefanie Powers stars as Jennifer Hart, a glamorous freelance journalist who just happens to be married to a millionaire. Jennifer and her husband, Jonathan (Robert Wagner), are inseparable, and along with their butler/chauffeur/friend Max (Lionel Stander) and pet pooch Freeway, have a penchant for finding murder wherever they go. In "Downhill to Death" (1980), Jennifer overhears a murder plot, and her plan to prevent the crime whisks the couple to snowy Vail for one of the most visually stunning entries in the series. Jennifer's resemblance to an ancient Egyptian princess (as happens often) leads to murder at the museum and possible entombment for Jennifer in "Murder Wrap" (1981). When a psychotic man dumps dangerous chemicals into their pool, Jennifer's quick action saves Jonathan's eyesight in "Hart of Darkness" (1981), showing that Mrs. H., in addition to being gorgeous, is smart, capable, and graceful under pressure.

See also: *Hart to Hart* (1979–1984, 110 episodes, USA)

Hart to Hart (1979–1984, 110 episodes, USA)

Created by: Sidney Sheldon
Production Co.: Columbia Pictures Television, Rona II, Spelling-Goldberg Productions
Originally Aired: ABC
Main Cast: Robert Wagner, Stefanie Powers, Lionel Stander

"When they met, it was murder."

Butler, chauffeur, and friend Max (Lionel Stander) rasps those words each week, introducing Jonathan and **Jennifer Hart**, putting viewers on notice that wherever the globetrotting duo goes, murder will follow. Jonathan (Robert Wagner), a self-made millionaire, and Jennifer (Stefanie Powers), a sometimes freelance journalist, attend museum openings, take luxury cruises, hit the slopes, and frequent charity galas, all the while stumbling upon murder in true amateur sleuth fashion. The Harts are gorgeous, their clothes are gorgeous, their house is gorgeous—everything is gorgeous with the possible exception of Max, who has a gorgeous (if crusty) soul. While solving crimes and dodging danger, the Harts maintain a playful, sexy, loving relationship, brought to life by the scintillating chemistry between Wagner and Powers. The sparks between the leads, in fact, are the truly exceptional aspect of this light mystery series.

See also: **Hart, Jennifer** (*Hart to Hart*)

Haven (2010– , 52 episodes, USA/Canada)

Based on: The novel *The Colorado Kid* by Stephen King
Created by: Jim Dunn, Sam Ernst
Production Co.: Entertainment One, Big Motion Pictures Productions, Piller Segan Shepherd, Universal Networks International
Originally Aired: Syfy
Main Cast: Emily Rose, Lucas Bryant, Eric Balfour, Richard Donat, John Dunsworth

When FBI Agent Audrey Parker (Emily Rose) chases an escaped prisoner to the picturesque, seaside town of Haven, Maine, little does she know that her life is about to change forever. It turns out that Haven is home not only to the fishing industry, but also to "The Troubles," psychic and supernatural powers that manifest in a large group of the townspeople every few decades, usually causing, well, troubles. It also turns out that Parker possesses the ability to help those who are "troubled," so she stays in Haven, joining the local police department. There she can also investigate her own murky past, when a photo surfaces of her look-alike mother, whom she had never known. It further turns out that the photo may actually be of Audrey herself, who has not aged over the decades, hinting that her memory has somehow been erased. All of this is just the tip of the iceberg, as information about cyclical meteor storms, time travel, and an alternate world is revealed. Helping Audrey sort through these exotic mysteries are two handsome hunks, who are also rivals for her affection. Nathan Wuornos (Lucas Bryant), Audrey's detective partner, has no sense of touch due to The Troubles, but is able to feel Audrey, giving them a unique connection. Duke Crocker (Eric Balfour), a suspected smuggler and charming bad boy, learns via an old diary that his late father wanted him to kill Audrey, but even Duke isn't that bad.

Obviously Haven, despite its name and its breathtaking beauty (the series is actually filmed in Nova Scotia), should not be your destination for a quiet vacation.

Havers, Barbara (*The Inspector Lynley Mysteries*)
Working-class New Scotland Yard detective with an aristocratic partner. See: ***The Inspector Lynley Mysteries* (2001–2008, 23 episodes, UK)**

Hawaii Five-0 (2010– , 93 episodes, USA)
Based on: The TV series *Hawaii Five-O* created by Leonard Freeman
Production Co.: Kurtzman Orci Paper Products, CBS Productions, 101st Street Television
Originally Aired: CBS
Main Cast: Alex O'Loughlin, Scott Caan, Daniel Dae Kim, Grace Park, Lauren German

A reimagining of the classic 60s series that ran on CBS for 12 seasons with Jack Lord. In the reboot, Alex O'Loughlin is Steve McGarrett, now a Lieutenant Commander in the U.S. Navy Reserve, called upon by Hawaii's governor to head a small task force devoted to solving major crimes. McGarrett chooses Danny "Danno" Williams (Scott Caan) as his partner, a recent transplant from New Jersey who sticks out like a sore thumb on the laid-back islands. Backing up the high-octane pair is Chin Ho Kelly (Daniel Dae Kim), a disgraced former member of the Honolulu Police Department, who is later reinstated and cleared of corruption charges. Kelly's cousin, Kono Kalakaua (Grace Park), another member of McGarrett's unit, leaves behind her career as a professional surfer to become a rookie with the HPD. Park's slim, athletic character is in stark contrast to the burly, male Kono of the original series, portrayed by Hawaiian actor Zulu. Together, the Five-0 team battles kidnappers, terrorists, killers and especially master criminal Wo Fat (Mark Dacascos), who seems to have a hand in every illegal activity on the islands. They also help McGarrett search for his father's killer, and arch-nemesis Wo Fat may be behind the murder. Sprinkle in political assassinations, the Japanese Yakuza, corrupt officials, undercover operatives, and a few surprises out of the past, and you have *Hawaii Five-0*.

If you're looking for a relaxing Island breeze, you're in the wrong place.

Hawaiian Eye (1959–1963, 134 episodes, USA)
Created by: Roy Huggins
Production Co.: Warner Bros. Television
Originally Aired: ABC
Main Cast: Anthony Eisley, Robert Conrad, Connie Stevens, Poncie Ponce, Grant Williams, Troy Donahue

Tom Lopaka (Robert Conrad) and Tracy Steele (Anthony Eisley) are partners in a Honolulu detective agency known as Hawaiian Eye, which they operate from posh surroundings at the Hawaiian Village Hotel. Helping the "eyes" to investigate tropical mysteries and provide security for the hotel are two colorful characters, Kazuo "Kim" (Poncie Ponce), a cab driver with helpful relatives spread throughout the islands, and Chryseis "Cricket" Blake (Connie Stevens), a photographer and singer at the hotel.

Cricket, a graduate of the oft-attended beach bimbo school of the early 60s, nonetheless manages to make herself useful during the boys' investigations. In "Blackmail in Satin" (1962), Cricket goes undercover as a photographer, working with new agency partner Greg MacKenzie (Grant Williams), who poses as a writer, to look into a woman's large payments to a suspicious stranger. Cricket accepts an undercover assignment again, this time as a hula-skirted greeter at the airport, placing herself in jeopardy to help foil a smuggling operation in "Aloha, Cricket" (1962).

Sometimes characters from ABC's hit series *77 Sunset Strip*, such as Stu Bailey (Efrem Zimbalist, Jr.), crossed over to *Hawaiian Eye* for brief appearances. The most famous juxtaposition of actors from the two series, however, came in the musical realm, when Edd Byrnes, alias parking valet "Kookie" from the Strip, paired with Connie Stevens for the pop hit "Kookie, Kookie, Lend Me Your Comb" in 1959. That's ginchy, Dad.

Hawk, Janis (*FlashForward*)
FBI agent investigating a brief, worldwide loss of consciousness.
See: *FlashForward* (2009–2010, 22 episodes, USA)

Hayden, Jessie (*Jessie*)
Psychiatrist who uses her medical training to assist law enforcement in Southern California.
See: *Jessie* (1984, 10 episodes, USA)

Hayes, Maddie (*Moonlighting*)

A reversal of fortune propels sophisticated ex-model Maddie Hayes (Cybill Shepherd) into an unlikely partnership with fast-talking P. I. David Addison (Bruce Willis) in the City of Angels. Along with rhyming receptionist Ms. DiPesto (Allyce Beasley) and an office full of people who never have anything to do, they become Blue Moon Investigations. Maddie and David never see eye to eye on anything, filtering clues, decisions, and observations through their respective feminist and guy's points of view. This disparity is especially clear in "The Dream Sequence Always Rings Twice" (1985), an evocative homage to film noir, in which Maddie and David each dream their solutions (in black and white) to a 1940s murder, where Maddie favors a man as the killer, and David a woman. The battle of the sexes continues in *Moonlighting's* most famous episode, "Atomic Shakespeare" (1986), a fantasy send-up of Shakespeare's *The Taming of the Shrew*, with Shepherd and Willis as embattled (and anachronistic) spouses Kate and Petruchio. While Maddie and David actually solve a case from time to time, the focus is often on romantic tension, which finds some resolution in "I Am Curious.... Maddie" (1987).

See also: ***Moonlighting* (1985–1989, 66 episodes, USA)**

Henson, Angela (*Angela's Eyes*)

FBI agent who can accurately detect when people are telling lies.
See: ***Angela's Eyes* (2006, 13 episodes, USA)**

Hetty Wainthropp Investigates (1996–1998, 27 episodes, UK)

Based on: The novel *Missing Persons* by David Cook
Production Co.: BBC
Originally Aired: Public Television
Main Cast: Patricia Routledge, Derek Benfield, Dominic Monaghan, John Graham Davies

The sleuthing life begins at 60 for Hetty Wainthropp (Patricia Routledge), who takes a job at the local Lancashire post office, but finds mystery more intriguing than mail. With her new calling, Hetty opens a private detective agency, although her retired husband (Derek Benfield) thinks she should be taking it easy with him. Hetty recruits down-on-his-luck teenager Geoffrey Shawcross (Dominic Monaghan) as her assistant and sidekick, and off they go, hunting bad guys on cases which have fallen off the police radar. In due course they are flushing out arsonists, searching for missing persons, and investigating organ trafficking. "Super Gran Sleuth" Hetty shows that you can be a gumshoe in sensible pumps.

Highlander: The Raven (1998–1999, 22 episodes, France/Canada)
Based on: A character from *Highlander: The Series*
Production Co.: Gaumont Television, Fireworks Entertainment, Davis-Panzer Productions, Chum Television, et al.
Originally Aired: In Syndication
Main Cast: Elizabeth Gracen, Paul Johansson

Short-lived spinoff from *Highlander: The Series*, starring Elizabeth Gracen as immortal Amanda, a 1200-year-old thief who, like others of her kind, can die only if she is beheaded. Amanda's daring capers bring her to the attention of Detective Nick Wolfe (Paul Johansson), who later leaves the police force for private security work and learns of Amanda's immortality. Together, they battle evil immortals, help the helpless, solve crimes, and deal with ghosts from Amanda's past, while keeping the secrets of immortality safe. Amanda's talent for grand larceny proves useful along the way, as in "Immunity" (1998), when she and Nick attempt to steal documents from an embassy. But her amazing propensity to run into vengeful immortals does tend to slow them down, and she has a surprise in store for Nick, who has been poisoned by one of her immortal enemies, in series finale, "Dead on Arrival" (1999).

Hill Street Blues (1981–1987, 146 episodes, USA)
Created by: Steven Bochco, Michael Kozoll
Production Co.: MTM Enterprises, 20th Century–Fox Television
Originally Aired: NBC
Main Cast: Daniel J. Travanti, Veronica Hamel, Michael Conrad, Bruce Weitz, Joe Spano, Charles Haid, Michael Warren, James B. Sikking, Betty Thomas, Kiel Martin, Taurean Blacque, Rene Enriquez, Barbara Bosson

"Let's be careful out there."
Groundbreaking and award-winning police drama about the lives (and sometimes loves) of the detectives and officers of a single inner-city police precinct. The large ensemble cast is led by Daniel J. Travanti as Captain Frank Furillo, who presides over the barely controlled chaos that is his precinct house, while pursuing a romance with public defender Joyce Davenport (Veronica Hamel) and managing requests from ex-wife Fay (Barbara Bosson). Gangs are a particular problem in this corner of the (unnamed) city, and beat cops, such as Bobby Hill (Michael Warren) and Lucille Bates (Betty Thomas) must contend with violence, turf wars, drug deals, and all manner of unsavoriness. Yet there is room for growth even here, and an inexperienced rookie like Lucy can move on to become a sergeant, and a gang leader like Jesus Martinez (Trinidad Silva) can go on to become a paralegal.
That's life on the Hill.

Hoffs, Judy (*21 Jump Street*)

Judy Hoffs (Holly Robinson) is assigned to a special police unit at 21 Jump Street, whose youthful-looking members go undercover at high schools, colleges, and local hangouts to catch both adolescent wrongdoers and those who prey upon the young. Judy works in an office full of men, including Tom Hanson (Johnny Depp), Doug Penhall (Peter DeLuise), and Captain Adam Fuller (Steven Williams), but holds her own among the boys with her intelligence and professionalism. She brings sensitivity and empathy to her work with troubled teens, as in "16 Blown to 35" (1987), when she jeopardizes her job by destroying evidence, a pornographic film, rather than ruining a girl's life. In "The Worst Night of Your Life" (1987), Judy befriends both "the wild girl" and "the plain girl" while undercover at a Catholic girls' school, not knowing which is responsible for a recent rash of arsons. Judy remains with the unit even after all the original members, including Hanson (Depp) have moved on to better things. Hoffs/Robinson also sings the *21 Jump Street* theme song. A trooper in every sense of the word.

See also: *21 Jump Street* (1987–1991, 103 episodes, USA)

Holiday (*Secret Agent Man*)

Beautiful, but no-nonsense operative for the mysterious "Agency."
See: *Secret Agent Man* (2000, 12 episodes, USA)

Holland, Cassie (*Cassie & Co.*)

Sassy cop turned private investigator in the City of Angels.
See: *Cassie & Co.* (1982, 13 episodes, USA)

Holliday, Dawn "Holli" (*One West Waikiki*)

State of Hawaii's Medical Examiner, who solves crimes with a hunky cop.
See: *One West Waikiki* (1994–1996, 20 episodes, USA)

Holmes, Shirley (*The Adventures of Shirley Holmes, Detective*)

Amateur sleuth and 12-year-old great-grandniece of Sherlock Holmes.
See: *The Adventures of Shirley Holmes, Detective* (1997–2000, 52 episodes, Canada)

Holt, Laura (*Remington Steele*)

"Try this for a deep, dark secret. The great detective Remington Steele? He doesn't exist. I invented him."

Private investigator Laura Holt, a modern woman of the early 80s, inhabits a world where clients don't take female detectives seriously, so she invents a male superior, Remington Steele, puts his name on her agency and goes to work. A quick kink in the plan develops, however, when a suave and mysterious man (Pierce Brosnan) appears, assuming Remington Steele's identity in series opener "License to Steele" (1982). Laura (Stephanie Zimbalist) begins a precarious business relationship with this charming rogue, trying not to mix business with pleasure, ever the conscientious, efficient professional. In the new arrangement, Laura does the legwork, while Mr. Steele serves as the flashy front man, although a true partnership begins to develop as Laura teaches Steele the tricks of the detective trade. Hints of staid Laura's wilder past surface in "Vintage Steele" (1983), when Laura runs across a former lover and his rowdy business associates while investigating a murder at a winery. She continues to assess and battle her feelings for Mr. Steele, while the glamorous duo pursues exciting cases in Mexico, Malta, England, and Ireland. Hints of a happy ending for the two spark the series finale, "Steeled with a Kiss–Part 2" (1987), but Laura stays true to herself until the very end, requiring honesty, respect, and trust before she'll give her heart away.

Laura Holt remains one of TV's most revered female detectives, a role model for professional women at a time when the concept was new both on television and in the world.

See also: *Remington Steele* (1982–1987, 94 episodes, USA)

Homeland (2011– , 36 episodes, USA)

Based on: The TV series *Prisoners of War* created by Gideon Raff
Created by: Alex Gansa, Howard Gordon
Production Co.: Teakwood Lane Productions, Fox 21 Television Studios, Keshet Media Group, Cherry Pie Productions, Showtime Networks
Originally Aired: Showtime
Main Cast: Claire Danes, Damian Lewis, Morena Baccarin, David Harewood, Diego Klattenhoff, Jackson Pace, Morgan Saylor, Mandy Patinkin, Rupert Friend, Tracy Letts

Claire Danes stars as Carrie Mathison, a brilliant, but troubled CIA agent, who struggles to cope with bipolar disorder, while working in a complex, demanding, and sometimes dangerous profession. When Nicholas Brody (Damian Lewis), a U.S. Marine sergeant, is rescued after eight years of captivity in Iraq, Carrie suspects that he has been turned into a sleeper agent by Al Qaeda. Since she has no real evidence against Brody, Carrie begins her own personal investigation, making contact with Brody, and eventually entering into a sexual relationship with him. This is all the tip of the iceberg, of course, as Carrie is discredited, dismissed, and reinstated, while receiving some electroconvulsive therapy for her condition in between. Meanwhile, Brody aborts his planned terrorist attack, but helps to kill Vice President William Walden (Jamey Sheridan), although he gains an unexpected protector in Carrie after their romance is reignited. More twists and turns, both personal and professional, ensue in this espionage thriller, which has netted Claire Danes two Emmy Awards and two Golden Globes for her lead performance.

Although *Homeland* has received numerous such accolades, including a Peabody Award in 2011, it is not without its detractors, and has been criticized in venues such as *Salon* and *The Guardian* for biased depictions of Muslims. Whatever your viewpoint, it's clear we've come a long way from *The Girl from U.N.C.L.E.*

Honey West (1965–1966, 30 episodes, USA)
Based on: The novels of G.G. Fickling
Created by: Gwen Bagni, Paul Dubov
Production Co.: Four Star Television
Originally Aired: ABC
Main Cast: Anne Francis, John Ericson, Irene Hervey

Ahead-of-its-time crime/action series starring Anne Francis as **Honey West**, proprietor of her own detective agency and a woman who uses her wits, courage, sex appeal, and martial arts skills in whatever combination necessary to get the job done. "The company" in Honey West & Co. is hotheaded, but devoted Sam Bolt (John Ericson), who furnishes Honey with an array of gadgets, including walkie-talkie sunglasses, teargas earrings, and an exploding compact. Honey's life is frequently in jeopardy, and, while Sam rushes to the rescue, cool-as-a-cucumber Honey is never a damsel in distress, always giving the bad guys as good as she gets. Honey's life is her work, although in her infrequent spare time, she enjoys chatting with Aunt Meg (Irene Hervey) and wrestling with her pet ocelot, Bruce (himself).

See also: **West, Honey (*Honey West*)**

Hudson, Kate (*Dear Detective*)
Head of a police homicide unit, who juggles single motherhood and the dating scene.
See: ***Dear Detective*** (1979, 4 episodes, USA)

Hunted (2012, 8 episodes, UK)
Created by: Frank Spotnitz
Production Co.: Kudos Film and Television, Big Light Productions, BBC
Originally Aired: Cinemax
Main Cast: Melissa George, Adam Rayner, Stephen Dillane, Stephen Campbell Moore, Adewale Akinnuoye-Agbaje, Morven Christie, Lex Shrapnel, Oscar Kennedy, Patrick Malahide

Sam Hunter (Melissa George), an elite operative for private security firm Byzantium, is ambushed and wounded while executing a mission in Tangiers. A now-recovered Sam suddenly reappears at work one year later, asking for her job back and determined to find out if someone at Byzantium is a traitor. Her new assignment is to infiltrate the home of rich bad guy Jack Turner (Patrick Malahide), which she accomplishes by saving his grandson from a mock kidnapping and becoming the boy's tutor. As multinational corporate conspiracies swirl around her, Sam continues to protect the boy while learning that the key to her betrayal resides in a tragic incident from her past.

Hunter (1977, 12 episodes, USA)

Created by: William Blinn
Production Co.: Lorimar Productions
Originally Aired: CBS
Main Cast: James Franciscus, Linda Evans, Ralph Bellamy

James Franciscus portrays James Hunter, a Santa Barbara bookstore owner, who doubles as a spy for a top-secret U.S. agency. Linda Evans is Marty Shaw, an operative who works with Jim, using her high-fashion modeling career as a cover for her espionage activities. The good-looking pair receives their assignments from General Howard Baker (Ralph Bellamy), who sets them on the trail of assassins, rogue agents, and terrorist groups. In the "Lysenko Syndrome," a brainwashing plot puts the duo in jeopardy, when Hunter is presumed dead and Marty is programmed to kill her uncle, an admiral. No "will they or won't they" romantic teasings on this short-lived series—Jim and Marty are already a sometimes couple, managing to find time for lovemaking during their dangerous adventures.

Hunter (1984–1991, 153 episodes, USA)

Created by: Frank Lupo
Production Co.: Stephen J. Cannell Productions
Originally Aired: NBC
Main Cast: Fred Dryer, Stepfanie Kramer, Charles Hallahan, Perry Cook, Garrett Morris, John Amos, Bruce Davison, Lauren Lane

When Clint Eastwood's *Dirty Harry* Callahan gained popularity on the big screen, it was inevitable that TV would create a small-screen doppelgänger of the "make my day" cop. Enter Sgt. Rick Hunter (Fred Dryer), a lanky LAPD detective who plays by his own rules and doesn't mind bucking his superiors when proper procedure gets in the way of bringing down bad guys. Hunter's partner is Sgt. **Dee Dee McCall** (Stepfanie Kramer), nicknamed "the brass cupcake," a beautiful cop who gives Rick a run for his money in the toughness department. Hunter and McCall respond to homicide calls in one beat-up jalopy after another, inspiring an inordinate number of chases which end with the launch of a flaming car into the sky.

This long-running series went through a number of cast changes, including a revolving set of precinct captains, finally settling on Captain Charlie Devane (Charles Hallahan) in season three. A reunion series, starring both Dryer and Kramer, ran for a few weeks in 2003, but the heart of this quintessentially 80s show remained in the earlier era.

See also: **McCall, Dee Dee** (*Hunter*)

Hunter, Samantha "Sam" (*Hunted*)

Elite operative for a private security firm which may contain a traitor.
See: *Hunted* (2012, 8 episodes, UK)

Hunter-Coddington, Ashley (*Acapulco H.E.A.T.*)

A former MI6 operative now working with the Hemisphere Emergency Action Team.
See: *Acapulco H.E.A.T.* (1993–1994, 1997–1998, 48 episodes, USA/Mexico/France)

The Huntress (2000–2001, 29 episodes, USA)

Based on: The book by Christopher Keane
Production Co.: USA Network
Originally Aired: USA Network
Main Cast: Annette O'Toole, Jordana Spiro, Luis Antonio Ramos, James Remar

Annette O'Toole and Jordana Spiro star as **Dottie and Brandi Thorson**, a suburban mother and daughter who just happen to be bounty hunters. Dottie and Brandi are novices, having taken over the business from their late husband and father, Ralph "Papa" Thorson (Craig T. Nelson), who was killed in a car bombing. The neophytes learn on the job, managing to capture Tiny Bellows (James Remar), a charming criminal who helps with later cases and sparks Dottie's amorous interest. The huntresses receive frequent assignments from bail bondsman Ricky Guzmán (Luis Antonio Ramos), and their lives are often in jeopardy, as they deal with desperate fugitives and their own inexperience. Even as business picks up, however, Dottie and Brandi seldom seem to get ahead, since another of Papa Thorson's debts always surfaces.

See also: **Thorson, Dottie and Brandi** (*The Huntress*)

Hurst, Annabelle (*Department S*)

Agent and computer expert for a special branch of Interpol.
See: *Department S* (1969–1970, 28 episodes, UK)

In Plain Sight (2008–2012, 61 episodes, USA)

Created by: David Maples
Production Co.: Pirates' Cove Entertainment, Universal Media Studios, Universal Cable Productions
Originally Aired: USA Network
Main Cast: Mary McCormack, Frederick Weller, Nichole Hiltz, Lesley Ann Warren, Paul Ben-Victor

Mary McCormack stars as **Mary Shannon**, a misanthropic U.S. Marshal with the Federal Witness Security Program (WITSEC) in Albuquerque, New Mexico. Mary and her know-it-all, but caring partner Marshall Mann (Frederick Weller) work to relocate witnesses, protect them, find them jobs, and help them acclimate to their new lives. Since upheaval is part of their profession, it's no surprise that Mary, Marshall, and their boss, Stan McQueen (Paul Ben-Victor), are constantly dealing with pushback, both from the witnesses themselves and those who would see the witnesses dead. Mary's life is further complicated by a dysfunctional and crime-prone family and her own trust and abandonment issues. It's small wonder that Mary is cranky most of the time and prefers the life of a loner. Still, Marshall is her best friend, and a new baby, along with overdue family reconciliations, may help Mary to reconnect with the world.

See also: **Shannon, Mary (*In Plain Sight*)**

The Inside (2005, 13 episodes, USA)

Created by: Tim Minear, Howard Gordon
Production Co.: Imagine Television, 20th Century–Fox Television
Originally Aired: Fox
Main Cast: Rachel Nichols, Adam Baldwin, Katie Finneran, Nelsan Ellis, Jay Harrington, Peter Coyote

Short-lived series starring Rachel Nichols as Rebecca Locke, a rookie agent assigned to the FBI's Violent Crimes Unit in Los Angeles. Locke has little field experience, so she appears underqualified, but she has a secret known to the unit's manipulative supervisor, Virgil "Web" Webster (Peter Coyote), that makes her a unique asset. Rebecca was abducted and held captive for 18 months as a young girl, but managed to escape, giving her rare insight as an adult into the minds of both victims and perpetrators. She now uses her "gift" to investigate heinous, serial crimes, working with Special Agent Paul Ryan (Jay Harrington), a genuine good guy who serves as a counterbalance to boss Webster's mysterious darkness. This interesting premise wasn't allowed to play itself out, as Fox canceled the series before airing all the produced episodes, a serial crime oft committed by networks.

The Inspector Lynley Mysteries (2001–2008, 23 episodes, UK)
Based on: The novels of Elizabeth George
Production Co.: British Broadcasting Corp.
Originally Aired: Public Television
Main Cast: Nathaniel Parker, Sharon Small

Detective Inspector Thomas Lynley (Nathaniel Parker) and Detective Sergeant Barbara Havers (Sharon Small) are mis-matched partners for New Scotland Yard. Lynley is an Oxford-educated peer of the realm, while Havers has a working-class background and more bad hair-days than anyone of whatever class should be allowed. Somehow, though, their partnership works, and they solve murders, even while personal issues threaten to intrude. In "Missing Joseph" (2002), the crime-solvers investigate the poisoning of a vicar in a peaceful village, while Lynley faces rejection from his lover. Havers finds herself demoted after firing a flare gun at a colleague, but Lynley gets her back for "In Pursuit of the Proper Sinner" (2004), a complex case involving the death of a retired policeman's daughter. Soon enough Havers is out of uniform and back in her usual drab detective's attire, closing cases with her aristocratic partner.

Irons, Vallery (*V.I.P.*)

Accidental and famous bodyguard/operative living in Los Angeles. See: **V.I.P.** (1998–2002, 88 episodes, USA/Germany)

Ironside (1967–1975, 199 episodes, USA)
Created by: Collier Young
Production Co.: Harbour Productions Unlimited, Universal TV
Originally Aired: NBC
Main Cast: Raymond Burr, Don Galloway, Don Mitchell, Barbara Anderson, Elizabeth Baur

The story of former SFPD Chief of Detectives Robert T. Ironside (Raymond Burr), wounded by a sniper's bullet and now a paraplegic, who continues to work for the San Francisco police as a special consultant. Ironside must navigate his new world in a wheelchair, but still solves cases with his own brand of grumpy determination and intelligence. Assisting the Chief are Detective Sgt. Ed Brown (Don Galloway) and ex-con turned bodyguard/caregiver Mark Sanger (Don Mitchell). Plainclothes officer Eve Whitfield (Barbara Anderson), a socialite who wanted to do more with her life than attend parties, is part of Ironside's original entourage. Ironside recalls his initial meeting with Eve and her subsequent recruitment in "Reprise" (1968), while he searches for the person who wounded her during a holdup. Officer Fran Belding (Elizabeth Baur) replaces Eve for later cases, while Ironside and company try to remain relevant during a time when the cops weren't very popular.

Isis (1975–1976, 22 episodes, USA)
Created by: Marc Richards
Production Co.: Filmation Associates
Originally Aired: CBS
Main Cast: JoAnna Cameron, Brian Cutler

Andrea Thomas is just your average high school science teacher until she finds an ancient Egyptian amulet on an archaeological dig. With this amazing talisman, Andrea (JoAnna Cameron) can transform herself into the goddess Isis, gaining limitless abilities, such as superhuman strength or command of earth, air, fire and water. Andrea uses these gifts to fight evil, but since she's a long way from ancient Egypt, the evil she confronts tends to be less exotic and more sophomoric, often involving poor judgment by her students. In "Scuba Duba" (1975), Andrea/Isis must save a student, when the boy flouts SCUBA diving safety rules and is trapped underwater. "Fool's Dare" (1975) brings the goddess to the rescue of a girl who, after accepting a dare, stumbles upon a ring of car thieves. "Oh, Mighty Isis!"

Isles, Maura (*Rizzoli & Isles*)

Dr. Maura Isles (Sasha Alexander) is the Chief Medical Examiner for the Commonwealth of Massachusetts. She works closely with homicide detective Jane Rizzoli (Angie Harmon), and the two have developed an unlikely friendship, given Maura's love of fashion and scientific minutiae vs. Jane's no-nonsense approach to clothing, work, and life in general. Maura excels at her job, although she has a few problems in the people skills department, such as a tendency to offer her encyclopedic knowledge, whether someone has asked for it or not. She has a tangled family history, learning that her biological father is an Irish crime boss, that her biological mother believes she died shortly after birth, and that her biological half-sister needs a kidney transplant. Maura manages to sort out most of these issues, although the checkered history and associations of her father, Paddy Doyle (John Doman), remain a dark mist that creeps out from the shadows when she least suspects it. She tends to be unlucky in love, most notably in "Melt My Heart to Stone" (2012), when her serial killer boyfriend hopes to make her his next victim. Still, her intelligence and resilience, as well as the help of Jane and the rest of the Rizzoli clan, continue to keep her among the forces of light.

See also: *Rizzoli & Isles* (2010– , 67 episodes, USA)

Jack of All Trades (2000, 22 episodes, USA/New Zealand)
Created by: Eric Morris
Production Co.: Renaissance Pictures

Originally Aired: In Syndication
Main Cast: Bruce Campbell, Angela Dotchin, Stuart Devenie

Campy comedy-adventure starring Bruce Campbell as American spy Jack Stiles and Angela Dotchin as Emilia Rothschild, his British counterpart, who work together on a South Pacific island in the early 1800s to thwart Napoleon's imperialistic designs. Emilia supplies the brains and Jack the brawn, as their madcap escapades take them from rescuing Ben Franklin in "The Floundering Father" (2000) to searching for King George's crown on the Marquis de Sade's island in "X Marquis the Spot" (2000). Emilia is also an inventor, furnishing miraculous creations when the need arises, while Jack calls upon his alter ego, The Daring Dragoon, a masked hero who swashes his buckle when secrecy is required. Add a dash of romantic tension, a sprinkling of anachronisms, and a soupçon of satire, and you have the bouillabaisse known as *Jack of All Trades*.

Jane Doe (2005–2008, 9 episodes, USA)

Created by: Dean Hargrove
Production Co.: Alpine Medien Productions, Larry Levinson Productions, Hallmark Entertainment, MAT IV
Originally Aired: Hallmark Channel
Main Cast: Lea Thompson, Joe Penny, William R. Moses, Jessy Schram, Zack Shada

Lea Thompson stars as Cathy Davis, a typical suburban housewife and mother of two, but this stay-at-home-mom has a secret past. Cathy was once an operative for the Central Security Agency, which finds itself once again in need of her services, especially her ability to solve intricate puzzles. Under the codename "Jane Doe," Cathy takes on cases part-time for the agency, while trying to convince her family, especially suspicious husband Jack (William R. Moses), that she's just out running a few more errands than usual. In "Now You See It, Now You Don't" (2005), Cathy's puzzle-solving skills are centerstage, when a thief steals The Declaration of Independence, leaving behind clues in the form of riddles (as thieves often do). Spying runs in the family when Cathy's mom, a former agent, comes to visit in "Yes, I Remember It Well" (2006), and mother (Donna Mills) must work with daughter to solve a kidnapping while reconciling some personal differences.

Jane Doe was part of a revolving "wheel" of mystery movies on The Hallmark Channel that included *Mystery Woman* and *McBride*.

Jareau, Jennifer "JJ" (*Criminal Minds*)

Communications Liaison and later profiler for the FBI's Behavioral Analysis Unit.

See: *Criminal Minds* (2005– , 209 episodes, USA)

Jenkins, Charlene (*Detective School*)
Housewife with an attitude who wants to become a private investigator.
See: *Detective School* (1979, 13 episodes, USA)

Jennings, Elizabeth (*The Americans*)
A KGB sleeper agent with a husband and kids in '80s suburban Virginia.
See: *The Americans* (2013– , 26 episodes, USA)

Jessie (1984, 10 episodes, USA)
Based on: The book *Psychologist with a Gun* by Harvey Schlossberg, Lucy Freeman
Production Co.: MGM/UA Television
Originally Aired: ABC
Main Cast: Lindsay Wagner, Tony Lo Bianco, J.D. Hinton, Tom Nolan, Renée Jones, Celeste Holm

Short-lived crime drama starring Lindsay Wagner as Dr. Jessie Hayden, a psychiatrist who uses her medical training to assist law enforcement. Jessie works with a Southern California police department, doing behavioral profiling to help catch criminals, but also counseling police personnel and crime victims alike. In "The Lady Killer" (1984), Jessie tries to convince a spousal abuse victim that she should press charges against her husband. Jessie's department liaison is Lieutenant Alex Ascoli (Tony LoBianco), who is often at odds with Jessie over her methods, but in "King of the Streets" they work together to get a burnt out cop off of the street.

This series reportedly went through several retoolings to find the right balance between action and braininess. Too bad there are no therapists like Jessie to counsel TV series with identity issues.

Johnson, Brenda Leigh (*The Closer*)
Deputy Chief of the LAPD's Priority Homicide Division whose interrogation techniques close cases.
See: *The Closer* (2005–2012, 109 episodes, USA)

Johnson, Rosie (*Strike Force*)
Beautiful, but tough detective in an elite LAPD unit.
See: *Strike Force* (1981–1982, 20 episodes, USA)

Johnson, Vivian (*Without a Trace*)
Vivian Johnson (Marianne Jean-Baptiste) is a special agent for the FBI's Missing Persons Squad in New York City. Working with other team members, such as unit chief Jack Malone (Anthony LaPaglia) and agent **Samantha Spade**

(Poppy Montgomery), Viv balances her home life of husband and teenage son with the grueling and often gut-wrenching task of tracking down missing persons. Vivian's good work gains her a promotion to squad supervisor, but her tenure as boss is short-lived when Jack takes his old job back, causing office tension in "Thou Shalt Not" (2004). When a heart condition starts to interfere with her work, she undergoes open-heart surgery in "Endgame (Part 1)" (2005). Dedicated Vivian, always the consummate professional, returns to duty in "Safe" (2005), and continues the team's mission of tracking down students, deli workers, prostitutes, child prodigies, attorneys—anyone who has gone missing seemingly "without a trace."

See also: *Without a Trace* (2002–2009, 160 episodes, USA)

Jonathan Creek (1997– , 31 episodes, UK)

Production Co.: British Broadcasting Corp.
Originally Aired: BBC America
Main Cast: Alan Davies, Caroline Quentin, Julia Sawahla, Stuart Milligan, Sheridan Smith, Sarah Alexander

Jonathan Creek (Alan Davies) invents brilliant illusions for professional magician Adam Klaus (Stuart Milligan). Jonathan's genius at working out puzzles brings him to the attention of investigative journalist **Madeline Magellan** (Caroline Quentin), who has a seemingly impossible murder to unravel. The unlikely duo, Jonathan, with his sheepdog hair and duffel coat, and Maddy, with her pushy ways and nose for trouble, partner to confront evil in the form of the "locked room mystery" and its implausible cousins. In addition to crime puzzles, Jonathan and Maddy must solve the riddle of their strange attraction and ultimately answer the "will they or won't they" relationship question.

Carla Borrego (Julia Sawahla) later replaces Maddy as agitator-in-chief, arriving at amateur-sleuth status by way of her gig as a crime show host. Carla is Jonathan's now married ex-girlfriend, so his life remains complicated, working with womanizing Adam and struggling with cases that no one else can close.

See also: **Magellan, Madeline** (*Jonathan Creek*)

Jones, Betty (*Barnaby Jones*)

Daughter-in-law of a folksy, milk-drinking P.I., who works as his secretary and later fellow sleuth.

See: *Barnaby Jones* (1973–1980, 178 episodes, USA)

Joplin, Trudy (*Miami Vice*)

Undercover detective nicknamed "Big Booty," who specializes in working the street.

See: *Miami Vice* (1984–1989, 111 episodes, USA)

Jordan, Carol (*Wire in the Blood*)

Detective Chief Inspector who works with an eccentric clinical psychologist in northern England.
See: *Wire in the Blood* (2002–2008, 31 episodes, UK)

Kalakaua, Kono (*Hawaii Five-0*)

Honolulu Police Department rookie working with a major crimes task force.
See: *Hawaii Five-0* (2010– , 93 episodes, USA)

Kane, J.Z. (*Dog and Cat*)

Hip, rookie LAPD officer who works with a conservative male partner.
See: *Dog and Cat* (1977, 6 episodes, USA)

Karen Sisco (2003–2004, 10 episodes, USA)

Based on: The novel *Out of Sight* by Elmore Leonard
Production Co.: Jersey Television, Universal Television, Eighty D Productions
Originally Aired: ABC
Main Cast: Carla Gugino, Bill Duke, Robert Forster

Gone-in-the-blink-of-an-eye series starring Carla Gugino as Karen Sisco, a Deputy U.S. Marshal based on Miami's Gold Coast (and on Jennifer Lopez's character in the film *Out of Sight*). Karen tracks down fugitives in southern Florida, displaying a toughness designed to win the respect of her fellow marshals and boss, Amos Andrews (Bill Duke). Karen's advisor and friend is her father, Marshall Sisco (Robert Forster), a private investigator. Both are taken hostage during a bank robbery in "Dog Day Sisco" (2004), and must work together to defuse the situation on the inside, while Amos tries to hold back the overeager FBI on the outside. In addition to fugitive-hunting, Karen also protects witnesses, does undercover drug work, and wears sexy clothes.

Keen, Elizabeth (*The Blacklist*)

Rookie FBI profiler who works with a criminal mastermind to track down a blacklist of baddies.
See: *The Blacklist* (2013– , 22 episodes, USA)

Kelly, Chris (*Pacific Blue*)

Ambitious member of the Santa Monica Police Department's bicycle unit.
See: *Pacific Blue* (1996–2000, 101 episodes, USA)

Kenzi (*Lost Girl*)

Petty criminal who opens a detective agency with a succubus.
See: *Lost Girl* (2010– , 61 episodes, Canada)

Killer Women (2014, 8 episodes, USA)

Based on: The Argentine TV series *Mujeres Asesinas*
Created by: Hannah Shakespeare
Production Co.: Electus, Latin World Entertainment, Pol-Ka Producciones, ABC Studios
Originally Aired: ABC
Main Cast: Tricia Helfer, Marc Blucas, Alex Fernandez, Marta Milans, Michael Trucco

Molly Parker (Tricia Helfer) is a Texas Ranger with the ability to get into the minds of female murderers, a skill that comes in handy within the male-dominated investigative unit. While she hunts killer women of various stripes, including a serial killer who murders women after shaving their heads and eyebrows, Molly deals with a complex personal life. She is trying to divorce State Senator Jake Colton (Jeffrey Nordling), who is not cooperating, and in "Some Men Need Killing" (2014), she saves him from a killer who singles out abusive husbands. In the meantime, Molly is pursuing a relationship with undercover DEA agent Dan Winston (Marc Blucas), but things get sticky when Dan picks up Molly's brother Billy (Michael Trucco) for drug smuggling.

The complications of this surprisingly small world within such a BIG state were mercifully short-lived, as ABC quickly axed the series, airing only six of the eight episodes produced.

The Killing (2011–2014, 44 episodes, USA/Canada)

Based on: The TV series *Forbrydelsen* created by Søren Sveistrup
Created by: Veena Sud
Production Co.: Fox Television Studios, Fuse Entertainment, KMF Films
Originally Aired: AMC
Main Cast: Mireille Enos, Joel Kinnaman, Liam James, Billy Campbell, Michelle Forbes, Brent Sexton, Kristin Lehman, Eric Ladin, Jamie Anne Allman

Seattle police detective Sarah Linden (Mireille Enos) is about to relocate to Sonoma with her son Jack (Liam James) when a possible murder case and a rookie homicide detective are dropped into her lap. The case turns into a true murder investigation, when the body of teenager Rosie Larson (Katie Findlay) is found in the trunk of a car at the bottom of a local lake. The rookie detective, Stephen Holder (Joel Kinnaman), turns out to be more of a hindrance than a help, falsifying evidence to implicate mayoral candidate Darren Richmond (Billy Campbell) in the crime. Sarah, believing the culprit has been found, is on a plane waiting to take off for her new life in California, when she learns about the false evidence, and must postpone her move. Sarah and Holder continue with the Larson murder in season two of this mystery serial, but now with much distrust between them.

Almost as dramatic as the plot twists and turns were the two resurrections this series received, one at the end of season two, when AMC reversed its cancellation decision, and the second at the end of season three, when the series was rescued for a final short season by Internet streaming service Netflix. Apparently there was more than one way to make a killing on *The Killing*.

King, Amanda (*Scarecrow and Mrs. King*)

Divorced housewife, mother, PTA volunteer, SPY. Amanda King's life changes forever when a handsome stranger enters it, carrying a small package and big trouble. Portrayed with great comic flair by Kate Jackson, Amanda is as homespun as they come, but drawn to a life of intrigue because she can serve her country, work with dashing agent Lee Stetson, code-named Scarecrow, and commute to spy headquarters, which are close to the place where she buys produce. But Amanda's skill set extends beyond the making of brownies and helping her sons with homework. She is observant, analytical, intelligent, loyal, and never does what Scarecrow (Bruce Boxleitner) tells her to do, which usually is a good thing. She saves Stetson from certain death in the hilarious "Saved by the Bells" (1983), when enemy spies mistake her for the great agent Scarecrow. When her domestic skills should be on best display during a mother-of-the-year contest, she gets involved in a murder investigation, creating an amusingly wrong impression for the judges in "A Little Sex, a Little Scandal" (1985). Although Amanda and Scarecrow seem to inhabit different worlds, they learn ever so slowly that they are soulmates, and secretly marry during the fourth and final season of the series in "Do You Take This Spy?" (1987).

See also: *Scarecrow and Mrs. King* (1983–1987, 88 episodes, USA)

King & Maxwell (2013, 10 episodes, USA)

Based on: The novels of David Baldacci
Created by: Shane Brennan
Production Co.: CBS Television Studios, Shane Brennan Productions
Originally Aired: TNT
Main Cast: Jon Tenney, Rebecca Romijn, Michael O'Keefe, Chris Butler, Ryan Hurst

Two former Secret Service agents, fired for their professional lapses, partner as private detectives in our nation's capital. Jon Tenney is Sean King, a decent guy who has trouble keeping track of his gun and won't ask the agency's deadbeat clients for money. Rebecca Romijn portrays Michelle Maxwell, who is fit as a fiddle, often rowing to their lake house office, but resembles Oscar Madison when it comes to keeping her work and living spaces clean. Rounding out the team is Ryan Hurst as Edgar Roy, an autistic savant, whose hacking prowess and high-tech skills come in handy in the P.I. biz. While the mysteries and mistakes of their Secret Service pasts continue to intrude into the present, King and Maxwell search for kidnap victims, solve murders, and investigate con men, while trying not to run afoul of tightly wound FBI Agent Frank Rigby (Michael O'Keefe). Alas, the secrets and conspiracies the good-looking duo encounter in the cliffhanger "Pandora's Box" (2013) will remain forever shrouded in the mists of premature series cancellation.

King, Anita (*Angel Street*)

Black detective partnering with a white rookie in an otherwise all-male precinct.
See: *Angel Street* (1992, 4 episodes, USA)

King, Tara (*The Avengers*)

Novice British agent who investigates outré crimes with a dapper veteran.
See: *The Avengers* (1961–1969, 161 episodes, UK)

Kinsey, Samantha (*Mystery Woman*)

Proprietor of a mystery bookstore, photographer, and amateur detective.
See: *Mystery Woman* (2003–2007, 11 episodes, USA)

Kovak, Sydney (*Partners in Crime*)

Former pickpocket who inherits a San Francisco detective agency from her ex-husband.
See: *Partners in Crime* (1984, 13 episodes, USA)

Kowalski, Abby (*Against the Wall*)

Chicago Internal Affairs Detective in conflict with her family members, all cops.
See: *Against the Wall* (2011, 13 episodes, USA)

Krebs, Mildred (*Remington Steele*)

An agent for the IRS fraud squad, Mildred Krebs begins *Remington Steele's* season two opener, "Steele Away with Me" (1983), by investigating the Remington Steele Agency for tax irregularities, but ends up working for private detectives Remington Steele (Pierce Brosnan) and **Laura Holt** (Stephanie Zimbalist) after a rollicking adventure in Mexico involving murder and smuggled diamonds. Mildred (Doris Roberts) puts her research skills and computer experience to good use in her new position as secretary/receptionist, but yearns for more action, as in "Hounded Steele" (1984), when she sets out by herself to find a missing pooch, only to become embroiled with Interpol and a retired jewel thief. She learns the secret of Remington's identity in "Steele Searching–Part 1" (1985), sealing her position as both indispensable employee of the Steele Agency and friend/confidante to Remington and Laura.

See also: *Remington Steele* (1982–1987, 94 episodes, USA)

Kyle, Helena (*Birds of Prey*)

The daughter of Batman and Catwoman, who protects New Gotham as superhero Huntress.

See: *Birds of Prey* (2002–2003, 13 episodes, USA)

Lacey, Mary Beth (*Cagney & Lacey*)

Mary Beth Lacey is a working-class wife and mother of the 80s, who just happens to be a detective for the New York City Police Department. As portrayed by Tyne Daly, Mary Beth partners with fellow detective **Christine Cagney** (Sharon Gless) to solve major crimes while blazing a trail for women in the male-dominated police force. Although Mary Beth's husband, Harvey Lacey (John Karlen), is a supportive mate, she frequently finds herself, like most working mothers, being pulled in too many directions at once. "Burnout" (1983) sees Mary Beth absent without leave from both precinct and home, when her long-awaited vacation is canceled at the last minute. Lacey spends the day at the beach, trying to sort through her emotions and find some perspective. She resumes work, but is often this side of frazzled, especially after her third child is born in "Family Connections" (1986). Lacey loves her job and is good at it, balancing her partner's irreverence and brashness with respectfulness and compassion.

Tyne Daly won the Emmy Award four times for her portrayal of Mary Beth Lacey, a character which, along with Gless's Cagney, continues to be the gold standard for female detectives on television.

See also: *Cagney & Lacey* (1982–1988, 125 episodes, USA)

Lady Blue (1985–1986, 14 episodes, USA)

Production Co.: MGM/UA Television
Originally Aired: ABC
Main Cast: Jamie Rose, Danny Aiello

Violent crime drama starring Jamie Rose as Chicago homicide detective Katy Mahoney. Tough-as-nails Katy tends to have excessive force issues, a reaction to the on-the-job killings of her father, brother, and lover, all local cops. While dodging the reprimands of new boss Lt. Terry McNichols (Danny Aiello), Katy pursues hit-men, thrill-murderers, serial killers, and gang-bangers with her usual enthusiasm. In "Willow's Cowboy" (1986), she's hot on the trail of some buckaroos who will stop at nothing to acquire a valuable shipment of ... bull semen. Just business as usual for Katy and the other members of the "Matron Squad."

Lance, Dinah (*Birds of Prey*)

Teenager with telekinetic abilities who works with female superheroes.
See: *Birds of Prey* (2002–2003, 13 episodes, USA)

Lance, Rita Lee (*Silk Stalkings*)

Police Sergeant who solves sex-based crimes with a handsome partner in Palm Beach, Florida.
See: *Silk Stalkings* (1991–1999, 176 episodes, USA)

Lane, Lois (*Adventures of Superman*)

Lois Lane is a reporter for *The Daily Planet* in Metropolis, working alongside newsman Clark Kent (George Reeves), who just happens to lead a double-life as Superman, the man of steel. Lois likes to beat Clark to scoops, and, as

The Man of Steel (George Reeves) and reporter Lois Lane (Phyllis Coates) investigate strange mysteries in the "dark series" of *Adventures of Superman* (Motion Pictures for Television Inc./Photofest).

portrayed by Phyllis Coates in the first season, is one tough cookie, who doesn't back down even when confronted by killers or kidnappers. Her nose for news involves her in dark investigations, such as "Mystery of the Broken Statues" (1952), where her inquisitiveness gets her abducted, but leads to the recovery of a priceless gem. Coates's Lois doesn't wait for Superman to rescue her, using a nearby statue as a bludgeon, when threatened by her kidnapper. For all her trailblazing, Phyllis Coates turned down a second season of *Adventures of Superman* due to other commitments.

Her successor, Noel Neill, portrays a softer Lois Lane, still inquisitive and out to best Clark in the newsroom, but more demure and with a developing romantic attraction to Superman. In "The Wedding of Superman" (1956), Lois marries the man of steel, but wakes up to find it was only a heartbreaking dream.

But tough or soft, in black-and-white or color, Lois Lane breaks new TV ground, because it takes a real superman to beat this newswoman to a byline.

See also: *Adventures of Superman* (1952–1958, 104 episodes, USA)

Law & Order (1990–2010, 456 episodes, USA)

Created by: Dick Wolf
Production Co.: Wolf Films, NBC Universal Television, Studios USA Television, et al.
Originally Aired: NBC
Main Cast: Jerry Orbach, S. Epatha Merkerson, Jill Hennessy, Sam Waterston, Steven Hill, Jesse L. Martin, George Dzundza, Chris Noth, Dann Florek, Michael Moriarty, Leslie Hendrix, Fred Dalton Thompson, Benjamin Bratt, Angie Harmon, Jeremy Sisto, Milena Govich, et al.

"In the criminal justice system, the people are represented by two separate yet equally important groups: the police who investigate crime and the district attorneys who prosecute the offenders. These are their stories."

With 456 episodes, 20 seasons and a seeming cast of thousands, *Law & Order* is a television institution and the progenitor of a franchise that includes *Law & Order: Criminal Intent*, *Law & Order: Special Victims Unit*, and even *Law & Order: UK*. The original series features an unusual, two-part format, with the first half of most episodes devoted to the investigation of a crime by NYPD homicide detectives, and the second half dedicated to the prosecution of the alleged perpetrator by the Manhattan District Attorney's office. Most of the field detectives throughout the series are men, the most notable of whom is Lennie Briscoe (Jerry Orbach), a native New Yorker who makes wisecracks over dead bodies and brings criminals to justice for 12 seasons. Back at the precinct, however, Lennie and the boys, including his partner Ed Green (Jesse L. Martin), report to a woman, and a woman of color at that, Lt. **Anita Van Buren** (S. Epatha Merkerson), commander of the detective squad and the longest-running character on the series. Van Buren supervises the work of the detectives, instructing them on which leads to pursue and how to handle suspects, while also conferring with District Attorney Jack McCoy (Sam Waterston) and a bevy of young, pretty ADAs, including Abbie Carmichael (Angie Harmon) and Claire Kincaid (Jill Hennessy). *Law & Order's* iconic clang, sounded at the beginning of each episode and in between scenes, heralds stories "ripped from the headlines," and viewers answered the call for two decades.

See also: **Van Buren, Anita (*Law & Order*)**

Law & Order: Criminal Intent (2001–2011, 195 episodes, USA)
Created by: Dick Wolf
Production Co.: Wolf Films, Universal Network Television, NBC Universal Television, et al.
Originally Aired: NBC (2001–2007), USA Network (2007–2011)
Main Cast: Vincent D'Onofrio, Kathryn Erbe, Jamey Sheridan, Courtney B. Vance, Chris Noth, Annabella Sciorra, Julianne Nicholson, Eric Bogosian, Alicia Witt, Jeff Goldblum, Saffron Burrows, Mary Elizabeth Mastrantonio, Leslie Hendrix

"In New York City's war on crime, the worst criminal offenders are pursued by the detectives of the Major Case Squad. These are their stories."

This gritty police procedural, a spinoff from *Law & Order*, follows partners Robert Goren (Vincent D'Onofrio) and **Alexandra Eames** (Kathryn Erbe) as they tackle high-profile crimes, many of which are taken from real news stories of the day. Brilliant, but quirky "Bobby" Goren is the Holmes to Eames's cool and professional Watson, a pairing of disparate personalities who somehow function better as a unit, doing whatever it takes to catch their criminal quarry. Assistant District Attorney Ron Carver (Courtney B. Vance) pushes the detectives to find evidence that will stick, while Captain James Deakins (Jamey Sheridan) supervises the unit, engaging in damage control on the occasions when Goren runs wild. In later years, Goren and Eames alternate with other duos as the focus of each episode, most notably Mike Logan (Chris Noth) and Megan Wheeler (Julianne Nicholson). But whoever the personnel (and there are many roster changes), the Major Case Squad always confronts the dark side of humanity, facing grim crimes and their depraved perpetrators, all in a day's work.

See also: **Eames, Alexandra (*Law & Order: Criminal Intent*)**

Law & Order: Special Victims Unit (1999– , 343 episodes, USA)
Created by: Dick Wolf
Production Co.: Wolf Films, Universal Television, NBC Studios, et al.
Originally Aired: NBC
Main Cast: Mariska Hargitay, Christopher Meloni, Richard Belzer, Dann Florek, Michelle Hurd, Stephanie March, Ice-T, BD Wong, Tamara Tunie

"In the criminal justice system, sexually based offenses are considered especially heinous. In New York City, the dedicated detectives who investigate these vicious felonies are members of an elite squad known as the Special Victims Unit. These are their stories."

The first spinoff from *Law & Order*, and one of television's longest-running scripted dramas, *Law & Order: Special Victims Unit* stars Mariska Hargitay as **Olivia Benson**, a detective in Manhattan's 16th precinct, which is devoted solely to the investigation of sex crimes. Benson's partner for the first 12 years is Detective Elliott Stabler (Christopher Meloni), and the two deal with the nasty nature of the job in their own ways—Benson tends to be overly sympathetic to the victims, sometimes to the point of unprofessionalism, while Stabler has anger issues, which lead to excessive force and Internal Affairs investigations. Still, they are effective case-closers, whose work is appreciated by their boss, Captain Donald Cragen (Dann Florek), even if both are on the high-maintenance side. Other detectives investigating the rapes, molestations, necrophilia, and sex-related murders that are the dark province of SVU include Fin Tutuola (Ice-T), a combat veteran who keeps to himself, and John Munch (Richard Belzer), a sarcastic conspiracy theorist.

This show's long run has seen many cast changes, including the departure of Christopher Meloni after 12 seasons, but the one constant has been Mariska Hargitay in her Emmy Award–winning role as Olivia Benson, defender of victims of sexual crimes.

See also: **Benson, Olivia** (*Law & Order: Special Victims Unit*)

Lawson, Holly (*Vera*)

Young detective with the Northumberland & City Police Department.
See: *Vera* (2011– , 16 episodes, UK)

Lee, Anna (*Anna Lee*)

Young cop who joins a private detective agency and deals with a colorful neighbor.
See: *Anna Lee* (1994, 5 episodes, UK)

Leg Work (1987, 10 episodes, USA)

Created by: Frank Abatemarco
Production Co.: 20th Century–Fox Television
Originally Aired: CBS
Main Cast: Margaret Colin, Patrick James Clarke, Frances McDormand

Margaret Colin stars as Claire McCarron, a former assistant D.A. turned private investigator, in this short-lived mystery series. Claire enjoys her new job as a detective, but finds it hard to pay the bills, and while visiting a client to collect an overdue fee, she witnesses the man's murder. Still cash-strapped, she hires on with a high-powered law firm, but clashes with her bosses over the apparent suicide of their wealthy client in "All This and a Gold Card Too." Other cases involve Claire's brother Fred (Patrick James Clarke), an NYPD cop, and her friend Willie Pipal (Frances McDormand), a prosecutor at the D.A.'s office. Claire's "leg work" often finds her in a Porsche, but taking the subway might have helped with the bottom line.

Lehman, Emily (*Standoff*)

Brainy FBI Agent with the bureau's Crisis Negotiation Unit in Los Angeles.

See: *Standoff* (2006–2007, 18 episodes, USA)

Level 9 (2000–2001, 13 episodes, USA)

Created by: Michael Connelly, John Secret Young, Josh Meyer
Production Co.: Level Nine Productions, Paramount Television
Originally Aired: UPN
Main Cast: Fab Filippo, Kate Hodge, Michael Kelly, Romany Malco, Max Martini, Kim Murphy, Susie Park, Esteban Powell

Level 9 is an elite and secret task force within the U.S. government charged with solving and preventing cyber crimes. Leading the motley crew of government agents, techno geeks, and former hackers is Annie Price (Kate Hodge), an obsessive FBI agent whose name could just as easily be "Any Price." Annie rides herd over team members with cool names, such as Jargon (Esteban Powell), a former high school hacker, Sosh (Kim Murphy), a former Internet model, and Shootin' Hooten (Romany Malco), late of the U.S. Postal Inspection Service. Together these cyber detectives pursue blackmailers, sleeper assassins, kidnappers, mercenary hackers, and villains with (not surprisingly) cool names such as Mailman and CrayZhorse.

Too bad Annie and crew didn't write some code to forge a renewal order from UPN.

Life (2007–2009, 32 episodes, USA)

Created by: Rand Ravich
Production Co.: Universal Media Studios, Ravich-Shariat Productions
Originally Aired: NBC
Main Cast: Damian Lewis, Sarah Shahi, Brent Sexton, Donal Logue, Adam Arkin, Brooke Langton, Robin Weigert

Damian Lewis portrays Charlie Crews, an ex-cop serving a life sentence for murders he did not commit. DNA evidence clears Charlie after 12 years in prison, and he returns to the LAPD, with a hefty settlement from the city, a new Zen philosophy, and a burning desire to solve the mystery which nearly ruined his life. Charlie's new partner is Detective Dani Reese (Sarah Shahi), a recovering drug addict and alcoholic, who is pressured by Lieutenant Karen Davis (Robin Weigert) to assist in a campaign to remove ex-con Crews from the force. But Reese becomes a loyal and supportive, if not always patient, partner, and the detectives battle many of their personal demons, while solving murders and trying to unravel the conspiracy that put Charlie in prison.

Linden, Sarah (*The Killing*)

Seattle police detective who postpones her move to California because of a difficult murder case.

See: *The Killing* (2011–2014, 44 episodes, USA/Canada)

Line of Fire (2003–2004, 13 episodes, USA)

Created by: Rod Lurie
Production Co.: DreamWorks Television, Battleplan Productions, Touchstone Television
Originally Aired: ABC
Main Cast: Leslie Bibb, Anson Mount, Leslie Hope, Jeffrey D. Sams, Julie Ann Emery, Brian Goodman, Michael Irby, David Paymer

Well-staffed crime drama juxtaposing the stories of two opposed, but linked "businesses"—the Richmond, Virginia FBI office, led by Special Agent Lisa Cohen (Leslie Hope), and the Richmond crime syndicate, headed by boss Jonah Malloy (David Paymer). When an agent dies during a shootout with Malloy's goons, Agent-in-charge Cohen is spoiling for a fight, and two newly assigned rookie agents, Paige Van Doren (Leslie Bibb) and Todd Stevens (Jeffrey D. Sams), join the fray. Dangerous Malloy and determined Cohen knock heads in "Take the Money and Run" (2003), when both try to intercept a shipment of illegal drugs.

Alas, this "*The Sopranos*-meets-*The Wire*" knockoff aired only 11 of the 13 episodes produced.

Lisbon, Teresa (*The Mentalist*)

Teresa Lisbon (Robin Tunney) heads a team of California Bureau of Investigation agents, including former con man and "psychic" Patrick Jane (Simon Baker). Lisbon is a petite, but formidable force, intelligent, tough, and by-the-book, but she becomes more of a rule-bender under Jane's influence, realizing that his unorthodox tactics help to close cases. In "Red Badge" (2009), Lisbon demonstrates a knack for the con herself when she stages a violent fit at CBI headquarters to trap her psychiatrist, who has framed her for murder. Agent Lisbon isn't much of a girly girl—when she tries on a pink bridesmaid's gown in "Strawberries and Cream: Part 1" (2011), she is so agitated by the experience that Jane says she looks like "an angry little princess." Lisbon's relationship with

Jane remains peculiarly intense yet solely professional for six years, until she decides to fly off to Washington to be with another man in "Blue Bird" (2014). Jane makes a dramatic, last-minute profession of love to Lisbon, and the two finally share a passionate kiss.

The series narrowly escaped cancellation at this point, leaving the fate of this beautiful, but mismatched couple to be resolved in the seventh and final season on CBS.

See also: *The Mentalist* (2008– , 138 episodes, USA)

Liu-Tsong, Madame (*The Gallery of Madame Liu-Tsong*)

Art gallery owner who becomes involved in mystery and foreign intrigue.
See: *The Gallery of Madame Liu-Tsong* (1951, 10 episodes, USA)

Locasto, Joanna (*Deception*)

SFPD detective who infiltrates the wealthy family of her deceased childhood friend.
See: *Deception* (2013, 11 episodes, USA)

Locke, Rebecca (*The Inside*)

Former child abductee, now a rookie agent with the FBI's Violent Crimes Unit in Los Angeles.
See: *The Inside* (2005, 13 episodes, USA)

London, Maxine "Max" (*Spy Game*)

Rookie spy at the Emergency Counter-Hostilities Organization (E.C.H.O.).
See: *Spy Game* (1997, 13 episodes, USA)

Longmire (2012–2014, 33 episodes, USA)

Based on: The novels of Craig Johnson
Production Co.: Warner Horizon Television, The Shephard/Robin Company, Two Boomerangs Productions
Originally Aired: A&E
Main Cast: Robert Taylor, Katee Sackhoff, Bailey Chase, Adam Bartley, Cassidy Freeman, Lou Diamond Phillips

Walt Longmire (Robert Taylor) is the sheriff of (fictional) Absaroka County in Wyoming. Laconic Longmire grieves for his wife, who was murdered in Denver one year earlier, although most people, including Walt's daughter Cady (Cassidy Freeman), believe Cady's mother died from cancer. While secrets surrounding the murder come to light, as is the way of secrets in a small town, Walt runs for reelection, and relies on his deputies to pick up the slack at work, especially new arrival Victoria "Vic" Moretti (Katee Sackhoff). Vic, a big-city girl from Philadelphia and a former homicide detective, is a fish out of water in wild Wyoming, where one day she pursues a sex trafficker, and the next a killer bear. Deputy Moretti is loyal to her new boss, and in "8 Seconds" (2012), she interrupts lovemaking with her husband to retrieve Walt, who has had too much to drink at the Red Pony Café. Longmire also receives support from his best friend, Henry Standing Bear (Lou Diamond Phillips), who owns the Red Pony and is Walt's liaison with the local Cheyenne Reservation.

Although the tone of this series harks back to classic Westerns, the plots are modern-day complex, leaving many twisted motivations, like shallow graves on Boot Hill, ready for exhumation.

Lost Girl (2010– , 61 episodes, Canada)
Created by: Michelle Lovretta
Production Co.: Prodigy Pictures
Originally Aired: Syfy
Main Cast: Anna Silk, Kris Holden-Ried, Ksenia Solo, K. C. Collins, Zoie Palmer, Rick Howland, Cle Bennett

"Life is hard when you don't know who you are. It's harder when you don't know what you are."

A succubus detective—talk about a high concept. The succubus in question is Bo (Anna Silk), a young woman raised by humans, who begins to suspect she is "different," when she accidentally kills her boyfriend during her first sexual encounter. On the run for years, and leaving behind a trail of dead bodies after she has drained their life force, Bo learns who she really is from The Fae, an ancient, supernatural society. Bo is supposed to decide which side to serve in the Fae world, "Light" or "Dark," but instead she remains neutral, preferring the company of humans, especially her new friend Kenzi (Ksenia Solo), a fast-talking thief. Bo and Kenzi decide to open a private investigation business, catering to both humans and Fae, while Bo continues to learn more about her origins and the ways of the multi-specied Fae. In "(Dis)Members Only" (2010), Bo and Kenzi investigate a missing person at a country club, where Bo and her wolf-shapeshifter boyfriend, Dyson (Kris Holden-Ried), a homicide detective in the human world, go undercover as just your average married couple. Bo also has a romantic relationship with Lauren (Zoie Palmer), a doctor and scientist in service to the Light Fae, who teaches Bo the handy talent of self-control, the practice of which allows Bo's human and Fae partners to remain alive after sexual encounters with her. Bo continues to face challenges, both in her ultra-complicated sex life and in her chosen middle ground between Light and Dark Fae, whose truce is always tenuous and whose adherents are hatching plots at every turn.

The life of a succubus isn't easy.

Loud, Jenny (*MacGruder and Loud*)
One half of a pair of married cops, who must keep their wedding secret from the department.
See: *MacGruder and Loud* (1985, 14 episodes, USA)

Love, Christie (*Get Christie Love!*)
Karate aficionado and the first African American female undercover cop on the LAPD.
See: *Get Christie Love!* (1974–1975, 22 episodes, USA)

Lovejoy (1986–1994, 71 episodes, UK)
Based on: The novels of Jonathan Gash
Created by: Ian La Frenais
Production Co.: BBC Drama Productions, Tamariska Productions, WitzEnd Productions, McShane Productions
Originally Aired: A&E
Main Cast: Ian McShane, Phyllis Logan, Dudley Sutton, Chris Jury, Caroline Langrishe, Diane Parish

Lovejoy, just "Lovejoy" (not "Mr."), is an antiques dealer, con artist, and amateur detective living in East Anglia. Lovejoy (Ian McShane) loves beauty for its own sake, but isn't averse to taking advantage of "punters," out to make a quick buck on antiques or art. In the course of his adventures, Lovejoy is often called upon to solve crimes, such as robberies or cons, either because he is a suspect himself or because someone has taken advantage of a friend. His partner in crime (either perpetrating or solving) is Lady Jane Felsham (Phyllis Logan), an upper-class interior designer who accepts Lovejoy for who he is and bails him out when he's in trouble. Jane and Lovejoy share a mutual romantic attraction, but since Jane is married to someone else, Lovejoy's fantasies are never fulfilled.

In later episodes, Charlotte Cavendish (Caroline Langrishe), a local auctioneer, becomes reluctantly involved in Lovejoy's shenanigans, and proves unable to resist his roguish charms.

Lowell, Terri (*The Agency*)
Documents forger and field operative for the CIA.
See: *The Agency* (2001–2003, 44 episodes, USA)

Lupo, Josefina "Jo" (*Eureka*)
Deputy Sheriff Jo Lupo works in a small town with a quaint main street, which sounds like an easy gig, but the small town is Eureka, home to a bevy of geniuses, who have a tendency to get into catastrophic, sometimes cosmic trou-

ble. Jo (Erica Cerra) assists Sheriff Jack Carter (Colin Ferguson) in keeping the peace, using her skills as a former U.S. Army Ranger and a no-nonsense attitude to combat the craziness around her. Her relationship with Zane Donovan (Niall Matter) is short-circuited by a shift in the timeline, wherein they have never dated and she is head of security at Global Dynamics, Eureka's giant scientific research facility. Love finds a way, however, in series finale, "Just Another Day" (2012), when Zane accepts Josefina's marriage proposal.

See also: *Eureka* (2006–2012, 77 episodes, USA)

MacGruder and Loud (1985, 14 episodes, USA)
Production Co.: Aaron Spelling Productions
Originally Aired: ABC
Main Cast: John Getz, Kathryn Harrold

Malcolm MacGruder and Jenny Loud are partners on a big-city police force, but there's a twist to their working relationship. Malcolm (John Getz) and Jenny (Kathryn Harrold) are married and must keep their wedded bliss a secret if they want to stay partners, because of the department's anti-fraternization regulations. While the couple dodges questions from their colleagues and develops a creative living arrangement, they pursue bad guys, sometimes in uncomfortable ways, as in "On the Wire" (1985), when Jenny must date a mobster in the course of a gambling investigation. These two are always in the line of fire, whether it's Malcolm, who becomes the target of kidnappers, or Jenny, who's a shooting victim. Not much of a honeymoon for these two dedicated cops.

Macready, Sharron (*The Champions*)
Secret agent with enhanced powers bestowed by an ancient civilization.
See: *The Champions* (1968–1969, 30 episodes, UK)

Madeline (*La Femme Nikita*)
Manipulative strategist for anti-terrorist organization Section One.
See: *La Femme Nikita* (1997–2001, 96 episodes, Canada)

Madsen, Rebecca (*Alcatraz*)
SFPD detective investigating the mass disappearance and reappearance of Alcatraz inmates.
See: *Alcatraz* (2012, 13 episodes, USA)

Magellan, Madeline (*Jonathan Creek*)
Madeline Magellan is an investigative journalist who specializes in covering miscarriages of justice. As portrayed by Caroline Quentin, Maddy is pushy,

impatient, and sometimes rude, but she usually gets what she wants, and in "The Wrestler's Tomb" (1997), she wants help from Jonathan Creek. Maddy thinks that Jonathan (Alan Davies), a magician's consultant who creates dazzling illusions, is just the man to prove that a publisher with an airtight alibi is actually guilty of murder. Writer and conjurer enter into an unholy alliance, unraveling impossible riddles, such as the mystery of "Ghost's Forge" (1999), where Maddy pulls off an illusion of her own while investigating a murder. In "Time Waits for Norman" (1998), Maddy and Jonathan try to fathom how the husband of Maddy's literary agent could seemingly be in two places at once, and England and America at that. The character of Madeline Magellan last appears in "The Three Gamblers" (2000), while Jonathan goes on to find new, but not necessarily less annoying, detective partners.

See also: *Jonathan Creek* (1997– , 31 episodes, UK)

Mahoney, Katy (*Lady Blue*)

Chicago homicide detective with excessive force issues.
See: *Lady Blue* (1985–1986, 14 episodes, USA)

Major Crimes (2012– , 39 episodes, USA)

Created by: James Duff
Production Co.: The Shephard/Robin Company, Warner Bros. Television
Originally Aired: TNT
Main Cast: Mary McDonnell, G. W. Bailey, Tony Denison, Michael Paul Chan, Raymond Cruz, Phillip P. Keene, Kearran Giovanni, Graham Patrick Martin

Captain Sharon Raydor (Mary McDonnell) takes over the LAPD's Major Crimes Division from departing Deputy Chief Brenda Leigh Johnson (Kyra Sedgwick) in this spinoff from *The Closer*. Raydor is immediately mistrusted by many of her new colleagues, because she was formerly posted to the Force Investigation Division, popularly known as Internal Affairs, habitual enemy of rank-and-file officers. When Raydor does not receive her promised promotion to Commander because of a personnel freeze, increasing her competition with high-ranking member of the unit Lieutenant Louie Provenza (G.W. Bailey), matters are made even worse. Captain Raydor works hard to win over Provenza and the crew, while closing high-profile cases with an emphasis on plea bargains to avoid costly trials for the city. The professional turns personal for Sharon when she agrees to take in Rusty Beck (Graham Patrick Martin), a teenage witness in a murder case, who has run away from his foster family. Sharon becomes both protector and mother to the boy, helping him deal with many stresses, including the pressure of being a witness, the reappearance of his irresponsible parents, and the issues of starting out at a new school. As if Sharon doesn't have enough on her plate, she also must contend with her estranged husband,

Jack Raydor (Tom Berenger), a charming lawyer who likes to gamble in Las Vegas. They should give her that promotion already.

Makepeace, Harriet "Harry" (*Dempsey and Makepeace*)

British noblewoman and member of an elite police unit, who is forced to partner with a Yank.
See: *Dempsey and Makepeace* (1985–1986, 30 episodes, UK)

Makutsi, Grace (*The No. 1 Ladies' Detective Agency*)

Secretary and later assistant detective at Botswana's only female-owned detective agency.
See: *The No. 1 Ladies' Detective Agency* (2008–2009, 7 episodes, UK/USA)

Manimal (1983, 8 episodes, USA)

Created by: Glen A. Larson, Donald R. Boyle
Production Co.: 20th Century–Fox Television, Glen A. Larson Productions
Originally Aired: NBC
Main Cast: Simon MacCorkindale, Melody Anderson, Michael D. Roberts, Reni Santoni

Dr. Jonathan Chase (Simon MacCorkindale) has a secret ... a BIG secret. Jonathan has learned a technique whereby he can transform himself into any animal—a hawk, a panther, a dolphin, or a bear. The handsome doctor uses this ability to fight crime, assisting beautiful police detective Brooke McKenzie (Melody Anderson) with her cases. Rounding out the exotic detective team is Ty Earl (Michael D. Roberts), Jonathan's buddy from the Vietnam War.

"Night of the Scorpion" (1983) pits Jonathan, Brooke, and Ty against Russian agents, who are searching for a mysterious list and an heiress who may hold the key to its whereabouts. While at the beach in "Scrimshaw," the trio discovers a skeleton with a scrimshaw clutched in its bony fingers and sets out to investigate the mystery.

Alas, Manimal's crime-fighting days were short-lived, with only eight adventures on record. To add insult to injury, *TV Guide* ranked *Manimal* as number 15 on its list of the "50 Worst TV Shows of All Time" in 2002. Grr....

Mann & Machine (1992, 9 episodes, USA)

Created by: Robert De Laurentiis, Dick Wolf
Production Co.: Wolf Films, Universal TV
Originally Aired: NBC
Main Cast: Yancy Butler, David Andrews, S. Epatha Merkerson

Cop shows love the mismatched-partners premise, and this one took it to the hilt, pairing an off-the-shelf wisecracking maverick with a female ROBOT. Yancy Butler is Sgt. Eve Edison, to all appearances a sexy (of course) female officer, who under the skin is a sophisticated robot capable of learning and emotion. Her none-too-willing partner is Detective Bobby Mann (David Andrews), who must teach Eve not only about police work, but also about what it means to be human. In "Billion Dollar Baby" (1992), Eve starts to develop maternal instincts, when she cares for a genetically engineered child sought by baby brokers. She learns about death and dying in "Cold, Cold Heart," when her case involves a terminally ill cryonics scientist.

Alas, her life lessons were cut short when this series went offline after only a handful of episodes.

Manners, Kate (*Most Wanted*)

LAPD officer working with an elite unit to catch the city's most wanted criminals.

See: *Most Wanted* (1976–1977, 21 episodes, USA)

Mannix (1967–1975, 194 episodes, USA)

Created by: Richard Levinson, William Link, Bruce Geller
Production Co.: Paramount Television, Desilu Productions, Norway Corporation
Originally Aired: CBS
Main Cast: Mike Connors, Gail Fisher, Ward Wood

Joe Mannix (Mike Connors) is a Los Angeles private detective of the hardboiled school. After a short (one season) stint with a large, progressive agency which relies upon computers to solve crimes, Mannix sets out on his own, setting up a small office in West L.A. There he accepts cases that get him shot at and beat up on a weekly basis, somehow immune to the peace and love vibe of late 60s. Assisting trouble-prone Joe is Peggy Fair (Gail Fisher), his secretary and gal Friday, who runs background checks via the phone and on rare occasion does undercover work. In "Out of the Night" (1973), Peggy goes against Joe's wishes to pose as a prostitute in hopes of breaking up a narcotics ring. Peggy is a single mother, the widow of a slain police officer, whose name Mannix clears of corruption charges in "Medal for a Hero" (1970).

Gail Fisher won two Golden Globe Awards and one Emmy Award for her portrayal of Peggy Fair and was an African American TV trailblazer throughout the 60s.

Marlowe, Gloria (*Bring 'Em Back Alive*)

U.S. vice consul in 1939 Singapore, who gets involved in intrigue with an adventurer/trapper.

See: *Bring 'Em Back Alive* (1982–1983, 17 episodes, USA)

Marple
See: *Agatha Christie's Marple* (2004–2013, 23 episodes, UK)

Marple, Jane (*Agatha Christie's Marple*)
Iconic amateur sleuth in a modern, non-canon adaptation of Christie's mysteries.
See: *Agatha Christie's Marple* (2004–2013, 23 episodes, UK)

Marple, Jane (*Agatha Christie's Miss Marple*)
Octogenarian amateur sleuth in a faithful adaptation of the source Christie novels.
See: *Agatha Christie's Miss Marple* (1984–1992, 12 episodes, UK/USA)

Mars, Veronica (*Veronica Mars*)
High school student and apprentice private investigator in a California seaside community.
See: *Veronica Mars* (2004–2007, 64 episodes, USA)

Marvel's Agents of S.H.I.E.L.D.
See: *Agents of S.H.I.E.L.D.* (2013– , 22 episodes, USA)

Mastriani, Jess (*Missing*)
Young psychic whose visions help the FBI locate missing people.
See: *Missing* (2003–2006, 56 episodes, Canada/USA)

Mathison, Carrie (*Homeland*)
CIA operative who battles bipolar disorder while chasing an Al Qaeda sleeper agent in the United States.
See: *Homeland* (2011– , 36 episodes, USA)

Matt Houston (1982–1985, 67 episodes, USA)
Created by: Lawrence Gordon
Production Co.: Aaron Spelling Productions, Largo Productions, Matt Houston Company
Originally Aired: ABC
Main Cast: Lee Horsley, Pamela Hensley, George Wyner, Lincoln Kilpatrick, Buddy Ebsen

Matlock Houston (Lee Horsley) is a Texas oilman now based in Los Angeles, who works as a private investigator, because making millions isn't as interesting as it sounds. C.J. Parsons (Pamela Hensley), a Harvard-educated lawyer, works as Matt's right-hand woman, assisting with investigative work and operating "Baby," an Apple computer that seems to have information on EVERYTHING (useful in the days before the Internet). The great-looking pair use Matt's helicopter for their "legwork" and frequently find their cases among the rich and famous, as in "Who Would Kill Ramona?" (1982), when a fading movie queen appears to be the target for murder. Sometimes they are victims themselves, as when C.J. is almost killed by Laurel and Hardy look-alikes in "Here's Another Fine Mess" (1983). Matt and C.J. are not just business associates, but also friends, who understand each other. C.J. understands Matt so well, in fact, that she narrates these adventures which bear his name (in the first season, at least), giving us little insights into his personality, such as, "He'll charm the socks off you."

Maxwell, Michelle (*King & Maxwell*)

Former Secret Service agent, now a private investigator with a lake house office.

See: *King & Maxwell* (2013, 10 episodes, USA)

May, Melinda (*Agents of S.H.I.E.L.D.*)

Pilot and weapons expert for a unit that investigates weird phenomena around the world.

See: *Agents of S.H.I.E.L.D.* (2013– , 22 episodes, USA)

McBain, Cassie (*She Spies*)

Jailed con artist turned undercover operative for Uncle Sam.

See: *She Spies* (2002–2004, 40 episodes, USA)

McBride, Ryan (*Baywatch Nights*)

Part of a team of private investigators who like to stick close to the beach.

See: *Baywatch Nights* (1995–1997, 44 episodes, USA)

McCafferty, Kate (*The Division*)

Police captain heading a team of officers in the Felony Division of the SFPD.

See: *The Division* (2001–2004, 88 episodes, USA)

McCall, Dee Dee (*Hunter*)

Sgt. Dee Dee McCall (Stepfanie Kramer), a homicide detective, works with partner Rick Hunter (Fred Dryer) to rid Los Angeles of its worst riffraff.

Nicknamed the "brass cupcake," beautiful Dee Dee is one tough cookie (brass cupcake, some kind of hard-to-bite baked good), unafraid to tackle a perp by jumping off the hood of a car and unflinching when a hulking good ol' boy harasses her. Dee Dee's husband was a police officer killed in line of duty, and in "The Shooter" (1985), she must relive those painful memories while searching with Hunter for a cop-killer who uses armor-piercing bullets. Sometimes McCall goes undercover, as in "The Snow Queen" (parts one and two, 1985), displaying a professional singing voice while posing as a chanteuse in a mobster's nightclub. Things turn dark on a later assignment, however, when Dee Dee is raped by a psychopath in "Rape and Revenge" (parts one and two, 1985), an episode controversial at the time for its violent depiction of the crime. McCall leaves Hunter and the LAPD behind to move away with her new husband in "Street Wise" (parts one and two, 1990), but continues to pursue her career with the San Diego Police Department, where Hunter joins her 13 years later for a short-lived revival of the series.

One good thing about brass cupcakes—they don't get stale.

See also: *Hunter* **(1984–1991, 153 episodes, USA)**

McCarron, Claire (*Leg Work*)

Former assistant district attorney turned private investigator who can't pay the bills.

See: *Leg Work* **(1987, 10 episodes, USA)**

McCormick, Ali (*Cold Squad*)

Police detective with a homicide unit in Vancouver specializing in cold cases.

See: *Cold Squad* **(1998–2005, 98 episodes, Canada)**

McIntyre, Paula (*Wire in the Blood*)

Detective Constable on a team which tracks down serial killers in northern England.

See: *Wire in the Blood* **(2002–2008, 31 episodes, UK)**

McKay, Gina (*Dangerous Curves*)

Miniskirt-wearing operative for a security and investigation firm in Dallas.

See: *Dangerous Curves* **(1992–1993, 34 episodes, USA)**

McKenzie, Brooke (*Manimal*)

Police detective who receives assistance from a doctor with a big secret.

See: *Manimal* **(1983, 8 episodes, USA)**

McLean, Evelyn (*Strange Report*)

Artist/model who assists a police consultant in investigating bizarre cases. See: *Strange Report* (1969–1970, 16 episodes, UK)

McMillan and Wife (1971–1977, 40 episodes, USA)

Created by: Leonard Stern
Production Co.: Talent Associates, Norton Simon Inc., Universal Television
Originally Aired: NBC
Main Cast: Rock Hudson, Susan Saint James, John Schuck, Nancy Walker

San Francisco Police Commissioner Stewart "Mac" McMillan solves mysteries with the help of his young, hip, slightly flaky, but insightful wife, **Sally**

Mac and Sally McMillan (Rock Hudson and Susan Saint James) join the venerable club of adorable sleuthing couples in *McMillan and Wife* (NBC/Photofest).

McMillan, while committing numerous 70s crimes against fashion and engaging in a love/hate relationship with their sardonic housekeeper Mildred. As portrayed by Rock Hudson, Susan Saint James, and Nancy Walker respectively, the cast has charisma to burn, and the domestic scenes make this series sparkle, especially romantic scenes between Mac and Sally, and physical comedy with "the commish" and Mildred, emphasizing the height disparity between Hudson and Walker. (The Hudson-Walker tango in "Cross & Double Cross" [1974] is a series standout.) Another comedy of opposites is played out between handsome, urbane Mac and his pudgy, plodding, but loyal assistant, Sgt. Charles Enright (John Schuck), who is on call 24/7, and never seems to get a good night's sleep or a decent meal. In between all the screwball comedy moments, the occasional murder gets solved, with Sally, the daughter of a policeman, somehow always in the thick of things.

One spoke of the *NBC Mystery Movie* "wheel" of rotating series, *McMillan and Wife* is light on mystery but abundant in charm.

See also: **McMillan, Sally (*McMillan and Wife*)**

McMillan, Sally (*McMillan and Wife*)

Sally McMillan volunteers at the hospital, organizes charitable events, and frequently stumbles upon crimes, so it helps that the Police Commissioner of San Francisco is her husband, Stewart "Mac" McMillan (Rock Hudson). As portrayed by Susan Saint James, Sally is spunky and bright with an infallible nose for trouble and good crime-solving instincts, though it is usually Mac who puts the final pieces of the puzzle together. In "The Devil, You Say" (1973), Sally is targeted by a coven, which believes that she is the reincarnation of a dead goddess, to genuinely creepy Halloween effect. An earthquake "Aftershock" (1975) reveals a dead body behind the bricks of the McMillans' fireplace, and Sally must fend off repeated suspicious offers for their damaged home. A very pregnant Sally competes in a road rally with Mac and some wealthy (or are they?) friends, where murder crosses the finish line in "Downshift to Danger" (1974).

Sally is killed off (reportedly due to a contract dispute with Saint James) in the last season of the series, renamed *McMillan*, a sad end for a charming, quintessentially 70s character.

See also: *McMillan and Wife* **(1971–1977, 40 episodes, USA)**

McNally, Andrea "Andy" (*Rookie Blue*)

Andy McNally (Missy Peregrym) leaves the police academy with four other rookies to begin work at 15 Division in a large (unnamed) city. Her academy training isn't much help on her first day, when she accidentally outs an undercover cop, blowing months of work, but she redeems herself by catching a killer. Andy has police work in her blood, but she is also aware of the toll the job takes, since her father, Tommy McNally (Peter MacNeill), burnt out as a homicide detective. In "Fite Nite" (2010), Andy is embarrassed by her father's drunken, belligerent behavior at a department event, especially since he had promised to stop drinking for the night. While Andy continues to learn the ropes at division, navigating a sea of grouchy training officers, she finds a sympathetic ear (not to mention a handsome face) in Detective Luke Callaghan (Eric Johnson), with whom she begins a romantic relationship. Love, however, seems to be a constantly moving target for Andy, as she is also attracted to Sam Swarek (Ben Bass), the cop whose cover she had earlier blown, setting up a seemingly eternal triangle. Although Andy survives a bomb blast at the station in "Everlasting" (2014), the problems of her love life may be harder to escape.

See also: *Rookie Blue* (2010– , 63 episodes, Canada)

McNamara, Cory (*Pacific Blue*)

By-the-book police officer who patrols Santa Monica's beaches by bicycle.
See: *Pacific Blue* (1996–2000, 101 episodes, USA)

Me and Mom (1985, 6 episodes, USA)

Created by: Hal Sitowitz
Originally Aired: ABC
Main Cast: Lisa Eilbacher, Holland Taylor, James Earl Jones, Henry Darrow

Barely a blip on the TV radar, *Me and Mom* stars Lisa Eilbacher as Kate Morgan, criminologist and owner of her own private detective agency. Kate's mother, Zena Hunnicutt (Holland Taylor), is a mink-wearing socialite with too much time on her hands, who gets involved in Kate's cases. Sometimes Zena is even the focus of her daughter's investigations, as when Zena's new beau is the main suspect in an art robbery or when Zena's late husband's murderer is murdered. Alas, even the presence of James Earl Jones as Kate's REAL partner, ex-cop Lou Garfield, wasn't enough to extend the life of this series.

Mears, Nikita (*Nikita*)

Trained operative and assassin, trying to bring down her former employer for killing her fiancé.
See: *Nikita* (2010–2013, 73 episodes, USA)

Medium (2005–2011, 130 episodes, USA)

Based on: The real-life experiences of Allison DuBois
Created by: Glenn Gordon Caron

Production Co.: Picturemaker Productions, Grammnet Productions, CBS Paramount Network Television (2006–2009), et al.
Originally Aired: NBC (2005–2009), CBS (2009–2011)
Main Cast: Patricia Arquette, Jake Weber, Miguel Sandoval, Sofia Vassilieva, Maria Lark, David Cubitt

Patricia Arquette stars as **Allison DuBois**, a clairvoyant who uses her psychic gifts to help the Phoenix District Attorney's Office prosecute cases and solve murders. Allison's visions arrive by way of her dreams, which jolt her awake, causing sleepless nights for her and dutiful husband Joe (Jake Weber). Although Allison develops a great track record, D. A. Manuel Devalos (Miguel Sandoval) and Detective Lee Scanlon (David Cubitt) are frequently skeptical, seemingly forgetting each week that it takes five or six nights of dreams for Allison to sort through the misleading and jumbled visions to get at the truth. In the meantime, Allison and Joe struggle to provide their three daughters, all of whom seem to have inherited Allison's gifts, with some semblance of a normal life.

See also: **DuBois, Allison (*Medium*)**

Memphis Beat (2010–2011, 20 episodes, USA)
Created by: Joshua Harto, Liz W. Garcia
Production Co.: Warner Horizon Television, Smokehouse (Pictures)
Originally Aired: TNT
Main Cast: Jason Lee, Alfre Woodard, Sam Hennings, DJ Qualls, Celia Weston, Leonard Earl Howze

Dwight Hendricks (Jason Lee) is a Memphis police detective, who loves everything about his city, especially the blues and Elvis, but loves his mother (Celia Weston) perhaps a bit too much. Dwight takes a laid-back approach to crime-solving, which sometimes brings him into conflict with his by-the-book boss, Lieutenant Tanya Rice (Alfre Woodard). Rice's squad, including Dwight's partner Charles "Whitehead" White (Sam Hennings), searches for missing beauty queens, confronts hostage situations, and investigates murders in episodes such as "Love Her Tender," "Baby, Let's Play House," and "Don't Be so Cruel," whose titles reference Presley's songs. In "Polk Salad Annie" (2010), the team investigates the attempted murder of a BBQ king, while Lieutenant Rice deals with personal problems when her son runs afoul of the law.

Alas, the show's network, TNT, was "nothin' but a hound dog," canceling this fresh series after two short seasons. Elvis has left the building (again).

The Mentalist (2008– , 138 episodes, USA)
Created by: Bruno Heller
Production Co.: Primrose Hill Productions, Warner Bros. Television
Originally Aired: CBS

136 • Mentalist

Main Cast: Simon Baker, Robin Tunney, Tim Kang, Owain Yeoman, Amanda Righetti, Rockmond Dunbar

Patrick Jane (Simon Baker) is a private consultant for the California Bureau of Investigation in Sacramento. In his prior career, Jane had been a con man and "psychic," and he now uses the keen observational skills acquired in that line of work to help the CBI catch criminals. His main interest in helping the CBI, however, is catching the serial killer known as Red John, who killed Jane's wife and daughter. Jane's immediate supervisor is Agent **Teresa Lisbon** (Robin Tunney), who tolerates Jane's often unprofessional antics, such as hypnotizing suspects or running mini-cons on them, because he helps to close cases, even while causing headaches for Lisbon with the higher-ups. Other members of the team include Kimball Cho (Tim Kang), an unsmiling former gang member, Wayne Rigsby (Owain Yeoman), the overcompensating son of a career criminal, and Grace Van Pelt (Amanda Righetti), the naive rookie of the crew, who eventually marries Rigsby. Red John snakes in and out of their lives for years, leaving behind a pile of dead bodies, some of them close to CBI's home, and jeopardizing the team's careers, but his machinations never break the bonds of loyalty between the members of Lisbon's quirky crew.

See also: **Lisbon, Teresa (*The Mentalist*)**

Former con man Patrick Jane (Simon Baker) meets his match in no-nonsense Agent Teresa Lisbon (Robin Tunney) on *The Mentalist* (CBS/Photofest).

Merren, Alice (*The Bletchley Circle*)
Former Bletchley Park codebreaker who solves crimes with her ex-coworkers.
See: *The Bletchley Circle* (2012–2014, 7 episodes, UK)

Miami Vice (1984–1989, 111 episodes, USA)
Created by: Anthony Yerkovich
Production Co.: Michael Mann Productions, Universal TV
Originally Aired: NBC
Main Cast: Don Johnson, Philip Michael Thomas, Saundra Santiago, Olivia Brown, Edward James Olmos, Michael Talbott, John Diehl

An iconic 80s series which reflected and influenced the music and styles of its era, and, coincidentally, was a cop show, *Miami Vice* stars Don Johnson as pastels-clad vice detective Sonny Crockett. Crockett works undercover as drug runner Sonny Burnett and lives on a sailboat with his pet alligator, "Elvis," while finding time to keep an eye on the hottest fashion trends. Crockett's partner in Vice is former New York detective Rico Tubbs (Philip Michael Thomas), whose undercover alter ego is Rico Cooper, a wealthy drug buyer.

While Crockett and Tubbs tool around town in Ferraris, chasing drug dealers, terrorists, and mobsters, Detective Gina Navarro Calabrese (Saundra Santiago) gets to walk the street, posing as a prostitute to capture unsuspecting johns. Gina's partner, "Big Booty" Trudy Joplin (Olivia Brown), also does the streetwalking routine, gaining the confidence of prostitutes, who often have valuable tales to tell.

Going to the mat for these cool detectives is Commander Marty Castillo (Edward James Olmos), whose stare says more than most people's speeches. Castillo's squad pursues good-looking bad guys, such as Tony Amato (Bruce Willis), a gun runner, "La Muerta" (Bianca Jagger), an assassin, Sean Carroon (Liam Neeson), an Irish terrorist, "Silk" (Wesley Snipes), a pimp, Christine Von Marburg (Melanie Griffith), a madam, and Esteban Montoya (Ian McShane), a drug dealer. The cast and innumerable guest stars shine so brightly, in fact, that *Miami Vice* is best viewed with iconic Ray-Ban sunglasses à la Sonny Crockett.

Miller, Kat (*Cold Case*)
Member of a Philadelphia homicide team specializing in unsolved cases.
See: *Cold Case* (2003–2010, 156 episodes, USA)

Mills, Abbie (*Sleepy Hollow*)
Abbie Mills (Nicole Beharie) is a police lieutenant in the not-so-sleepy hamlet of Sleepy Hollow. Upon meeting Ichabod Crane (Tom Mison), a resurrected

Revolutionary war soldier, Abbie learns that Sleepy Hollow is ground zero for the coming apocalypse, and that she and Crane are the two biblically prophesied witnesses with the ability to stop Armageddon. As a child, Abbie and her sister Jenny (Lyndie Greenwood) had seen something nasty in the woods, specifically the demon Moloch, ringleader for the forces of evil in the coming showdown. The incident and its aftermath had led to an estrangement between the sisters and repeated institutionalizations for Jenny, but in "The Lesser Key of Solomon" (2013), Abbie and Jenny become allies in the fight against Moloch and his minions. Abbie's work takes her out of the real world and into purgatory, where she is trapped in "Bad Blood" (2014), but later escapes with Ichabod's help.

Time for an update to Lt. Mills's job description and, perhaps, a hefty raise.

See also: *Sleepy Hollow* (2013– , 13 episodes, USA)

Miss Fisher's Murder Mysteries (2012– , 26 episodes, Australia)

Based on: The novels and short stories of Kerry Greenwood
Created by: Deb Cox, Fiona Eagger
Production Co.: Every Cloud Productions
Originally Aired: Public Television
Main Cast: Essie Davis, Nathan Page, Hugo Johnstone-Burt, Ashleigh Cummings, Richard Bligh, Travis McMahon, Anthony Sharpe

The Honourable Miss **Phryne Fisher** (Essie Davis) is a thoroughly modern woman living in the not-so-modern Melbourne of the 1920s. Miss Fisher is a lady of means, which gives her the freedom to be unconventional, and she exercises that freedom by becoming a private detective. In the course of her investigations, which are never run-of-the-mill, involving everything from Latvian anarchists to possible formulas for alchemy, Miss Fisher often crosses paths with Inspector Jack Robinson (Nathan Page), who is not delighted to watch this tornado of a woman swirl through his crime scenes, unconcerned about red tape and police protocol. But as Jack learns more about Phryne and her methods, a burgeoning professional partnership forms, which may turn into something more if straight-arrow Jack can find some common ground with bohemian Phryne. In the meantime, Miss Fisher pursues her cases, working with adorable maid/companion Dot Williams (Ashleigh Cummings), a demure and religious woman, just as brave as Phryne, but otherwise her perfect foil. With Phryne, Jack, Dot, and earnest Constable Hugh Collins (Hugo Johnstone-Burt) on the case, Melbourne's criminals don't stand a chance.

See also: **Fisher, Phryne** (*Miss Fisher's Murder Mysteries*)

Miss Marple

See: *Agatha Christie's Miss Marple* (1984–1992, 12 episodes, UK/USA)

Missing (2003–2006, 56 episodes, Canada/USA)
Based on: The *1-800-WHERE-R-YOU* series of novels by Meg Cabot
Created by: Glenn Davis, William Laurin
Production Co.: NDG Productions, Lions Gate Television, Missing Productions II
Originally Aired: Lifetime
Main Cast: Caterina Scorsone, Gloria Reuben, Vivica A. Fox, Mark Consuelos, Justina Machado, Dean McDermott, Justin Louis

Originally titled *1–800-Missing*, this crime/paranormal drama stars Caterina Scorsone as Jess Mastriani, a young woman whose psychic visions help to locate missing people. In the first season, Jess works as a consultant for the FBI, partnering with Brooke Haslett (Gloria Reuben), who is highly skeptical of Jess's abilities, especially since her visions are more like puzzles, which are almost as difficult to solve as the crimes themselves. A major reboot occurred in season two, with not only the change in title, but also a new lead for the series in Vivica A. Fox as FBI Agent Nicole Scott. Caterina/Jess becomes the second banana, now a full-fledged, if junior, agent, but there's less emphasis on her visions and more attention to her partnership with rule-breaking, sassy, supercop Nicole. As an iconoclast, Nicole does immediately accept the validity of Jess's visions, and finds the information gained from them useful, when she can slow down long enough to hear it. With a new boss, John Pollock (Justin Louis), who loves to grab all the credit, and a partner who has problems with authority, rookie Jess certainly has her hands full.

Missing (2012, 10 episodes, USA)
Created by: Gregory Poirier
Production Co.: Upcountry Productions, Little Engine Productions, Stillking Films, ABC Studios
Originally Aired: ABC
Main Cast: Ashley Judd, Cliff Curtis, Sean Bean, Adriano Giannini, Nick Eversman

Rebecca Winstone (Ashley Judd) reluctantly sends her 18-year-old son Michael (Nick Eversman) to a summer architecture program in Rome, while she tends to her flower shop at home. When Michael goes missing, Becca flies to Europe to track him down, but she has more than the average American's resources at hand, since Rebecca is a retired CIA agent. The usual assortment of twists and turns ensues, including the reappearance of Becca's husband, Paul (Sean Bean), thought dead in a car bombing; an international chase through France, Croatia, the Czech Republic, Austria, and Bulgaria; and rounds of "who do you trust" with CIA, French, Russian, and Interpol agents. Becca is tenacious in mowing down obstacles to locate Michael, but the happy ending is short-lived when Becca herself goes missing, now forever lost due to the abrupt cancellation of this espionage series.

Mission: Impossible (1966–1973, 171 episodes, USA)

Created by: Bruce Geller
Production Co.: Desilu Productions, Paramount Television
Originally Aired: CBS
Main Cast: Steven Hill, Barbara Bain, Greg Morris, Peter Lupus, Peter Graves, Martin Landau, Leonard Nimoy, Lynda Day George

"As always, should you or any of your I.M. Force be caught or killed, the Secretary will disavow any knowledge of your actions."

Fast-paced espionage series chronicling the exploits of the Impossible Missions Force (IMF), a team of secret agents led by Jim Phelps (Peter Graves), who receives instructions via a tape-recording which self-destructs seconds after reaching its conclusion. Phelps selects operatives for each sensitive and dangerous assignment based on their unique skills, and his favorites include master of disguise Rollin Hand (Martin Landau), top model turned undercover specialist **Cinnamon Carter** (Barbara Bain), and (later) disguise expert Lisa Casey (Lynda Day George). The team topples dictators, rescues hostages, and prevents assassinations, using impossibly intricate plans and split-second timing, aided by the skills of electronics genius Barney Collier (Greg Morris) and strongman Willy Armitage (Peter Lupus). Most missions involve an elaborate ruse, such as an impersonation, culminating in a big reveal, where one of the agents rips off a mask to display their true identity to the startled mark.

Mission: Impossible, as its title suggests, is all about the mission, and we learn little about the personal lives of the IMF or who their bosses might be. That just adds to the intrigue and élan of this imaginative series.

See also: **Carter, Cinnamon** (*Mission: Impossible*)

Mission: Impossible (1988–1990, 35 episodes, USA)

Created by: Bruce Geller
Production Co.: Paramount Network Television
Originally Aired: ABC
Main Cast: Peter Graves, Thaao Penghlis, Tony Hamilton, Phil Morris, Jane Badler, Bob Johnson

Peter Graves reprises his role as Jim Phelps in this sequel to the 1966 TV series of the same title. Phelps comes out of retirement to lead the Impossible Missions Force, with a new dossier of agents and more advanced high-tech gadgets at his disposal. Joining Phelps for dangerous duty around the world are Thaao Penghlis as Nicholas Black, master of disguise; Phil Morris as Grant Collier, electronics expert and son of Barney Collier (Phil's real-life father Greg Morris) from the original series; and Jane Badler as Shannon Reed, a former Secret Service Agent and role-playing specialist. The IMF fights neo–Nazis, thwarts invasions, destroys druglords, and even saves the planet, as in "Target

Earth," when Shannon finds herself trapped on an orbiting spacecraft hijacked by terrorists. In short, the new team is much like the old team, just with better toys for a digital age.

Mr. & Mrs. North (1952–1954, 57 episodes, USA)
Based on: The novels of Richard and Frances Lockridge
Production Co.: Bernard L. Schubert Productions, Federal Telefilms
Originally Aired: CBS (1952–1953), NBC (1954)
Main Cast: Richard Denning, Barbara Britton, Francis De Sales

Mr. and Mrs. North are Jerry (Richard Denning) and Pamela (Barbara Britton), a cosmopolitan couple living in New York's Greenwich Village, who stumble upon crimes and solve them, while keeping the mood light with their sophisticated wit. Danger seems to follow publisher Jerry and housewife Pamela, whether it's to a fashion show where a model dies on stage or to the racetrack, where a jockey's body turns up in the trunk of their car. When they need official help, the Norths turn to their friend, homicide Lieutenant Bill Weigand (Francis De Sales), but Pam is the natural detective of the three, paying attention to details and practicing the art of reading people.

Married sleuths Jerry and Pamela set the (TV) stage for later crime-solving couples with charm to spare, such as Mac and Sally in *McMillan and Wife* and Jonathan and Jennifer in *Hart to Hart*.

Mr. & Mrs. Smith (1996, 13 episodes, USA)
Created by: John J. Sakmar, Kerry Lenhart
Production Co.: Page Two Productions, Bakula Productions, Warner Bros. Television
Originally Aired: CBS
Main Cast: Scott Bakula, Maria Bello, Roy Dotrice

Short-lived series about a pair of sexy operatives who work for an international private intelligence firm known as The Factory. Mr. Smith (Scott Bakula) and Mrs. Smith (Maria Bello) have never met, but, after a case pushes them together, they are assigned to pose as a suburban couple, while pursuing missions around the world. The Smiths try to discern the secrets of each other's pasts (including their real names), as they ferret out assassins, search for kidnappers, and, in "The Grape Escape" (1996), save the European grape crop from genetically engineered insects.

In an interesting "will they or won't they" twist, she seems willing, but he is reluctant, a reverse of forerunner *Remington Steele's* romantic dynamic.

The Mod Squad (1968–1973, 123 episodes, USA)
Created by: Bud Ruskin
Production Co.: Thomas-Spelling Productions

142 • Mod

Originally Aired: ABC
Main Cast: Michael Cole, Clarence Williams III, Peggy Lipton, Tige Andrews

Hipper than hip crime series about three troubled youths who get a second chance by working undercover for the police, going where "the fuzz" can't and "keeping it real." With Michael Cole as Pete Cochran, Clarence Williams III as Linc Hayes, and Peggy Lipton as **Julie Barnes**, this drama tackles many hot issues of the 60s, such as Vietnam, LSD, radicals, and race relations. Captain Adam Greer (Tige Andrews) hands out assignments and serves as surrogate father to these sometimes reluctant cops. Probably the most sensitive squad of law enforcement officials ever mustered, this trio cries, frets, and wrestles with

(Left to right) Pete Cochran (Michael Cole), Julie Barnes (Peggy Lipton) and Linc Hayes (Clarence Williams III) are sensitive, groovy cops in *The Mod Squad* (ABC/Photofest).

their consciences, while walking the fine line between working for the man and becoming the man. As Linc would say, "solid."
See also: **Barnes, Julie** (*The Mod Squad*)

Monk (2002–2009, 125 episodes, USA)

Created by: Andy Breckman
Production Co.: Mandeville Films, Touchstone Television (2002–2007), ABC Studios (2007–2009), et al.
Originally Aired: USA Network
Main Cast: Tony Shalhoub, Bitty Schram, Jason Gray-Stanford, Ted Levine, Traylor Howard

Obsessive-compulsive detective Adrian Monk works as a consultant for the San Francisco Police Department, using his almost supernatural gifts of observation and analysis to solve crimes when the police can't. Mr. Monk (Tony Shalhoub) has difficulty navigating the world due to his intense phobias and quirks, so he employs an assistant to hand him disinfecting wipes, drive him to crime scenes, and help when he gets stuck in unending compulsive loops. First **Sharona Fleming** (Bitty Schram) and later **Natalie Teeger** (Traylor Howard) serve as his gal Fridays, providing advice, moral support, and, yes, an unending series of towelettes, so Monk can get to the point where he says, "here's what happened."

See also: **Fleming, Sharona** (*Monk*); **Teeger, Natalie** (*Monk*)

Monroe Messer, Lindsay (*CSI: NY*)

Montana native with an amazing head for detail, who becomes a detective in New York City.
See: *CSI: NY* (2004–2013, 197 episodes, USA)

Montenegro, Angela (*Bones*)

Forensic artist who helps to solve crimes via craniofacial reconstruction and holograms.
See: *Bones* (2005– , 190 episodes, USA)

Moonlight (2007–2008, 16 episodes, USA)

Created by: Ron Koslow, Trevor Munson
Production Co.: Warner Bros. Television, Silver Pictures Television
Originally Aired: CBS
Main Cast: Alex O'Loughlin, Sophia Myles, Jason Dohring, Shannyn Sossamon

Alex O'Loughlin stars as Mick St. John, a Los Angeles private detective with a bloody little secret—he's a vampire. At a murder scene, Mick runs into

Internet reporter **Beth Turner** (Sophia Myles), and vampire and mortal find themselves drawn together in crime, while flashbacks reveal a prior (un)deadly connection between the two that Beth only partially remembers. Soon Beth learns Mick's secret and is introduced to the shadowy underworld of L.A. vampiredom, which includes Mick's is-she-or-isn't-she-undead late wife Coraline (Shannyn Sossamon) and his boyish but wealthy friend Josef (Jason Dohring), a 400-year-old vampire. In the meantime, tortured Mick and spirited Beth continue to hear the call of forbidden love, while finding time to solve crime and fight evil in both their worlds.

See also: **Turner, Beth** (*Moonlight*)

Moonlighting (1985–1989, 66 episodes, USA)

Created by: Glenn Gordon Caron
Production Co.: Picturemaker Productions, ABC Circle Films
Originally Aired: ABC
Main Cast: Cybill Shepherd, Bruce Willis, Allyce Beasley, Curtis Armstrong

When former model **Maddie Hayes** (Cybill Shepherd) learns that her embezzling accountant has flown the coop, she resolves to liquidate her few remaining assets, including a struggling detective agency which had been used as a tax write-off. Fast-talking agency honcho David Addison (Bruce Willis) has other ideas, however, and convinces Maddie to give the P.I. biz a try, where they will work together as partners to solve cases. A wisecracking, yammering battle of the sexes ensues, masquerading as a business called Blue Moon Investigations. Allyce Beasley co-stars as loyal receptionist Ms. DiPesto, who answers the agency's phones with her trademark original rhymes. Maddie and David's "leg work" often finds them in the car, and, as the dueling investigators discuss a case, each drowns out the other, Maddie with the feminist viewpoint, and David with the guy's perspective. It's no surprise, then, that romantic sparks fly as the series progresses, and the duo dances the will-they-or-won't-they pas de deux.

See also: **Hayes, Maddie** (*Moonlighting*)

Moreno, Nina (*New York Undercover*)

NYPD detective who deals with more than her share of violence and tragedy.

See: *New York Undercover* (1994–1998, 89 episodes, USA)

Moretti, Kate (*Perception*)

Special Agent for the FBI in Chicago, who works with a schizophrenic neuropsychiatrist.

See: *Perception* (2012– , 34 episodes, USA)

Moretti, Victoria "Vic" (*Longmire*)
Transplanted Philadelphia homicide detective, now a sheriff's deputy in wild Wyoming.
See: *Longmire* (2012–2014, 33 episodes, USA)

Morgan, Debra (*Dexter*)
Miami homicide detective and adoptive sister of a blood-spatter analyst/serial killer.
See: *Dexter* (2006–2013, 96 episodes, USA)

Morgan, Kate (*Me and Mom*)
Criminologist and private detective who gets unwanted help from her mother.
See: *Me and Mom* (1985, 6 episodes, USA)

The Most Deadly Game (1970–1971, 12 episodes, USA)
Created by: Morton S. Fine, David Friedkin
Production Co.: Aaron Spelling Productions
Originally Aired: ABC
Main Cast: Ralph Bellamy, Yvette Mimieux, George Maharis

"Murder is the most deadly game. These three criminologists play it."

Three detectives join forces to solve only the most unusual crimes in this short-lived mystery series. Ralph Bellamy is Ethan Arcane, experienced criminologist and father figure to Vanessa Smith (Yvette Mimieux) and Jonathan Croft (George Maharis). In "Photo Finish" (1970), the team must deal with a serial killer named "Scorpio, Mars in the Eighth House," who is sending photos of murder victims to Arcane and begging to be stopped. Vanessa uncovers that 70s staple, a satanic cult, during an investigation of her friend's grisly murder in "Witches' Sabbath" (1970). As she and Jonathan begin to pursue their mutual romantic interest, they delve into the murder of a foreign spy during a fox hunt in "Lady from Praha" (1970).

While mostly a forgettable whodunit, *The Most Deadly Game* is known for its tragic association with the suicide of Inger Stevens, who was originally set to star as the female lead.

Most Wanted (1976–1977, 21 episodes, USA)
Production Co.: Quinn Martin Productions
Originally Aired: ABC
Main Cast: Robert Stack, Shelly Novack, Jo Ann Harris, Hari Rhodes

Dan Stoddard (Hari Rhodes), the Mayor of Los Angeles, creates an elite unit within the LAPD to capture criminals on his most-wanted list. Stoddard taps square-jawed Captain Linc Evers (Robert Stack) to lead the task force with a mandate to focus on one case at a time, ensuring that the job will get done right. Assisting Evers in the Most Wanted unit are Sgt. Charlie Benson (Shelly Novack) and Officer Kate Manners (Jo Ann Harris), and the team pursues hijackers, kidnappers, revolutionaries, arsonists, burglars and others who would wreak havoc in the city of Angels. In "The White Collar Killer" (1977), Linc, Charlie and Kate go undercover as inmates in a minimum-security prison to determine who is killing convicted government officials.

Even with Stack's star power, Harris's good looks and a bevy of guest stars, including Ian McShane, Lynda Day George, Stuart Whitman, John Saxon, Pernell Roberts, and Mariette Hartley, this one wasn't on ABC's most-wanted list the following fall.

Motive (2013– , 26 episodes, Canada)
Created by: Daniel Cerone
Production Co.: Foundation Features, Lark Productions
Originally Aired: ABC
Main Cast: Kristin Lehman, Louis Ferreira, Brendan Penny, Lauren Holly, Cameron Bright, Roger Cross, Valerie Tian, Warren Christie

Kristin Lehman portrays Angie Flynn, a working-class homicide detective in Vancouver, B.C. Flynn juggles single motherhood with her police investigations, and her ability to read people and situations is an asset in both roles. Assisting Flynn with work and life is her partner on the force, Detective Oscar Vega (Louis Ferreira), and the two interrogate suspects with a particular emphasis on the motives for a crime. Like *Columbo*, *Motive* reveals the identity of the killer at the beginning of each episode, so the emphasis is on why the murder was committed and how the detectives will bring the perpetrator to justice. Unlike *Columbo*, however, *Motive* mixes the professional with the personal, as when Sgt. Mark Cross (Warren Christie) becomes Flynn's team commander, and their immediate animosity reveals a former extramarital affair. But when Cross himself is suspected of murder in "For You I Die" (2014), Angie comes to his defense, and a long-buried secret about one of their cases may reveal the real motive behind the crime.

The Mrs. Bradley Mysteries (1998–2000, 5 episodes, UK)
Based on: The novels of Gladys Mitchell
Production Co.: British Broadcasting Corp., WGBH, BBC America
Originally Aired: Public Television
Main Cast: Diana Rigg, Neil Dudgeon

Diana Rigg portrays Adela Bradley, an amateur sleuth in the Miss Marple mold, if Miss Marple wore stunning Jazz Age couture and had a hunky chauffeur

(Neil Dudgeon) as a confidant. The twosome roams the English countryside in a Rolls Royce and stumbles upon excitement and mystery, as in "Death at the Opera" (2000), wherein Mrs. B.'s alma mater is the setting for murder. Mrs. Bradley uses her intelligence, observational skills, and psychological analysis to solve crimes, such as the case of "The Worsted Viper" (2000), where she finds that virginity and weddings are the factors linking murder victims. She also displays a keen wit, sharing it not only with suspects and victims, but also with viewers, when Diana Rigg turns to the camera and speaks her wry reflections directly to the audience.

Mrs. Columbo (1979–1980, 13 episodes, USA)

Production Co.: Universal TV, Gambit Productions
Originally Aired: NBC
Main Cast: Kate Mulgrew, Lili Hadyn, Henry Jones

Short-lived *Columbo* spinoff about the wife of the famed Los Angeles police lieutenant. Kate Mulgrew stars in the title role as a part-time reporter for neighborhood newspaper *The Weekly Advertiser*. In the course of researching her articles, which are used as filler for the newspaper's advertisements and coupons, Kate Columbo stumbles upon crimes that require her keen powers of observation for solution. Tenacious and fearless, she confronts murderers one-on-one, as she does with a psychotic ventriloquist in the creepy "A Riddle for Puppets" (1979). Mrs. Columbo is a multitasker, who also raises a nine-year-old daughter, cares for a troublemaking basset hound, and does this seemingly as a single mother, since her husband, the police lieutenant, is always mysteriously out of town.

This series went through three title changes, including *Kate Loves a Mystery*, dropped all ties to *Columbo*, and rechristened its main character "Kate Callahan," but to no avail. Kate may have loved a mystery, but viewers didn't love Kate's mysteries, whether she was Mrs. Columbo or Mrs. Callahan.

Mulligan, Hildy (*Murder in the First*)

Single mother and SFPD homicide detective who likes to play the good cop.

See: *Murder in the First* (2014– , 10 episodes, USA)

Munroe, Jill (*Charlie's Angels*)

Farrah Fawcett stars as Jill Munroe, one of three female private investigators at Charles Townsend's detective agency, hence "Charlie's Angels." With her blonde mane, brilliant smile, and toned body, Jill specializes in undercover assignments where she isn't exactly covered up, jobs which require skimpy clothes, such as a sexy masseuse, a playmate centerfold candidate, and a preacher's backwoods daughter. She is an excellent athlete in many sports, posing as a swimming instructor in "The Mexican Connection" (1976), a roller derby queen in "Angels on Wheels" (1976), and a tennis instructor in "The Killing Kind" (1976). Jill departs the agency after just one year, although she sometimes returns to lend a hand, as when her sister and replacement Angel Kris Munroe (Cheryl Ladd) is kidnapped in "Angel in a Box" (1979).

Despite her short tenure, Jill/Farrah remains the most iconic Angel, at least in part due to the fact that Farrah's now famous bathing suit poster, which sold 20 million copies, was released in the same year that *Charlie's Angels* debuted.

See also: ***Charlie's Angels*** **(1976–1981, 110 episodes, USA)**

Munroe, Kris (*Charlie's Angels*)

Beautiful P.I. who replaces her gorgeous sister at a wealthy man's detective agency.

See: ***Charlie's Angels*** **(1976–1981, 110 episodes, USA)**

Murder in the First (2014– , 10 episodes, USA)

Created by: Steven Bochco, Eric Lodal
Production Co.: TNT Originals
Originally Aired: TNT
Main Cast: Taye Diggs, Kathleen Robertson, Richard Schiff, James Cromwell, Ian Anthony Dale, Nicole Ari Parker, Raphael Sbarge, Lombardo Boyer, Tom Felton, Steven Weber

This crime drama follows a single case throughout the season, covering the investigation, arrest, and trial. SFPD homicide detectives Terry English (Taye Diggs) and Hildy Mulligan (Kathleen Robertson) investigate two seemingly unrelated murders, both of which eventually lead to Silicon Valley wunderkind Erich Blunt (Tom Felton). While questioning Blunt about the murder of a flight attendant, bereaved widower English plays bad cop, while single mother Mulligan does the good cop routine. Mulligan later gives the term "good cop" new meaning by obtaining Blunt's DNA sample via a kiss while on a romantic dinner-date. Inspector Mulligan isn't all candy hearts, however, later shooting and killing a knife-wielding suspect, but is cleared of any wrongdoing and returns to duty. After multiple twists and turns, bad-boy Blunt is found innocent of the flight attendant's murder, but is charged with homicide again, this time for killing his biological father. More twists ensue, and enough viewers enjoyed them to ensure a second season for this series on TNT.

Murder, She Wrote (1984–1996, 264 episodes, USA)

Created by: Peter S. Fischer, Richard Levinson, William Link
Production Co.: Universal Television, Corymore Productions
Originally Aired: CBS
Main Cast: Angela Lansbury, William Windom, Tom Bosley, Ron Masak

Murder, she writes ... murder, she finds. It's a wonder that mystery novelist **Jessica Fletcher** gets any writing done with all the murders that keep cropping up around her. But Cabot Cove resident Mrs. Fletcher (Angela Lansbury) is always ready to drop her work and assist the sheriff's office when murder rears its ugly head in the small Maine town. What's more, murder seems to follow her wherever she goes, on writing junkets, to family weddings, or on vacation, so Jessica always packs her skills of observation, analysis, and deduction, ready to put them to use when trouble strikes, as it always does. When Jessica rounds up the suspects each week, a cavalcade of guest stars drops in, from Julie Adams to Efrem Zimbalist, Jr., from Elizabeth Ashley to Adrian Zmed, accompanied by a multigenerational list of classic stars and fresh faces in between.

Miss Marple never solved this many cases.

See also: **Fletcher, Jessica (*Murder, She Wrote*)**

Angela Lansbury is successful mystery author and amateur sleuth Jessica Fletcher in *Murder, She Wrote* (CBS/Photofest).

Murphy, Connie (*The Dresden Files*)

Chicago police lieutenant who consults with a professional wizard on bizarre cases.

See: *The Dresden Files* (2007, 12 episodes, Canada/USA)

Murray, Gill (*Scott & Bailey*)

Detective Chief Inspector and head of the Manchester police department's Major Incident Team.

See: *Scott & Bailey* (2011– , 22 episodes, UK)

Myers, Nina (*24*)

Second-in-command and double agent at the Counter Terrorist Unit in Los Angeles.

See: *24* (2001–2010, 194 episodes, USA)

The Mystery Files of Shelby Woo (1996–1998, 41 episodes, Canada/USA)

Created by: Alan Goodman
Originally Aired: Nickelodeon
Main Cast: Irene Ng, Pat Morita, Adam Busch, Preslaysa Edwards, Steve Purnick, Ellen David, Noah Klar

High school student Shelby Woo (Irene Ng) is an intern at the Cocoa Beach Police Department, where she prefers crime-solving to performing her assigned office tasks. Shelby's innkeeper grandfather, Mike Woo (Pat Morita), disapproves of her detective work as do the police, but that doesn't stop Shelby and friends Noah Allen (Adam Busch) and Cindy Ornette (Preslaysa Edwards) from investigating mysteries big and small, such as the case of a dolphin missing from a marine lab or the report of suspicious injuries plaguing a touring theater company. Even Shelby's move to Boston in later years doesn't curb her sleuthing ways—she simply discovers new mysteries with a New England flair and finds local partners in crime-solving.

Mystery Girls (2014, 10 episodes, USA)

Created by: Shepard Boucher, Tori Spelling
Production Co.: ABC Family Original Productions, ProdCo
Originally Aired: ABC Family
Main Cast: Tori Spelling, Jennie Garth, Miguel Pinzon

Holly Hamilton (Tori Spelling) and Charlie Contour (Jennie Garth) once starred in a 90s TV series called *Mystery Girls*. When Nick Diaz (Miguel Pinzon), their number one fan, witnesses a murder in Los Angeles, he will talk only to his favorite "detectives," who are busy being a rich has-been star and a suburban housewife respectively. The women join forces to convince Nick to come clean about the murder he witnessed, inspiring Holly to hatch a plan to start a real detective agency in Beverly Hills with Charlie as her partner. Charlie comes on board, reluctantly at first, and Nick becomes their office assistant, the job of his dreams. Glamour-puss Holly and down-to-earth Charlie pursue their cases, such as stopping a high school prank and retrieving a high-fashion purse, investigations not exactly in the noir tradition, but understandable for a situation comedy, and a short-lived one at that.

Mystery Woman (2003–2007, 11 episodes, USA)
Created by: Michael Sloan
Production Co.: Alpine Medien Productions, Larry Levinson Productions, Hallmark Entertainment, MAT IV
Originally Aired: Hallmark Channel
Main Cast: Kellie Martin, Clarence Williams III

Kellie Martin stars in this series of TV-movie whodunits as Samantha Kinsey, proprietor of a mystery bookstore, photographer, and amateur detective. Assisting Samantha in her investigations is the bookstore's manager, Philby (Clarence Williams III), who just happens to be an ex-spy and a whiz at ferreting out secret information. Samantha uses the knowledge of motives, procedures, and criminal behavior gained from her reading of mystery books to solve crimes, as in "Wild West Mystery" (2006), where she must determine who shot a cowboy in a wild west show she has organized. Her photographic expertise is centerstage in "Snapshot" (2005), when a wealthy member of the store's book club is murdered after an inheritance dispute.

Sam is tenacious, pushy, and nosy—in other words, she's just like every other self-respecting member of the amateur sleuth's club.

NCIS (2003– , 258 episodes, USA)
Created by: Donald P. Bellisario, Don McGill
Production Co.: Belisarius Productions, Paramount Network Television, CBS Television Studios, et al.
Originally Aired: CBS
Main Cast: Mark Harmon, Michael Weatherly, Pauley Perrette, David McCallum, Sean Murray, Cote de Pablo, Lauren Holly, Rocky Carroll, Brian Dietzen, Sasha Alexander, Emily Wickersham

Another of TV's long-running and highly-populated (and popular) procedurals, *NCIS* adds a twist to the usual crime-solving—the cases here involve U.S. Navy and Marine Corps personnel. The unit in charge of such investigations is the Major Case Response Team of the Naval Criminal Investigative

Service, led by former Marine sniper Leroy Jethro Gibbs (Mark Harmon). An impatient and demanding supervisor, Gibbs sometimes slaps team members on the back of the head when they aren't performing up to his expectations. (Don't try this at YOUR workplace.) Assisting Gibbs in tracking down murderers and terrorists is Senior Special Agent Anthony "Tony" DiNozzo (Michael Weatherly), a womanizing manchild, who likes to use movie analogies when discussing cases.

The longest tenured-female on this colorful team is Abigail "Abby" Sciuto, a forensic scientist, who spends her days in the lab, examining DNA, analyzing ballistics, and searching for digital footprints. As portrayed by Pauley Perrette, who has appeared in every episode, Abby has a "goth" personal style, wearing dark clothing and displaying multiple tattoos, but she generally has a sunny personality and loves her geeky job. Unlike most of the other team members, Abby isn't afraid of Gibbs, and appears to be his favorite, a pigtailed daughter to his silver-haired dad, but with bodies in the next room.

Another long-standing member of the crew is Ziva David (Cote de Pablo), who begins as a Mossad (Israeli intelligence) liaison, but later becomes an agent for NCIS and a U.S. citizen. Ziva is loyal and fierce, killing her own half-brother, a double agent, to save Gibbs's life. Although fluent in 10 languages, Ziva provides moments of comic relief with her mangling of American idioms, which are called "Ziva-isms" by fans of the show.

Cote de Pablo departed the series after season 11, but this procedural juggernaut marches on. Although immensely popular, *NCIS* frequently contains graphic autopsy scenes, so, as they say on TV, viewer discretion is advised.

Nancy Drew (1995, 13 episodes, France/Canada)

Based on: The novels of Carolyn Keene
Production Co.: Nelvana, France 2, Marathon Productions, Westcom Entertainment Group
Originally Aired: In Syndication
Main Cast: Tracy Ryan, Jhene Erwin, Joy Tanner

Nancy Drew returns to the small screen in this short-lived series starring Tracy Ryan as the well-known amateur sleuth. Now a brunette, the older Nancy is a college student living in Manhattan with roommates Bess Marvin (Jhene Erwin) and George Fayne (Joy Tanner). When not busy studying, Nancy has a part-time job at a temp agency, in addition to her hobby of solving the mysteries which always seem to crop up around her. In "Exile," Nancy must investigate the disappearance of her professor, while "The Stranger by the Road" prompts Nancy and her friends to look into rumors of a haunted château in France. "The Long Journey Home," involving Russian mobsters and a stolen religious artifact, concludes the series with an apt if unintentionally prophetic title.

The Nancy Drew Mysteries
See: *The Hardy Boys/Nancy Drew Mysteries* (1977–1979, 46 episodes, USA)

Nash, Traci (*Rookie Blue*)
Black single mother trying to make it as a cop with four other rookies.
See: *Rookie Blue* (2010– , 63 episodes, Canada)

Nelson, Victoria "Vicki" (*Blood Ties*)
Toronto P.I. with failing eyesight, assisted in her investigations by a centuries-old vampire.
See: *Blood Ties* (2007–2008, 22 episodes, Canada)

The New Adventures of Wonder Woman
See: *Wonder Woman* (1975–1979, 59 episodes, USA)

The New Avengers (1976–1977, 26 episodes, UK/France/Canada)
Based on: The TV series *The Avengers* created by Sydney Newman
Created by: Brian Clemens, Albert Fennell
Production Co.: The Avengers Enterprises, IDTV Production, TF1
Originally Aired: CBS
Main Cast: Patrick Macnee, Gareth Hunt, Joanna Lumley

Patrick Macnee reprises his role as John Steed in this sequel to the 60s spy-fi series *The Avengers*, reimagined for 70s audiences. Joining Steed in stylish espionage are Gareth Hunt as Mike Gambit and Joanna Lumley as Purdey, two younger and more athletic agents who benefit from Steed's wisdom and starch. Ballet-trained, high-kicking Purdey and crack marksman Gambit assist their mentor on standard spy stuff, although bizarre cases still present themselves, such as "Gnaws" (1976), where the assignment is a giant rat. The pesky robots from the earlier series return in "The Last of the Cybernauts?" (1976), and the trio makes a valiant effort to pretend that no one is missing Mrs. **Emma Peel**.

New Tricks (2003– , 87 episodes, UK)
Created by: Nigel McCrery, Roy Mitchell
Production Co.: Wall to Wall Television, British Broadcasting Corp.
Originally Aired: Public Television
Main Cast: Alun Armstrong, James Bolam, Amanda Redman, Dennis Waterman, Denis Lawson, Nicholas Lyndhurst, Tamzin Outhwaite, Larry Lamb, Susan Jameson, Anthony Calf

Sandra Pullman (Amanda Redman) has her hands full with old police dogs (left to right) Brian Lane (Alun Armstrong), Gerry Standing (Dennis Waterman), and Jack Halford (James Bolam) in *New Tricks* (BBC/Photofest).

Long-running British procedural which examines the question of whether you really can teach an old (police) hound new tricks. After shooting a dog during a hostage rescue, **Sandra Pullman** (Amanda Redman), a forty-something Detective Superintendent, is assigned to a new and underfunded unit, the Unsolved Crime and Open Case Squad (UCOS). Ambitious Sandra isn't happy about moving down the career ladder, but she sets about assembling a squad of retired cops with the help of her mentor, former Detective Chief Superintendent Jack Halford (James Bolam). The old/new squad is quirky, to say the least. Brian Lane (Alun Armstrong) has exceptional memory and detail skills, allowing him to uncover clues others have missed, but suffers from OCD and has problems relating to people, making him a royal pain in the behind. Gerry Standing (Dennis Waterman) is an aging ladies man with three ex-wives, who likes to gamble and seems to be a little too friendly with gangsters. Pullman herself is a junk food-eating overachiever, who doesn't have much of a social life, although she's not struggling in the looks department. These detectives and their later replacements close unsolved cases in their inimitably scrappy way, breaking rules, bucking superiors, and showing, as Dennis Waterman sings in the opening theme, it "doesn't really matter if you're old and grey."

See also: **Pullman, Sandra** (*New Tricks*)

New York Undercover (1994–1998, 89 episodes, USA)

Created by: Kevin Arkadie, Dick Wolf
Production Co.: Cry Wolf, Universal Television, Wolf Films
Originally Aired: Fox
Main Cast: Malik Yoba, Michael DeLorenzo, Patti D'Arbanville-Quinn, Lauren Vélez

Police procedural distinguished by its hip, urban feel and use of contemporary music, a *Miami Vice* without boats or pastels. Malik Yoba is Detective J.C. Williams, a black undercover cop who must deal with professional and personal issues, and sometimes the intersection between the two, as when his fiancée is murdered on the day before their wedding. The professional also bleeds into the personal for J.C.'s partner, Detective Eddie Torres (Michael DeLorenzo), when his girlfriend, Detective Nina Moreno (Lauren Vélez), takes a bullet for Eddie in the line of duty. Nina recovers from temporary paralysis after the shooting, and later marries Eddie, but their happiness is short-lived when her new husband dies in a car bombing. (Weddings were a death sentence on this show.) The detectives report to Lieutenant Virginia Cooper (Patti D'Arbanville-Quinn), commander of the Fourth Precinct's detective squad, who loses her husband too, but by the (relatively) peaceful route of divorce. It's fortunate, then, that the detectives have a refuge from the violence and chaos—a place called Natalie's, a local club featuring R&B and hip-hop acts, including Mary

J. Blige, Boyz II Men, Chaka Khan, Gladys Knight, Aaron Neville, The Notorious B.I.G., and many more.

This distinctive crime drama won two NAACP Image Awards for Outstanding Drama Series.

Nikita (2010–2013, 73 episodes, USA)

Based on: The TV series *La Femme Nikita* created by Joel Surnow
Production Co.: Wonderland Sound and Vision, Sesfonstein Productions, Warner Bros. Television
Originally Aired: The CW
Main Cast: Maggie Q, Shane West, Lyndsy Fonseca, Aaron Stanford, Melinda Clarke, Xander Berkeley, Lyndie Greenwood, Dillon Casey, Noah Bean, Devon Sawa

A reimagining of USA Network's earlier series *La Femme Nikita* and Luc Besson's film *Nikita*. (Who says there are no new ideas in Hollywood?) This time out Maggie Q portrays Nikita, now with the last name Mears, a young woman awaiting execution for murder until a supersecret agency called Division fakes her death and trains her to become a spy and assassin. In a twist from the earlier series, however, Nikita is able to escape Division after the agency kills her fiancé (shades of *Alias*), and, as the series begins, she is out to bring down Division at any cost. To this end, she plants a mole in Division, one Alexandra "Alex" Udinov (Lyndsy Fonseca), a young woman whom Nikita had rescued after an assassination order from Division. Helping Nikita and Alex in the plot against Division is Michael Bishop (Shane West), who had trained Nikita in the fine art of assassination, but turned against the agency when he learned it was responsible for the death of his wife and daughter. Nikita and Michael become lovers, and manage to eliminate Percy Rose (Xander Berkeley), Division's nefarious leader, in "Homecoming" (2012). Things are seldom simple in spyville, however, and before long Nikita is on the run, accused of assassinating the President of the United States. The charge isn't true, of course, since Nikita has been framed by rogue agent Helen "Amanda" Collins (Melinda Clarke), Division's former interrogator and master manipulator (the analog of "Madeline" in the prior series), who's been Nikita's nemesis since the beginning. More twists and turns ensue, but Nikita and Michael battle their way to a happy ending in the aptly named series finale, "Canceled" (2013).

Nikita (*La Femme Nikita*)

Operative who exchanges a life sentence in prison for virtual slavery in an antiterrorist organization.

See: *La Femme Nikita* (1997–2001, 96 episodes, Canada)

North, Pamela (*Mr. & Mrs. North*)
Housewife who stumbles upon crimes and solves them with her publisher husband.
See: *Mr. & Mrs. North* (1952–1954, 57 episodes, USA)

The No. 1 Ladies' Detective Agency (2008–2009, 7 episodes, UK/USA)
Based on: The novels of Alexander McCall Smith
Created by: Richard Curtis, Anthony Minghella
Production Co.: The Weinstein Company, Home Box Office, British Broadcasting Corp., Mirage Enterprises, et al.
Originally Aired: HBO
Main Cast: Jill Scott, Anika Noni Rose, Lucian Msamati, Desmond Dube

Jill Scott stars as Precious Ramotswe, who opens Botswana's only female-owned detective agency after selling off her inherited cows. Precious proceeds to hire crackerjack secretary Grace Makutsi (Anika Noni Rose) as her assistant, and together they sip red-bush tea while empowering their female clients through the solution of cases big and small. In "The Big Bonanza" (2009), they deal with a disappearing dog and a demon dentist, while in "Poison" (2009), they investigate a possible poisoner and a feuding family's link to the ivory trade. The ladies continue to spread their wings, as Mma Makutsi tries on a new role (and hairstyle) as Assistant Detective, while Mma Ramotswe ventures along the relationship road with auto mechanic Mr. JLB Matekoni (Lucian Msamati). Even in facing the return of Ramotswe's abusive ex-husband and the machinations of an unscrupulous rival detective, these ladies are indomitable.

Numb3rs (2005–2010, 118 episodes, USA)
Created by: Nicolas Falacci, Cheryl Heuton
Production Co.: The Barry Schindel Company, Scott Free Productions, Paramount Network Television, CBS Television Studios
Originally Aired: CBS
Main Cast: Rob Morrow, David Krumholtz, Judd Hirsch, Alimi Ballard, Dylan Bruno, Diane Farr, Navi Rawat, Sophina Brown, Aya Sumika, Peter MacNicol

"We all use math every day."
Unique police procedural about an FBI agent, Don Eppes (Rob Morrow), and his brilliant brother, Charlie (David Krumholtz), who partner to solve crimes by using techniques of statistical and mathematical analysis. Don works for the FBI's Los Angeles office, while Charlie is a professor at the (fictitious) California Institute of Science. Charlie begins to consult for the Bureau when the brothers realize his blackboard scribblings and computer models can close cases. Assisting Don on the law-enforcement end, are, among others, Agents

David Sinclair (Alimi Ballard) and Megan Reeves (Diane Farr). On the brain trust side, Professors **Amita Ramanujan** (Navi Rawat) and Larry Fleinhardt (Peter MacNicol) suggest new mathematical or scientific approaches for Charlie's cases. Whether investigating murders, kidnappings, rapes, or robberies, Charlie and the team use math "to solve the biggest mysteries we know."

See also: **Ramanujan, Amita (*Numb3rs*)**

O'Brian, Chloe (*24*)

Computer nerd and loyal analyst at the Counter Terrorist Unit in Los Angeles.

See: *24* (2001–2010, 194 episodes, USA)

Ogbaa, Daisy (*Chase*)

U.S. Marshal, member of a crack fugitive apprehension team in Houston, Texas.

See: *Chase* (2010–2011, 18 episodes, USA)

O'Hara, Juliet "Jules" (*Psych*)

Juliet O'Hara (Maggie Lawson) is a detective with the Santa Barbara Police Department, partnered with hard-nosed Head Detective Carlton Lassiter (Timothy Omundson). Into their ordered lives breezes psychic detective Shawn Spencer (James Roday), who is no psychic at all, but a keen observer of detail and an inspired crime-solver. While "Lassie" is obsessively skeptical of Spencer's gifts, "Jules" is inclined to believe in Shawn's powers, and finds herself attracted to the talented, if sophomoric, "psychic." It takes years for Juliet and Shawn to find romance, and while things run smoothly at first, when Juliet learns that Shawn is not truly a psychic, she feels betrayed and breaks off their relationship. In "Juliet Wears the Pantsuit" (2013), Shawn moves out of their shared apartment, but Juliet shows she can take care of herself, using her wits and physical strength to take down a man who invades her home. When Juliet accepts an offer to be Head Detective for Chief Karen Vick (Kirsten Nelson), who is moving to the Bay Area, prospects look bleak for the couple. But Shawn follows his heart to San Francisco in series finale "The Break-Up" (2014), where Jules accepts his marriage proposal on a public street, but it's business as usual, when a robber snatches the ring and they give chase.

See also: *Psych* (2006–2014, 121 episodes, USA)

1-800-Missing

See: *Missing* (2003–2006, 56 episodes, Canada/USA)

One West Waikiki (1994–1996, 20 episodes, USA)
Created by: Glen A. Larson
Production Co.: Larson Entertainment, Rysher Television
Originally Aired: CBS
Main Cast: Cheryl Ladd, Richard Burgi, Kayla Blake, Paul Gleason, Ogie Zulueta

Dr. Dawn "Holli" Holliday (Cheryl Ladd) is the state of Hawaii's Medical Examiner, newly arrived from Los Angeles, where she used her forensics expertise at the Coroner's Office. Lt. Mack Wolfe (Richard Burgi) is a top homicide detective with the Honolulu P.D., just back from suspension after clearing his name when his partner is killed. Mack prefers to go with his gut when solving murders, while Holli relies on logic, science, and the latest forensic techniques to get at the truth. Opposites attract, of course, especially when they're gorgeous like these two, so romantic sparks fly, as Holli and Mack search for the Romanoff jewels, investigate the murder of a sumo wrestler, and stop the spread of a deadly virus.

Just another day in paradise.

Oskowski, Stephanie "Steve" (*Father Dowling Mysteries*)

Amateur sleuths are common on TV, but one of the most uncommon detective duos ever is the divine pairing of Father Frank Dowling (Tom Bosley) and Sister Stephanie "Steve" Oskowski (Tracy Nelson) of St. Michael's Parish in Chicago. Father Frank and Sister Steve stumble upon murders in, around, and related to the church, and manage to solve them before the police have a chance. Sister Steve is an amazing asset in these investigations, often going undercover, whether it be as an aerobics instructor, an expert card dealer, a flashy bartender, or even (the scandal!) a woman of ill repute. The young nun, it seems, grew up in the neighborhood and amassed a staggering array of useful, if not necessarily sanctified, skills. In "The Sanctuary Mystery" (1990), Sister Steve poses as a blackmailer to get the goods on a corrupt police captain who is framing her younger brother Mark (Stephen Dorff) for murder. Steve comes to the aid of an old flame who is being pursued by a killer, and has come conflicted feelings along the way, in "The Man Who Came to Dinner Mystery" (1989).

While she is not the most likely amateur detective ever to grace the small screen, Sister Steve is certainly a spirited original.

See also: *Father Dowling Mysteries* (1987–1991, 44 episodes, USA)

O'Toole, Danny (*Codename: Foxfire*)

Former CIA operative, recruited by the President's brother to conduct secret missions.

See: *Codename: Foxfire* (1985, 8 episodes, USA)

Over My Dead Body (1990–1991, 11 episodes, USA)
Created by: William Link, David Chisholm
Production Co.: Universal TV
Originally Aired: CBS
Main Cast: Edward Woodward, Jessica Lundy, Jill Tracy, Rick Fitts, Peter Looney

Nikki Page (Jessica Lundy), an obit writer for a newspaper in San Francisco, witnesses a murder through her window, but the police can find no body or evidence of a crime. Hoping to grab a scoop and raise her stature at the paper, fast-talking Nikki enlists the help of her favorite mystery writer, Maxwell Beckett (Edward Woodward). Beckett, a cranky, aging author enduring a two-book slump, agrees to help Nikki in hopes of getting his creative juices flowing. They join forces in true amateur sleuth tradition, solving the *Rear Window*–esque murder and developing a penchant for stumbling upon further crimes that will require their unique sleuthing abilities. In "No Ifs, Ands, or Butlers" (1990), Nikki asks Max to play butler for her friend's family, when the actual servant is accused of murder.

While this show was crafted to be a hipper *Murder, She Wrote*, Maxwell Beckett did not go on to become a household name like **Jessica Fletcher**.

Overseas Adventure
See: **Foreign Intrigue** (1951–1955, 156 episodes, USA)

Pacific Blue (1996–2000, 101 episodes, USA)
Created by: Bill Nuss
Production Co.: North Hall Productions, Gary Nardino Productions
Originally Aired: USA Network
Main Cast: Rick Rossovich, Jim Davidson, Darlene Vogel, Paula Trickey, Marcos Ferraez, David Lander, Mario Lopez, Jeff Stearns, Shanna Moakler, Amy Hunter

Frequently described as "*Baywatch* on bikes," *Pacific Blue* follows officers of the Santa Monica Police Department as they patrol the city's beaches on bicycles. Not surprisingly, it's a good-looking crew (bicycle shorts!), with Rick Rossovich leading the way in the first few seasons as Lieutenant Anthony Palermo, who serves as both commanding officer and father figure to the young cops. Cory McNamara (Paula Trickey) is a by-the-book officer from a police family, but her training and lineage can't save her dignity when she's chasing a perp and is thrown on stage during a wet T-shirt contest (as often happens), winning, no less, in "The Phoenix" (1996). Ambitious Chris Kelly (Darlene Vogel), formerly in public relations at the police department, thinks the way to the top is faster by bicycle, and joins the unit, later marrying T.C. Callaway (Jim Davidson), a fellow officer who does succeed in making lieutenant.

The usual cast changes ensued thereafter, but this unit of gorgeous cops continued to strike fear into the hearts of beach-going miscreants for five sunny seasons.

Page, Nikki (*Over My Dead Body*)

San Francisco obituary writer who doubles as an amateur sleuth with the help of an aging author.
See: *Over My Dead Body* (1990–1991, 11 episodes, USA)

Painkiller Jane (2007, 22 episodes, Canada/USA)

Based on: The comic book series by Jimmy Palmiotti, Joe Quesada
Created by: Gil Grant
Production Co.: Insight Film Studios, IDT Entertainment, Indestructible Productions, Kickstart Productions
Originally Aired: Syfy
Main Cast: Kristanna Loken, Alaina Huffman, Rob Stewart, Stephen Lobo, Noah Danby, Sean O. Roberts

Kristanna Loken is Jane Vasco, a DEA agent recruited by a top-secret government agency to hunt "neuros," neurological aberrants who have superhuman mental abilities, but have trouble distinguishing right from wrong. During the course of her investigations, Jane discovers that she has a special power of her own, the ability to heal her injuries, even mortal ones, although she still feels the pain of her wounds until the regeneration is complete. While trying to learn more about her own background and miraculous gift, Jane and the team, led by Andre McBride (Rob Stewart), look into all manner of weird and mysterious circumstances, from rapid aging to group amnesia, from time loops to mythical beasts, in search of a "neuro" connection. Jane finds that her new world is dark, violent, and full of illusion.

Paretsky, Dorothy (*Angel Street*)

Working-class, Polish American rookie detective in Chicago.
See: *Angel Street* (1992, 4 episodes, USA)

Parker, Audrey (*Haven*)

Former FBI agent, now a detective in a picturesque town with psychic and supernatural "troubles."
See: *Haven* (2010– , 52 episodes, USA/Canada)

Parker, Molly (*Killer Women*)

Texas Ranger who specializes in profiling female murderers.
See: *Killer Women* (2014, 8 episodes, USA)

Parras, Nancy (*The District*)

Elizabeth Marvel stars as Nancy Parras, a patrol officer in Washington, D.C., and one of Police Chief Jack Mannion's (Craig T. Nelson) inner circle. Although Nancy doesn't see the best of humanity in her work on the crime-ridden streets of the "District," she manages to retain her compassion for others, while being tough when she has to be. In "Lost and Found" (2001), Nancy must deal with the death of her boyfriend, Detective Danny McGregor (David O'Hara), before she can leave the safety of desk duty and return to the streets. She overcomes additional personal obstacles, including a diagnosis of Huntington's disease, and a rocky relationship with her father, who also has the disease, in "Passing Time" (2004). Officer Nancy Parras is a fighter and a survivor.

See also: *The District* (2000–2004, 89 episodes, USA)

Parsons, C.J. (*Matt Houston*)

Harvard-educated lawyer who assists a Texas oilman in private investigations.

See: *Matt Houston* (1982–1985, 67 episodes, USA)

Partners in Crime

See: *Agatha Christie's Partners in Crime* (1983–1984, 10 episodes, UK)

Partners in Crime (1984, 13 episodes, USA)

Created by: James Stark, Leonard Stern
Production Co.: Carson Productions
Originally Aired: NBC
Main Cast: Lynda Carter, Loni Anderson, Leo Rossi, Eileen Heckart, Walter Olkewicz

Carole Stanwyck (Lynda Carter) and Sydney Kovak (Loni Anderson) have an unusual connection. Each was married at one time to the same man, now deceased, who has willed them his San Francisco detective agency. Former spouse Raymond certainly did not have a "type." Carole is a brunette socialite fallen on hard times, who has taken up a career as a photographer to make ends meet. Sydney is a blonde pickpocket reared on the streets, who yearns to be a serious musician. After joining forces to solve their ex-husband's murder, Carole and Sydney decide to give the PI game a chance. While trying to bridge their differences, the women ferret out blackmailers, investigate murders, search for kidnappers, and in "Celebrity" (1984), provide protection for a rock star. It's all in a day's work for these unlikely partners in crime.

Patrick, Kate (*South Beach*)

Con artist/thief blackmailed into working for a mysterious government agent in Florida.
See: *South Beach* (1993, 7 episodes, USA)

Peck, Gail (*Rookie Blue*)

Tough chick with a goth streak, trying to make her way as a rookie cop.
See: *Rookie Blue* (2010– , 63 episodes, Canada)

Peel, Emma (*The Avengers*)

Leather-clad Emma Peel (Diana Rigg) fences her way into the fourth season of *The Avengers* in "The Town of No Return" (1965) and leaves an indelible imprint. Brilliant, witty, stylish, and accomplished in the martial arts, Mrs. Peel joins agent John Steed (Patrick Macnee) in pursuing spy-fi villains, such as "The Cybernauts" (1965), cybernetic assassins programmed to help a madman take over the world. Mrs. Peel has it all, and when judo chops won't do, her high IQ comes to the rescue, as in "The Master Minds" (1965), when she helps Steed pass a test to infiltrate a school for intellectuals. As busy as she is with her scientific pursuits, artistic hobbies, and, of course, her secret missions with Steed, Mrs. Peel somehow finds time for shopping, wearing the latest mod looks and a stunning array of catsuits. Emma Peel leaves behind the spy life, not to mention the repartee and innuendo with Steed, in "The Forget-Me-Knot" (1968), when her husband, presumed dead, returns to the living.

Although she may ride off into

The appealing but dangerous Mrs. Emma Peel (Diana Rigg) of *The Avengers* (ITV/ABC/Photofest).

the sunset with her hubby, the appeal of Emma Peel, as portrayed by Diana Rigg, endures.

See also: *The Avengers* (1961–1969, 161 episodes, UK)

Perception (2012– , 34 episodes, USA)

Created by: Kenneth Biller, Michael Sussman
Production Co.: Paperboy Productions, ABC Studios
Originally Aired: TNT
Main Cast: Eric McCormack, Rachael Leigh Cook, Kelly Rowan, Arjay Smith, LeVar Burton, Scott Wolf

Eric McCormack portrays Dr. Daniel Pierce, a neuropsychiatrist and university professor in Chicago, who himself suffers from paranoid schizophrenia. One of Pierce's former students, Kate Moretti (Rachael Leigh Cook), now a Special Agent with the FBI, seeks his help on a case, and Pierce becomes a consultant for the Bureau, working with Moretti. Pierce provides unique insight into the human mind, while Moretti goes wherever a case may lead, whether the FBI likes the direction or not. Daniel's hallucinations sometimes provide the key break in a case, which makes him a valuable but challenging partner for Moretti, since he sometimes has trouble distinguishing reality from fantasy. In "Light" (2012), Kate discounts one of Daniel's conspiracy theories, only to discover that he actually witnessed a murder. As their partnership and friendship continues to develop, complex romantic relationships intrude, including the return of Kate's ex-husband, Donnie Ryan (Scott Wolf), an assistant U.S. attorney, Daniel's affair with his former psychiatrist, Dr. Caroline Newsome (Kelly Rowan), and the reappearance of Daniel's imaginary friend, Natalie Vincent (also Kelly Rowan), who looks just like Caroline. It's a good thing Daniel has Max Lewicki (Arjay Smith), a live-in teaching assistant, to help him keep everyone, real and imaginary, straight in his life.

Perception definitely ups the ante on the "brilliant, but flawed" detective trope, but demonstrates that someone with schizophrenia can still contribute to society.

Person of Interest (2011– , 68 episodes, USA)

Created by: Jonathan Nolan
Production Co.: Bad Robot Productions, Kilter Films, Warner Bros. Television
Originally Aired: CBS
Main Cast: Jim Caviezel, Taraji P. Henson, Kevin Chapman, Amy Acker, Sarah Shahi, Michael Emerson

"You are being watched. The government has a secret system, a machine that spies on you every hour of every day. I know, because I built it."

Harold Finch (Michael Emerson), a brilliant software engineer, builds a computer system for the U.S. government which can predict acts of terror. When Harold finds that the machine also predicts one-off murders, and the government isn't interested in those potential victims, he uses his very deep pockets to finance private operations, recruiting down-on-his-luck black ops expert John Reese (Jim Caviezel), a one-man wrecking crew, to help prevent the predicted crimes. Finch sets up a techno-lair to do the necessary background research on each case, while Reese does surveillance and breaks arms (and more) when needed. Reese's vigilante activities bring him to the attention of Detective **Jocelyn "Joss" Carter** (Taraji P. Henson), who originally pursues the elusive "man in the suit," but eventually sees the value of his work with Finch, and becomes their eyes and ears on the police force. Another cop, Detective Lionel Fusco (Kevin Chapman), also joins the team through Reese's special brand of coercion, and ever so slowly finds he has a soul after years as a corrupt cop. Conspiracies within and without the government complicate matters further (they always do), and a woman called Root (Amy Acker), with an unusual connection to Harold's machine, becomes a particular thorn in his side, although (perhaps) an ally later. Sameen Shaw (Sarah Shahi), a government assassin, who gives Reese a run for his money in the head-butting department, is slowly pulled into the group's orbit, receiving regular assignments after a tragic loss for the team. Even when a competing machine called Samaritan is programmed to seek out and destroy Finch and company, they continue their work under new identities…. "Victim or perpetrator, if your number's up," they will find you.

See also: **Carter, Jocelyn "Joss"** (*Person of Interest*)

Pezzini, Sara (*Witchblade*)
New York City detective possessing an ancient, supernatural weapon.
See: *Witchblade* (2001–2002, 23 episodes, USA)

Phillips, Rose "Phil" (*Under Suspicion*)
The only female detective in a Portland police precinct.
See: *Under Suspicion* (1994–1995, 18 episodes, USA)

Phillips, Shane (*She Spies*)
Master thief working with two other beautiful women for U.S. intelligence.
See: *She Spies* (2002–2004, 40 episodes, USA)

Pirzad, Rachel (*Alphas*)
Defense Department consultant who can heighten any one of her five senses to help track criminals.
See: *Alphas* (2011–2012, 24 episodes, USA)

Plant, Dana (*Snoops*)
By-the-book ex-cop, working with other sexy private detectives in the city of Angels.
See: *Snoops* (1999, 13 episodes, USA)

Police Woman (1974–1978, 91 episodes, USA)
Created by: Robert L. Collins
Production Co.: Columbia Pictures Television, David Gerber Productions
Originally Aired: NBC
Main Cast: Angie Dickinson, Earl Holliman, Ed Bernard, Charles Dierkop

Trailblazing police procedural starring Angie Dickinson as Sgt. **Pepper Anderson**, a member of the Los Angeles Police Department's Criminal Conspiracy Unit. Under the supervision of Sgt. Bill Crowley (Earl Holliman), and backed up by detectives Pete Royster (Charles Dierkop) and Joe Styles (Ed Bernard), Pepper fights crime by going undercover, posing as a flight attendant, gym teacher, exotic dancer, or prison inmate to catch drug dealers, murderers, jewel smugglers and blackmailers. Pepper is smart and sexy, tough, but sensitive, and the cases she tackles are not only dangerous, but also grim, exposing her to white slavers, baby selling, and the death of informants and colleagues. But grit alone won't make you a 70s icon—you need some sartorial splendor, and Pepper dazzles in her super-studded pantsuit, while even Royster contributes with his funky patchwork cap.

Although there is undue emphasis on placing Dickinson in provocative clothing, occupations, and situations, *Police Woman* does help to pave the way for both female leads in drama series and women crimefighters on TV, such as *Cagney & Lacey* a few years later.

See also: **Anderson, Pepper** (*Police Woman*)

Police Woman Decoy
See: *Decoy: Police Woman* (1957–1958, 39 episodes, USA)

Powell, Dani (*P.S.I. Luv U*)
Grifter in witness protection, now working as a detective/bodyguard in Palm Springs.
See: *P.S.I. Luv U* (1991–1992, 13 episodes, USA)

Prentiss, Amy (*Amy Prentiss*)
San Francisco's first female Chief of Detectives.
See: *Amy Prentiss* (1974–1975, 3 episodes, USA)

Price, Annie (*Level 9*)
FBI agent in charge of an elite task force dealing with cyber crime. See: *Level 9* (2000–2001, 13 episodes, USA)

Prime Suspect (1991–2006, 15 episodes, UK/USA)
Created by: Lynda La Plante
Production Co.: Granada Television, ITV Productions, WGBH
Originally Aired: Public Television
Main Cast: Helen Mirren

Influential and multi-award–winning, *Prime Suspect* stars Helen Mirren as Detective Chief Inspector Jane Tennison in this dark police procedural set in London. As Series 1 opens, DCI Tennison is placed in charge of her first major murder investigation, much to the consternation of her all-male squad, especially Detective Sgt. Bill Otley (Tom Bell), who tries to sabotage her at every turn. Tennison and the team eventually solve the serial murder case, but Jane's obsession with her work, to the exclusion of everything else, costs her a relationship with boyfriend Peter Rawlins (Tom Wilkinson). Jane does earn the grudging respect and support of her squad and superiors, later receiving a promotion to Detective Superintendent, while tackling a case ("The Scent of Darkness," 1995) that calls into question the results of her first murder investigation. Battling her own personal problems, including alcoholism and a terminated pregnancy, Tennison soldiers on, doing what she does best—solving horrific crimes and finding a measure of justice for murder victims, whether country club manager or prostitute.

Prime Suspect (2011–2012, 13 episodes, USA)
Based on: The TV series *Prime Suspect* created by Lynda La Plante
Created by: Alexandra Cunningham
Production Co.: ITV Studios America, Film 44, Universal Media Studios
Originally Aired: NBC
Main Cast: Maria Bello, Brian O'Byrne, Kirk Acevedo, Peter Gerety, Tim Griffin, Damon Gupton, Kenny Johnson, Elizabeth Rodriguez, Aidan Quinn

Short-lived police procedural about the cases of Detective Jane Timoney (Maria Bello) at the elite Manhattan East Homicide Squad, where she is the only female detective. As a new transfer, Jane is an outsider, but acceptance proves even more difficult because she is sometimes reckless, often rude, and always averse to going with the flow. The Squad's commander, Lieutenant Kevin Sweeney (Aidan Quinn), recognizes Jane's character flaws, but also knows she closes cases, with her superior intellect and sharp instincts. Although Jane sometimes seems challenged in the personality department, she is managing a relationship with her boyfriend Matt Webb (Kenny Johnson) and his six-year-old son, but Matt's ex-wife is another matter. Good thing Jane can rely upon the support of her barkeeper dad Desmond (Peter Gerety) and can find salvation in her work when needed.

Prince, Diana (*Wonder Woman*)

Operative for the Inter-Agency Defense Command and alter ego of Wonder Woman.
See: *Wonder Woman* (1975–1979, 59 episodes, USA)

Prince, Kate (*Charlie's Angels*)

A former Miami cop who works as a private detective for a reclusive rich man.
See: *Charlie's Angels* (2011, 8 episodes, USA)

Profiler (1996–2000, 83 episodes, USA)

Created by: Cynthia Saunders
Production Co.: NBC Studios, The Sander/Moses Group, Three Putt Productions (1998–2000)
Originally Aired: NBC
Main Cast: Ally Walker, Robert Davi, Julian McMahon, Roma Maffia, Peter Frechette, Erica Gimpel, Dennis Christopher, Jamie Luner

Dr. Samantha "Sam" Waters (Ally Walker) is a forensic psychologist with the psychic ability to "see" a murder after inspecting a crime scene, a picture-show running just for her. As the series opens, Sam has retired from profiling, still traumatized by the murder of her husband three years earlier at the hands of the serial killer known as "Jack of All Trades" (Dennis Christopher). Sam's mentor, Bailey Malone (Robert Davi), coaxes her back to work at the FBI's Violent Crimes Task Force, where she and the team deal with all manner of grim and grisly crimes, but "Jack" is never far off their radar. Because of the omnipresent threat from Jack, Sam's home, a fortified firehouse, is guarded around the clock, and her friend, Angel Brown (Erica Gimpel), an artist, lives there for moral support and to help care for Sam's daughter, Chloe (Caitlin Wachs). After several years of playing cat and mouse, Jack kidnaps Sam in "Reunion" (parts one and two, 1999) and subjects her to psychological torture in hopes of turning her into a serial killer, his perfect mate. Sam manages to escape and finally prevail over Jack, leading her to retire for good this time.

A new profiler joins the team, Rachel Burke (Jamie Luner), but the dark spell cast by Sam and Jack had been broken, and the series was canceled after its fourth season.

The Protector (2011, 13 episodes, USA)
Created by: Michael Nankin, Jeffrey Bell
Production Co.: ABC Studios, Wass-Stein Productions
Originally Aired: Lifetime
Main Cast: Ally Walker, Tisha Campbell-Martin, Miguel Ferrer, Chris Payne Gilbert, Terrell Tilford, Thomas Robinson, Sage Ryan

Ally Walker stars as Gloria Sheppard, a woman who is expert at burning the candle at both ends. Gloria works as a robbery-homicide detective for the LAPD, while caring for twin sons as a single parent in her spare time. It's lucky, then, that Gloria has help in her two disparate worlds. Her partner, Detective Michelle Dulcett (Tisha Campbell-Martin) assists in solving crimes, while Gloria's brother and roommate, Davey Sheppard (Chris Payne Gilbert), holds down the homefront, although Davey is sometimes more like a third child. As Gloria and Michelle investigate the high-profile murders of plastic surgeons, fashionistas, and famous hairstylists, Gloria must deal with a gifted child, her brother's new role as neighborhood lothario, and visits from her ex-husband and mother.

The Lifetime network must have recognized that harried Gloria needed a break, because they sent her series on a permanent vacation after 13 episodes.

The Protectors (1972–1974, 52 episodes, UK)
Created by: Gerry Anderson
Production Co.: Incorporated Television Company
Originally Aired: In Syndication
Main Cast: Robert Vaughn, Nyree Dawn Porter, Tony Anholt

Fast-paced series chronicling the adventures of The Protectors, a group of jet-setting detectives who will assist anyone anywhere for a price. London-based Harry Rule (Robert Vaughn) leads the team as they foil kidnappings, locate Nazis, protect governments, thwart blackmailers and search for deadly viruses. Contessa Caroline di Contini (Nyree Dawn Porter) fights continental villains with Harry, while operating her own detective agency in Italy, which specializes in art crimes. Frenchman Paul Buchet (Tony Anholt) rounds out the roster, serving as answer man and gadget jockey. The Protectors' cases take them all over Europe, to Paris, Rome, Salzburg, Malta, and Madrid, as they solve crimes in true international man (and woman) of mystery style.

Psi Factor: Chronicles of the Paranormal (1996–2000, 88 episodes, Canada)
Created by: Peter Aykroyd, Christopher Chacon
Production Co.: Alliance Atlantis Communications, First Television, Paranormal Productions, Atlantis Films
Originally Aired: In Syndication

Main Cast: Paul Miller, Nancy Anne Sakovich, Barclay Hope, Colin Fox, Maurice Dean Wint, Matt Frewer, Nigel Bennett, Dan Aykroyd

Science fiction series documenting the cases of The Office of Scientific Investigation and Research, a covert organization which examines reports of paranormal activity. Dan Aykroyd introduces the episodes, explaining that they are based on "actual cases" of the OSIR, blurring the line between fact and fiction on this scripted show. Format changes and shifting plotlines pushed a lot of actors/characters in and out of this series (and back in again), but one mainstay was Nancy Anne Sakovich as data analyst Lindsay Donner. Lindsay and team members, like physicist Peter Axon (Barclay Hope), investigate mysterious phenomena, such as poltergeists, extraterrestrial encounters, psychic abilities, and demonic possessions, determining whether the weird occurrences have esoteric, but ultimately mundane explanations or are truly paranormal events. Hidden agendas and betrayals within OSIR complicate matters, as the group enters the realm of genetic engineering, alien DNA, and secret experiments.

P.S.I. Luv U (1991–1992, 13 episodes, USA)

Created by: Glen A. Larson, Bob Shayne
Production Co.: CBS Entertainment Production, Glen A. Larson Productions
Originally Aired: CBS
Main Cast: Greg Evigan, Connie Sellecca, Earl Holliman

Cody and Dani Powell are a married couple working as detectives/bodyguards for Palm Security and Investigations, except they aren't married and those aren't their real names. Cody (Greg Evigan) is NYPD cop Joey Paciorek and Dani (Connie Sellecca) is Wanda Talbert, a con woman. Both are in witness protection after a sting operation against organized crime in New York, so they come to Palm Springs as employees of P.S.I. boss Matthew Durning (Earl Holliman), while hiding out from the mob. The pairing of an honest cop with a sly grifter doesn't lead to harmonious exchanges, but their skill sets are complementary, so they get the job done. In "The Honeymooners" (1991), Cody and Dani must go undercover as newlyweds to ferret out the cause of a woman's death in a hotel swimming pool. When two children witness a murder in "Unmarried … with Children" (1991), Dani finds herself identifying with one of them, a girl who has come to the agency for protection and wants to pay with money stolen from the dead body.

The title of the series is a mnemonic for the agency's phone number, but apparently CBS forgot the number anyway, canceling the show after 13 episodes.

Psych (2006–2014, 121 episodes, USA)

Created by: Steve Franks
Production Co.: Pacific Mountain Productions, Tagline Pictures, Universal Cable Pro-

ductions, Universal Media Studios, NBC Universal Television Studio, GEP Productions
Originally Aired: USA Network
Main Cast: James Roday, Dulé Hill, Timothy Omundson, Maggie Lawson, Kirsten Nelson, Corbin Bernsen

Offbeat, comic police procedural starring James Roday as Shawn Spencer, a psychic detective for the Santa Barbara Police Department. Shawn has a big secret—he isn't really psychic—but his amazing powers of observation coupled with well-timed leaps of inspiration make him an indispensable consultant to the department. Shawn's partner in crime-solving and tomfoolery is Burton "Gus" Guster (Dulé Hill), a pharmaceutical salesman with a preposterously flexible work schedule, who is able to run off at a moment's notice to find adventure, shenanigans, funny nicknames, and snacks with Shawn. Head Detective Carlton "Lassie" Lassiter (Timothy Omundson), as straight an arrow as Shawn is bent, believes Shawn is a fake, attempting to expose him at every turn, but begins, albeit begrudgingly, to accept Shawn's remarkable crime-solving abilities. Detective **Juliet "Jules" O'Hara** (Maggie Lawson) is more open-minded than Lassiter and accepts that Shawn might be psychic, but Shawn's deception causes problems when he and Jules develop a romantic relationship in later years. Riding herd over this obstreperous group is Chief Karen Vick (Kirsten Nelson) with the informal (and sometimes formal) help of Shawn's father, former police sergeant Henry Spencer (Corbin Bernsen). Together this group solves murders, searches for stolen money, and even hunts for buried treasure, finding themselves in situations that bear a suspicious resemblance to the plots of movies and TV shows, such as *Jaws, Clue, Friday, the 13th,* and *Twin Peaks* (the most delicious of all their homages).

Solving crimes shouldn't be this much fun.

See also: **O'Hara, Juliet "Jules"** (*Psych*)

Pullman, Sandra (*New Tricks*)

Sandra Pullman (Amanda Redman) is a Detective Superintendent and head of the Unsolved Crime and Open Case Squad (UCOS) in Greater London. UCOS wasn't Sandra's first choice for an assignment, but when a kidnap victim is seriously injured because Sandra shoots an obstreperous dog during a rescue attempt, she becomes a laughingstock and is forced to take a step down the career ladder. Sandra must assemble a squad of retired cops for the new and underfunded unit, and the old guys are a handful, to say the least. In "Good Work Rewarded" (2004), Sandra returns after a trip to find the office a mess and the boys behaving like children, so she withholds the gifts she bought them until one after the other, they tow the line. In between the comic antics, the team solves the 20-year-old murder of a young boy on a golf course. Sandra likes to be the best at whatever she does, but finds herself attracted to unavailable men, as she reveals to her therapist in "ID Parade" (2004). She continues to wrangle her unruly boys and make a difference by solving open cases for 10 years, finally departing in "The One That Got Away" (2013) to work with a war crimes investigator. Although she didn't set out to do it, Sandra Pullman definitely taught a few old (police) dogs some brand new tricks.

See also: *New Tricks* (2003– , 87 episodes, UK)

Purdey (*The New Avengers*)

Ballet-trained secret agent who high-kicks her way through adventures with two male partners.

See: *The New Avengers* (1976–1977, 26 episodes, UK/France/Canada)

Pushing Daisies (2007–2009, 22 episodes, USA)

Created by: Bryan Fuller
Production Co.: The Jinks/Cohen Company, Living Dead Guy Productions, Warner Bros. Television
Originally Aired: ABC
Main Cast: Lee Pace, Anna Friel, Chi McBride, Field Cate, Ellen Greene, Swoosie Kurtz, Kristin Chenoweth

Inventive cross-genre series about a man who is able to bring the dead back to life, but finds there are a couple of CATCHES to his gift. Ned (Lee Pace) is a pie-maker who learned as a child that his touch could resurrect the dead. Now an adult, Ned works with local private investigator Emerson Cod (Chi McBride) to solve murders with a unique investigative technique—Ned raises the dead, so Emerson can ask who killed them, then touches the victim a second time, laying them to rest forever. Things get complicated, however, when Ned's childhood sweetheart, Charlotte "Chuck" Charles (Anna Friel), is murdered on a cruise ship. Ned revives her at the local funeral home, but can't bring himself to let her go permanently. Chuck (or "Dead Girl," as the grumpy Cod likes to call her) joins the detective team, making the interrogations even more challenging, since they have only one minute to question the murder victims or someone in the vicinity will die (another rule of Ned's gift). In the meantime, Chuck begins a romance with glum Ned, no easy task, since they can't touch lest Chuck be returned to the dead permanently. Throw in a perky waitress who is lovesick for Ned (Kristin Chenoweth), a couple of eccentric, synchronized-swimming aunts (Ellen Greene, Swoosie Kurtz) who mourn Chuck's loss, stunning visuals, including a kitschy-noir restaurant called The Pie Hole, and you have the flaky goodness known as *Pushing Daisies*.

Ramanujan, Amita (*Numb3rs*)

Amita Ramanujan (Navi Rawat) is not a sleuth in the traditional sense. She spends her days at the (fictitious) California Institute of Science, first as a grad student in mathematics and later as a professor. But Amita's academic mentor is Charlie Eppes (David Krumholtz), who helps to solves cases for the FBI by using the techniques of mathematical and statistical analysis. Amita joins Charlie in this work, and the two later become romantically involved. Most of her work is done in front of a computer or blackboard, but occasionally she finds herself in the line of fire, as in "Angels and Devils" (2009), when she is kidnapped by a cult leader. Her rocky relationship with Charlie, fraught with professional and cultural differences, sees a happy conclusion in series finale "Cause and Effect" (2010), when the two finally get married.

See also: *Numb3rs* (2005–2010, 118 episodes, USA)

Ramirez, Magda (*The Division*)

SFPD Inspector who juggles single motherhood and the amorous attentions of her married partner.

See: *The Division* (2001–2004, 88 episodes, USA)

Ramotswe, Precious (*The No. 1 Ladies' Detective Agency*)

Proprietor of Botswana's only female-owned detective agency.

See: *The No. 1 Ladies' Detective Agency* (2008–2009, 7 episodes, UK/USA)

Raydor, Sharon (*Major Crimes*)

Head of the LAPD's Major Crimes Division who must win over a mistrustful crew.

See: *Major Crimes* (2012– , 39 episodes, USA)

Reed, Shannon (*Mission: Impossible*)

Former Secret Service agent, now a member of the Impossible Missions Force.

See: *Mission: Impossible* (1988–1990, 35 episodes, USA)

Reese, Dani (*Life*)

LAPD detective and recovering drug addict with an ex-con for a partner.

See: *Life* (2007–2009, 32 episodes, USA)

Reeves, Megan (*Numb3rs*)

Los Angeles FBI agent who works on a unique crime-solving team with a math genius.

See: *Numb3rs* (2005–2010, 118 episodes, USA)

Remington Steele (1982–1987, 94 episodes, USA)

Created by: Robert Butler, Michael Gleason
Production Co.: MTM Enterprises
Originally Aired: NBC
Main Cast: Stephanie Zimbalist, Pierce Brosnan, Doris Roberts, James Read, Janet DeMay

When private investigator **Laura Holt** puts her name on an office, but no one beats down her door, she invents the perfect male detective, Remington Steele, to head her agency and answer the expectations of clients. Little does

A charming con man (Pierce Brosnan) forges an unusual partnership with private investigator Laura Holt (Stephanie Zimbalist) in *Remington Steele* (NBC/Photofest).

she know that a charming con man is about to assume Remington Steele's identity and take her on a wild ride of mystery, comedy, and romance. With Stephanie Zimbalist as Laura and Pierce Brosnan as Mr. Steele, these two solve cases with Laura's painstaking dedication to legwork and Mr. Steele's references to old movies, which always provide a spark of illumination at just the right time. Murphy Michaels (James Read), a professional detective at the agency, is unhappy about the arrival of this interloper, both because of Steele's history as a thief and because Murphy has as yet unfulfilled hopes for a romantic relationship with Laura. Janet DeMay rounds out the original team as receptionist Bernice Foxe, whom Mr. Steele persists in calling "Miss Wolfe," to continued humorous effect. Loyal assistant **Mildred Krebs** (Doris Roberts) joins the firm in season two, replacing both Michaels and Foxe, trying to fathom the complex professional and personal relationship between her bosses, while carving out her own niche in their work and hearts.

Stylish, witty, charming and exciting, *Remington Steele* is still fresh 30 years later.

See also: **Holt, Laura (***Remington Steele***)**; **Krebs, Mildred (***Remington Steele***)**

Rendezvous (1952, 4 episodes, USA)

Originally Aired: ABC
Main Cast: Ilona Massey

Ilona Massey stars as French singer and intelligence operative Nikki Angell in this short-lived adventure series. A member of the French resistance during World War II, Angell is a chanteuse at her own Paris nightclub, Chez Nikki, while covertly battling Communist agents and other elements who would subvert France and democracy. In addition to entertaining at the club and, of course, espionage, Nikki finds time for romance with a newspaper reporter (David McKay).

Although it seems barely a blip on the small screen's radar, *Rendezvous* is noteworthy for featuring TV's first female spy as a lead character.

Reyes, Monica (*The X-Files***)**

FBI agent assigned to investigate weird cases with paranormal overtones.
See: ***The X-Files*** (1993–2002, 202 episodes, USA)

Reynolds, Dani (*Cover Up***)**

Covert operative who travels the world posing as a fashion photographer.
See: ***Cover Up*** (1984–1985, 22 episodes, USA)

Rice, Tanya (*Memphis Beat*)

By-the-book Memphis police lieutenant supervising a laid-back, Elvis-loving detective.
See: *Memphis Beat* (2010–2011, 20 episodes, USA)

Richard Diamond, Private Detective (1957–1960, 77 episodes, USA)

Created by: Blake Edwards
Production Co.: Four Star Productions
Originally Aired: CBS (1957–1959), NBC (1959–1960)
Main Cast: David Janssen, Regis Toomey, Roxane Brooks, Mary Tyler Moore, Barbara Bain, Russ Conway

Richard Diamond (David Janssen) starts out as a private eye of the hard-boiled school, a former policeman accepting cases from a cramped New York office. Things get sunnier for Diamond, when he moves to Los Angeles in season three, working from a Hollywood Hills home with a panoramic view of the city. In keeping with the L.A. lifestyle, the handsome detective drives a convertible, using a car-phone, ultra-high-tech at the time, to keep in touch with his answering service. Enter "Sam" (Mary Tyler Moore and later Roxane Brooks), his operator at the answering service, who calls "Mr. D." with important messages, often catching him in the nick of time to avert danger and possible bodily injury at the hands of assorted bad guys. Sam is shown only from the waist down to emphasize her shapely legs and accentuate her sultry voice.

The show's portrayal of Sam was so distinctive, in fact, that *Richard Diamond, Private Detective* is best remembered for the operator rather than the detective, although neither Mary Tyler Moore nor Roxane Brooks were listed in the credits for the series at the time.

The situation for women in detective series could only improve from there, and it did, especially after *Honey West* came along a few years later.

Riland, Chris (*Crime with Father*)

Teenage daughter of a police captain who helps solve his cases.
See: *Crime with Father* (1951–1952, 16 episodes, USA)

Rizzoli & Isles (2010– , 67 episodes, USA)

Based on: The novels of Tess Gerritsen
Production Co.: Hurdler Productions, Ostar Productions, Warner Horizon Television
Originally Aired: TNT
Main Cast: Angie Harmon, Sasha Alexander, Lorraine Bracco, Jordan Bridges, Bruce McGill, Lee Thompson Young

Working-class detective Jane Rizzoli (Angie Harmon, left) and tony medical examiner Maura Isles (Sasha Alexander) are colleagues and unlikely friends in *Rizzoli & Isles* (Turner Network Television/Photofest).

Cagney & Lacey for the new century. Angie Harmon is **Jane Rizzoli**, a brilliant, working-class homicide detective for the Boston Police Department, who can't manage to escape her overprotective family members even at work. Sasha Alexander portrays Dr. **Maura Isles**, the socially awkward Chief Medical Examiner for the Commonwealth of Massachusetts, who can't refrain from spouting boring facts about EVERYTHING. The women work together to solve murders, where Jane's impatient, intuitive style often clashes, hilariously so, with Maura's precise, scientific method. But non-frilly Jane and fashion-conscious Maura are also unlikely best friends, supporting each other through prodigious family issues, violent encounters with criminals, unsuccessful romances, and life in general. A hurricane known as Angela Rizzoli (Lorraine Bracco), Jane's mother, a (mostly) positive force in both women's lives, waitresses at a café inside police headquarters and lives in Maura's guesthouse. Jane's brother Frankie Rizzoli (Jordan Bridges), also a cop, makes his way up from patrolman to detective, but isn't as sharp as his successful big sister. Jane works with her former partner and mentor, Vince Korsak (Bruce McGill), who once saved her from a serial killer, and Barry Frost (Lee Thompson Young), her new partner, who is later killed in a car accident (to deal with the tragic loss of actor Lee Thompson Young to suicide). Although their jobs are grisly, these folks remain a family, some related by blood, and some related by heart.

See also: **Isles, Maura (*Rizzoli & Isles*)**; **Rizzoli, Jane (*Rizzoli & Isles*)**

Rizzoli, Jane (*Rizzoli & Isles*)

Angie Harmon stars as Jane Rizzoli, a beautiful, but tough homicide detective for the Boston Police Department. Although "beautiful, but tough" is a female detective cliché, Harmon breathes real life into Jane Rizzoli, who never falls into caricature. Rizzoli works with Dr. Maura Isles (Sasha Alexander), the Commonwealth's Chief Medical Examiner, and the women have a friendship of opposites, with Jane's wisecracking impatience played, often comically, against Maura's pedantic sincerity. But their complementary worldviews are needed to close cases, and Jane's particular fortes, bravery and strength, save her from not one, but two serial killers in "See One. Do One. Teach One" (2010). Balancing a demanding profession with a romantic relationship proves difficult for both women, but Jane does find happiness for a time with Casey Jones (Chris Vance), a military man who proposes marriage. Jane breaks off the engagement, however, when Casey accepts a foreign assignment and it becomes clear that their careers will always pull them in different directions. At the same time, Jane finds that she is pregnant with Casey's baby, but a brutal attack while she is protecting a homeless teenager brings about a miscarriage in "It Takes a Village" (2014). Rizzoli, being Rizzoli, however, she is back on the job before the doctors clear her to work. Some people spend a lifetime searching for who they are, but Jane Rizzoli knows she is a detective.

See also: ***Rizzoli & Isles* (2010– , 67 episodes, USA)**

Roberts, Vicky (*The Event*)

Former CIA operative turned private security contractor/assassin.
See: ***The Event* (2010–2011, 22 episodes, USA)**

Rogers, Julie (*Charlie's Angels*)
One of three beautiful women working as private investigators for a wealthy, unseen boss.
See: *Charlie's Angels* (1976–1981, 110 episodes, USA)

Roget, Manouche "The Leopard" (*The Zoo Gang*)
Former World War II resistance fighter working with her comrades 30 years later to fight crime.
See: *The Zoo Gang* (1974, 6 episodes, UK)

Rookie Blue (2010– , 63 episodes, Canada)
Created by: Tassie Cameron, Morwyn Brebner, Ellen Vanstone
Production Co.: Shaw Media, Thump, Inc., CanWest, Entertainment One
Originally Aired: ABC
Main Cast: Missy Peregrym, Gregory Smith, Travis Milne, Enuka Okuma, Charlotte Sullivan, Ben Bass, Matt Gordon, Eric Johnson, Peter Mooney, Noam Jenkins

Another modern police procedural with a large cast, but this one focuses on uniformed officers, and rookies at that, giving it a brighter look and feel than the *Law & Order/Criminal Minds* crowd. Missy Peregrym leads the way as **Andrea "Andy" McNally**, a fresh-faced rookie who goes to work at 15 Division and quickly finds that her Academy training isn't much help on the street or with the precinct's unforgiving training officers. On her first day, Andy accidentally blows the cover of Officer Sam Swarek (Ben Bass), wasting months of his undercover work on a money-laundering operation, but the acrimonious start to their relationship leads to romance later, although a love triangle keeps their status prickly. Joining Andy in the rookie class at the station are Traci Nash (Enuka Okuma), a black single mother trying to find a balance between her new career and raising a young son, and Gail Peck (Charlotte Sullivan), a tough girl with a goth streak, hoping to make her way without using her family connections in the department. Traci arrives at 15 Division already in a secret relationship with one of the detectives, Jerry Barber (Noam Jenkins), while Gail becomes romantically involved with another rookie, Chris Diaz (Travis Milne) in an "opposites attract" pairing. Andy and the other rookies, including Dov Epstein (Gregory Smith), an over-eager, baby-faced recruit, collect defeats, embarrassments, and reprimands, but also the occasional victory, while trying to figure out what it means to be a cop and navigating the constantly shifting romantic landscape of 15 Division.
See also: **McNally, Andrea "Andy"** (*Rookie Blue*)

Rosemary & Thyme (2003–2007, 22 episodes, UK)
Created by: Brian Eastman, Clive Exton
Production Co.: Carnival Films, Yorkshire Television

Originally Aired: Public Television
Main Cast: Felicity Kendal, Pam Ferris

Who would have thought that gardening could be such a bloody business? Professional gardeners Rosemary Boxer and Laura Thyme travel around England and Europe planting beautiful gardens, while digging up skeletons wherever they go. Rosemary (Felicity Kendal) is a onetime botany professor sacked by her former lover and Laura (Pam Ferris) is a former policewoman left by her husband for a much younger woman. Their paths cross at a rustic hotel in "And No Birds Sing" (2003), and they join forces to uncover a sinister plot involving Rosemary's sick friend, poison, and diseased trees. With plenty of time now on their hands, the women accept gardening commissions together, but murder, that blighter, is like a weed, as in "The Tree of Death" (2003), when an impaled man is discovered during their churchyard restoration. These bright, brave, and sassy women solve botanical mysteries, such as why the roses are dying at a prep school in "The Invisible Worm" (2004), while answering the perennial question of who left the dead body in the undergrowth. Stunning locations add to the charm of this cozy, but not stodgy, mystery.

Rothschild, Emilia (*Jack of All Trades*)

British spy working with a cheeky American on a South Pacific island in the early 1800s.
See: ***Jack of All Trades* (2000, 22 episodes, USA/New Zealand)**

Rush, Lilly (*Cold Case*)

Kathryn Morris portrays Lilly Rush, a Philadelphia homicide detective whose specialty is unsolved crimes or "cold cases." Lilly looks fragile, with delicate features and porcelain skin, almost like she's from another era, perfectly suiting the tone of this series which spends so much of its time in the past. Detective Rush's looks, however, belie her toughness, as in "Torn" (2007), when she undertakes to solve an ancient case from 1919 about a murdered suffragette, while dealing with the problems of her alcoholic mother (Meredith Baxter), who has been imprisoned. In "WASP" (2009), women's rights are again centerstage, as Lilly and the team re-open a 1944 case about a female pilot who was murdered in the course of her work for a World War II Air Force program. "Fly Away" (2003) takes Lilly back to her own childhood of neglect and public assistance, as she investigates the death of a little girl who fell from a window. As each murder victim makes an evanescent appearance at the close of their case, Detective Rush knows that she has seen justice done.
See also: ***Cold Case* (2003–2010, 156 episodes, USA)**

Philadelphia homicide detective Lilly Rush (Kathryn Morris) tackles unsolved crimes in *Cold Case* (CBS/Photofest).

St. John, Cassandra (*Silk Stalkings*)

Palm Beach police detective who solves crimes of passion with her former spouse.

See: *Silk Stalkings* (1991–1999, 176 episodes, USA)

Sam (*Richard Diamond, Private Detective*)

Answering-service operator, known for her shapely legs and sultry voice, assisting a P.I. in Los Angeles.

See: *Richard Diamond, Private Detective* (1957–1960, 77 episodes, USA)

Sampson, Abby (*Charlie's Angels*)

Former thief who works as a private detective for a rich recluse.

See: *Charlie's Angels* (2011, 8 episodes, USA)

Saving Grace (2007–2010, 46 episodes, USA)

Created by: Nancy Miller
Production Co.: Fox Television Studios, Grand Productions, Paid My Dues Productions

Originally Aired: TNT
Main Cast: Holly Hunter, Leon Rippy, Kenny Johnson, Laura San Giacomo, Bailey Chase, Gregory Norman Cruz, Lorraine Toussaint, Dylan Minnette

Grace Hanadarko (Holly Hunter) is a police detective in Oklahoma City's Major Crimes division. Grace isn't exactly a paragon of virtue—she drinks too much, sleeps around, tells lots of lies, and her language would make a sailor blush. One night while intoxicated, Grace runs down and kills a pedestrian, and an angel appears in answer to her plea for God's help. The angel, a tobacco-chewing charmer named Earl (Leon Rippy), is a "last chance angel," who tells Grace it's time she found the Lord and that "God is using you for great things." Angel Earl cleans up (almost) all signs of the accident, but that doesn't mean Grace cleans up her act. She continues her wanton ways, including an affair with her married partner on the squad, Hamilton "Ham" Dewey (Kenny Johnson). In between bouts of bad behavior, Grace does get some police work done, but darkness always surrounds her, as in "Have a Seat, Earl" (2008), when she kidnaps the priest who molested her in her youth. She endures more trials, including accidentally killing a child, and in series finale, "I'm Gonna Need a Big Night Light" (2010), she finally accepts God, but whether she finds redemption in battling an evil entity is open to interpretation.

Scarecrow and Mrs. King (1983–1987, 88 episodes, USA)

Production Co.: Shoot the Moon Enterprises, B&E Enterprises (Episodes 1–11), Warner Bros. Television
Originally Aired: CBS
Created by: Brad Buckner, Eugenie Ross-Leming
Main Cast: Kate Jackson, Bruce Boxleitner, Beverly Garland, Mel Stewart, Martha Smith, Greg Morton, Paul Stout

Dashing spy Lee Stetson, code-named "Scarecrow," hands a package to suburban housewife **Amanda King** at a bustling train station and asks her to give it to the man in the red hat. Thus begins a rollicking, four-year adventure starring Kate Jackson as Amanda King, novice spy, who uses her native intelligence, common sense, and homespun experience to help catch international bad guys, and Bruce Boxleitner as the professional agent and quintessential (albeit sometimes cranky) good guy, who tries to resist his attraction to neophyte Amanda. Martha Smith adds zest as the competitive and office-bound **Francine Desmond**, while Mel Stewart portrays avuncular section chief Billy Melrose. This wholesome adventure/comedy/romance is at its best when highlighting the contrast between Amanda's suburban experience, especially life with Amanda's doting mother, Dotty (Beverly Garland), and the worldly ways of the government operatives, particularly Stetson, who is at home at embassy parties and Washington galas. A slow-burning will-they-or-won't-they plot line, with

Agency operatives Amanda King (Kate Jackson) and Lee Stetson (Bruce Boxleitner) are all dressed up with nowhere to go in *Scarecrow and Mrs. King* (CBS/Photofest).

leads Jackson and Boxleitner displaying crackling chemistry, simmers to a boil in season four, with the marriage of Scarecrow and Mrs. King.

See also: **Desmond, Francine** (*Scarecrow and Mrs. King*); **King, Amanda** (*Scarecrow and Mrs. King*)

Sciuto, Abigail "Abby" (*NCIS*)

Forensic scientist with a goth personal style, who investigates crimes related to U.S. Navy personnel.

See: *NCIS* (2003– , 258 episodes, USA)

Scott & Bailey (2011– , 22 episodes, UK)

Created by: Sally Wainwright, Diane Taylor
Production Co.: Red Production Company, Ingenious Broadcasting, Veredus Productions
Originally Aired: Public Television
Main Cast: Suranne Jones, Lesley Sharp, Amelia Bullmore, David Prosho, Tony Mooney, Delroy Brown, Nicholas Gleaves, Rupert Graves, Sean Maguire, Danny Miller

Scott & Bailey is a detective drama with three females in lead roles, but Charlie's Angels it isn't. This British police procedural, more like a modern Cagney & Lacey, has the gritty (and sometimes lurid) feel so popular with contemporary audiences. Suranne Jones stars as Rachel Bailey, a Detective Constable on the Manchester police department's Major Incident Team. Bailey is an ambitious and talented detective, but she sometimes behaves childishly when things don't go her way. Rachel's partner, Detective Constable Janet Scott (Lesley Sharp), is older and wiser than Bailey. Janet excels at her job, but has problems at home, especially with husband Adrian Scott (Tony Pitts). Scott and Bailey's boss is Detective Chief Inspector Gill Murray (Amelia Bullmore), who has enjoyed a friendship of many years with Janet, but whom Rachel refers to as "Godzilla." In "Futures" (2013), Rachel and Janet must pull together after a serious personal and professional falling-out, when Gill is kidnapped at knifepoint by a suicidal woman. Each of the three detectives, including victim Gill, uses her unique skill-set to try and reach a positive outcome. Positive turns out to be relative here, as it is in much of this series and in life.

Scott, Janet (*Scott & Bailey*)

Experienced and wise detective on the Manchester police department's Major Incident Team.
See: *Scott & Bailey* (2011– , 22 episodes, UK)

Scott, Nicole (*Missing*)

Sassy FBI agent whose partner has psychic visions that lead them to missing people.
See: *Missing* (2003–2006, 56 episodes, Canada/USA)

Scully, Dana (*The X-Files*)

Dana Scully (Gillian Anderson) is an FBI agent assigned to investigate weird, unsolved cases from the bureau's "X-Files," while keeping an eye on her partner, Fox "Spooky" Mulder (David Duchovny), who is obsessed with the paranormal. A medical doctor, Scully looks to science and rationality for explanations to strange phenomena, but is forced to become a believer, like Mulder, when she finds direct evidence of UFOs, alien abductions, and a global conspiracy. Although a skeptic when it comes to her otherworldly cases, Scully draws comfort from her Catholic faith and wears an iconic crucifix around her neck. Scully's involvement with the X-Files leads to major personal ramifications, including terminal cancer when an implanted microchip is removed from her neck, and a return to full health when a new chip is inserted. After a later diagnosis of infertility, Scully becomes pregnant under mysterious circumstances, and gives birth to a son in "Existence" (2001).

No one (in this world, at least) has a job description quite like that of FBI Agent Dana Scully.

See also: *The X-Files* (1993–2002, 202 episodes, USA)

The Secret Adventures of Jules Verne (2000, 22 episodes, UK/ Canada)

Created by: Gavin Scott
Production Co.: Filmline International, Talisman Crest
Originally Aired: Syfy
Main Cast: Michael Praed, Francesca Hunt, Michel Courtemanche, Chris Demetral

Steampunk adventure based on the premise that the novels of SF pioneer Jules Verne were taken from actual incidents in the author's life and not his imagination. Jules (Chris Demetral) sketches strange, futuristic contraptions while he should be paying attention to his law professor, but the evil League of Darkness wants to capture him and pick his brain (almost literally) for ideas that they might make a reality. Rebecca Fogg (Francesca Hunt) works as an undercover operative for the British Secret Service, a beautiful, intelligent young woman with well-honed fighting skills, a Victorian Emma Peel who sometimes plays the demure country lady to keep up appearances. Rebecca's second cousin Phileas Fogg (Michael Praed), who has resigned from the Secret Service, wins the dirigible airship Aurora in a poker game rigged by Queen Victoria and her ministers. The paths of these three exceptional individuals cross, leading them on a wild ride to do battle with extraordinary menaces, from rocket-propelled vampires to animated relics of the saints. Assisting them is Passepartout (Michel Courtemanche), also "won" by Phileas in the card game, but much more than a manservant, an accomplished inventor and navigator. The empire is in good hands.

Secret Agent

See: *Danger Man* (1960–1962, 39 episodes; 1964–1966, 47 episodes, UK)

Secret Agent Man (2000, 12 episodes, USA)

Created by: Barry Josephson, Richard Regen, Barry Sonnenfeld
Production Co.: Columbia TriStar Television, Sonnenfeld Josephson Worldwide Entertainment
Originally Aired: UPN
Main Cast: Costas Mandylor, Dina Meyer, Dondre Whitfield, Paul Guilfoyle, Musetta Vander

Although this series uses an updated version of the "Secret Agent Man" theme song made famous by the 60s show *Secret Agent* (a.k.a. *Danger Man*), this is not a remake of the earlier Patrick McGoohan vehicle. Costas Mandylor stars as Monk, an operative for the mysterious "Agency," who seems to attract a lot of female attention as he executes his clandestine missions. Dina Meyer is Holiday, a no-nonsense agent who seems to attract a lot of male attention in the course of her work for the same outfit. Monk and Holiday, along with their colleague Davis (Dondre Whitfield), report to Brubeck (Paul Guilfoyle), rounding out this spy team, all with the last names of jazz musicians (as often happens). These attractive operatives frequently run afoul of Prima (Musetta Vander), a spy with shifting loyalties, who seems to attract a lot of male attention, even (at one time) Monk's.

Alas, the series itself attracted neither male nor female attention, and UPN canceled it after 12 episodes.

The Secrets of Isis

See: *Isis* (1975–1976, 22 episodes, USA)

Shannon, Mary (*In Plain Sight*)

Mary Shannon is a U.S. Marshal attached to the Albuquerque office of the Federal Witness Security Program. As portrayed by Mary McCormack, Shannon is independent, stubborn, misanthropic, impatient, and highly skilled at her work, which involves the relocation and protection of witnesses whose lives are in jeopardy. Mary juggles her witness family and her own shady relatives, and the latter connection leads to her abduction in "Stan by Me" (2008). Along with pedantic, but loyal partner Marshall Mann (Frederick Weller), Mary again tries to straighten out family business in "The Art of the Steal" (2011), hoping to clear sister Brandi (Nichole Hiltz) of auto theft. A now pregnant Mary must deal with a crafty witness who has hidden her own pregnancy in "A Womb with a View" (2011). All's well that ends (well), as Mary comes to terms with the death of her long-absent father, her codependent relationship with Marshall, and at least some of her trust issues in series finale "All's Well That Ends" (2012).

See also: ***In Plain Sight*** (2008–2012, 61 episodes, USA)

Shaw, Marty (*Hunter*)

Spy who uses her high-fashion modeling career as a cover for espionage activities.

See: *Hunter* (1977, 12 episodes, USA)

Shaw, Sameen (*Person of Interest*)

A former government assassin now working as a private operative/vigilante.

See: *Person of Interest* (2011– , 68 episodes, USA)

She Spies (2002–2004, 40 episodes, USA)

Created by: Joe Livecchi, Steven Long Mitchell, Vince Manze, Craig W. Van Sickle
Production Co.: Reno & Osborn Productions, MGM Television
Originally Aired: NBC, In Syndication
Main Cast: Natasha Henstridge, Kristen Miller, Natashia Williams, Carlos Jacott, Jamie Iglehart, Cameron Daddo

"Every once in a while an elite crime fighting team emerges—highly sophisticated covert ops, specially trained in global intelligence maneuvers. This is not one of those teams."

A *Charlie's Angels*-meets-*White Collar* adventure/comedy about three beautiful female felons, who receive a get-out-of-jail-free card in exchange for working as undercover operatives for the U.S. government. Uncle Sam can always use another con artist, hacker, and master thief, so Cassie McBain (Natasha Henstridge), D.D. Cummings (Kristen Miller), and Shane Phillips (Natashia Williams) are happy to answer the call, as long as they can leave prison garb behind them. The lovely ladies set off to battle evildoers, and much of the action, especially in the first season, is tongue-in-cheek, with lots of winking at the camera and implausible violence where no one breaks a nail or gets their hair mussed. Skimpy attire is, of course, de rigueur for gorgeous operatives, so when the ladies go undercover in "Spies Gone Wild" (2004), they're not, in fact, under much cover, as they work to find a kidnapped princess on spring break. Needless to say, these "bad girls gone good" are a handful for their handlers, but, lucky for us, they're on our side.

Sheppard, Gloria (*The Protector*)

LAPD robbery-homicide detective who doubles as a single parent with twin sons.

See: *The Protector* (2011, 13 episodes, USA)

Sheridan, Stacy (*T.J. Hooker*)

Beautiful cop who shifts from desk duty to street patrol with a gorgeous partner.

See: *T.J. Hooker* (1982–1986, 91 episodes, USA)

She's the Sheriff (1987–1989, 44 episodes, USA)
Created by: Dan Guntzelman, Steve Marshall
Production Co.: Lorimar Productions
Originally Aired: In Syndication
Main Cast: Suzanne Somers, George Wyner, Pat Carroll, Lou Richards, Leonard Lightfoot, Guich Koock

Situation comedy starring Suzanne Somers as Hildy Granger, widow and mother of two, who replaces her late husband as sheriff of Lakes County, Nevada. Hildy battles not only crooks, but also her rambunctious family, and even her own deputies, especially Max Rubin (George Wyner), who constantly hatches plots against her because he was passed over for the sheriff's position. Although some of her job involves lightweight tourist matters, Hildy also does real police work, going undercover as a prostitute to get the goods on a notorious madam in "Call Me Madam" (1987), and even getting wounded in "Hildy Gets Shot" (1987). New career notwithstanding, there is still time for monkeyshines, soap opera, and even romance in Sheriff Granger's unlikely life.

Sidle, Sara (*CSI: Crime Scene Investigation*)
Materials and element analyst for a forensics team in Las Vegas, who copes with a traumatic past.
See: **CSI: Crime Scene Investigation** (2000– , 337 episodes, USA/Canada)

The Silent Force (1970–1971, 15 episodes, USA)
Created by: Luther Davis
Production Co.: Aaron Spelling Productions
Originally Aired: ABC
Main Cast: Ed Nelson, Lynda Day (George), Percy Rodrigues

Mission: Impossible–esque series about a secret band of government agents who work undercover to bring down bad guys, but instead of international wrongdoers, The Silent Force targets organized crime in the U.S. The team consists of Ward Fuller (Ed Nelson), Amelia Cole (Lynda Day), and Jason Hart (Percy Rodrigues), who strike out from Washington, D.C., to topple corrupt judges, clean up the recording industry, and capture loan sharks. In "The Octopus" (1970), Amelia poses as a gangster's wife to break the syndicate's stranglehold on the trucking business. When it comes to fighting the mob, The Silent Force definitely raises its voice.

Silk Stalkings (1991–1999, 176 episodes, USA)
Created by: Stephen J. Cannell
Production Co.: Stephen J. Cannell Productions Inc., Stu Segall Productions, Columbia Pictures Television, 20th Century–Fox Television, et al.

Originally Aired: CBS (1991–1993) , USA Network (1993–1999)
Main Cast: Mitzi Kapture, Rob Estes, William Anton, Charlie Brill, Tyler Layton, Nick Kokotakis, Chris Potter, Janet Gunn

Long-running series that premiered on CBS as part of its *Crimetime after Primetime* experiment, but later moved to USA Network for six more seasons. At the start, it follows Sgts. Rita Lee Lance (Mitzi Kapture) and Chris Lorenzo (Rob Estes), two detectives who specialize in solving sex-based crimes among the rich and famous in Palm Beach, Florida. Since crimes of passion, which the detectives refer to as "silk stalkings," appear to occur with amazing frequency among the sun-drenched (and scantily clad) set, Rita and Chris keep their minds on their work, and maintain a platonic relationship for four years, occasionally dating others. In season five, coinciding with the lead actors' desire to leave the series, a quick courtship leads to marriage for the pair, but, alas, they don't get to enjoy married life for long. (It's a dangerous job, after all.)

The new replacements, Detectives Michael Price (Nick Kokotakis) and Holly Rawlins (Tyler Layton), don't get to enjoy their jobs for long either, although no hail of bullets is involved—they simply disappear over the summer. The new, new replacements, Detective Sgts. Tom Ryan (Chris Potter) and Cassandra St. John (Janet Gunn), had shared a brief marriage, but vow not to let their personal history get in the way of their professional partnership. They pursue the sexy, but depraved denizens of Palm Beach for three more seasons, although they aren't the beneficiaries of a happy ending either, this time due to series cancellation.

Simmons, Jemma (*Agents of S.H.I.E.L.D.*)

Life sciences expert on a team that investigates threats to the U.S. and the world.
See: *Agents of S.H.I.E.L.D.* (2013– , 22 episodes, USA)

Simmons, Kay (*V.I.P.*)

Computer whiz who works with other gorgeous operatives in a Los Angeles protection agency.
See: *V.I.P.* (1998–2002, 88 episodes, USA/Germany)

Sirens (1993–1995, 35 episodes, USA/Canada)

Created by: Ann Lewis Hamilton
Production Co.: Gangbuster Films, Telescene Film Group Productions
Originally Aired: ABC (1993); In Syndication (1994–1995)
Main Cast: Jayne Brook, Adrienne-Joi Johnson, Liza Snyder, Jayne Heitmeyer, Ellen David

The sirens in question are three attractive female rookie cops who patrol the streets of Pittsburgh, and, yes, sometimes use their sirens. Jayne Brook plays Officer Sarah Berkezchuk, who has qualms about using physical force and is experiencing some stress in her marriage. Liza Snyder is Molly Whelan, a veteran of Desert Storm and second-generation cop with attitude issues. Adrienne-Joi Johnson portrays Officer Lynn Stanton, an African American single mother with a son and daughter. Despite the too-good-looking leads, the series was more *Hill Street Blues* than *Charlie's Angels*, but gritty reality wasn't enough to save it from ABC's chopping block after 13 episodes.

Sirens returned in first-run syndication, with Jayne Heitmeyer as Jessie Jaworski, replacing the departed Jayne Brook. There were several fatalities in the second season, including Jessie's fellow officer husband and the series itself.

Sisco, Karen (*Karen Sisco*)

Deputy U.S. Marshal who tracks down fugitives in southern Florida.
See: *Karen Sisco* (2003–2004, 10 episodes, USA)

Skouris, Diana (*The 4400*)

Jacqueline McKenzie portrays Diana Skouris, an agent with The National Threat Assessment Command (NTAC), who investigates the sudden reappearance of 4400 people abducted under mysterious circumstances. Diana partners with Tom Baldwin (Joel Gretsch) to interview and track the returnees, who have begun to exhibit special abilities, such as telekinesis, enhanced strength, and healing powers. Diana quickly forms a bond with one young abductee, Maia Rutledge (Conchita Campbell), who can accurately predict future events, and in "The New and Improved Carl Morrissey" (2004), Diana brings Maia home, later adopting her. Diana's loyalties are continually tested, as in "Mommy's Bosses" (2005), when she and Tom learn that NTAC is responsible for a plague affecting some of the returnees, including Maia.
See also: *The 4400* (2004–2007, 44 episodes, USA)

Skye (*Agents of S.H.I.E.L.D.*)

Former computer hacker investigating threats to the world and her own mysterious past.
See: *Agents of S.H.I.E.L.D.* (2013– , 22 episodes, USA)

Sledge Hammer! (1986–1988, 41 episodes, USA)

Created by: Alan Spencer
Production Co.: D'Angelo Productions, New World Television, Spencer Productions
Originally Aired: ABC
Main Cast: David Rasche, Anne-Marie Martin, Harrison Page

Sitcom spoof of *Dirty Harry*, *Hunter*, and cop characters of their ilk, who shoot their .44 Magnums first, and ask questions later (or never). Inspector Sledge Hammer (David Rasche) talks to his gun, shoots jaywalkers, blows up an entire building to foil a sniper, and thinks *The Deer Hunter* is a comedy. There isn't much time for THOUGHT in Sledge's worldview, so it's lucky he has partner Dori Doreau (Anne-Marie Martin) to help with the mental gymnastics of crime-solving, although she is adept with a karate kick when the occasion warrants. In "Brother, Can You Spare a Crime?"(1987), a jewel thief claims to be Hammer's long-lost brother, and Dori finds proof that it's a lie. Dori undergoes a temporary personality transplant, adopting the brutish mentality of Sledge, when she receives a blow to the head in "Desperately Seeking Dori" (1987). The partners pursue further adventures, whose titles riff on films and shows, such as, "The Spa Who Loved Me," "Death of a Few Salesmen," and "Jagged Sledge" under the watchful eye of Captain Trunk (Harrison Page), who has developed maladies such as migraines and indigestion thanks to close contact with Hammer. Season one ends with a Hammer-induced nuclear explosion, so season two takes place five years earlier.

Even Dirty Harry Callahan didn't achieve such rarefied heights of deadliness.

Sleepy Hollow (2013– , 13 episodes, USA)

Based on: The short story *The Legend of Sleepy Hollow* by Washington Irving
Created by: Alex Kurtzman, Roberto Orci
Production Co.: 20th Century–Fox Television, Sketch Films, K/O Paper Products
Originally Aired: Fox
Main Cast: Tom Mison, Nicole Beharie, Orlando Jones, Katia Winter, Lyndie Greenwood, John Noble

Ichabod Crane (Tom Mison) rises from the dead (literally) in this reimagining of Washington Irving's famous story. Handsome Crane, a former spy for General George Washington, is resurrected in modern-day Sleepy Hollow at the same time as the Headless Horseman, soon revealed to be one of the Four Horsemen of the Apocalypse. When Sheriff August Corbin (Clancy Brown) is beheaded by the Horseman, Lt. **Abbie Mills** (Nicole Beharie), Corbin's protégé and surrogate daughter, begins to investigate, learning that Sleepy Hollow will be ground zero for the coming apocalypse, and that she and Crane, the prophesied witnesses, are the only two people who can stop it. Helping, but sometimes complicating, matters is Katrina Crane (Katia Winter), Ichabod's wife, a witch stuck in purgatory, who can communicate with Ichabod through dreams. Captain Frank Irving (Orlando Jones), Abbie's boss, is also an ally, but pays a high price when the evil touches his own daughter. Family connections, in fact, are pivotal in the haunted Hollow. Abbie's sister, Jenny Mills (Lyndie Greenwood), has been institutionalized for being honest about the weird things she's seen, and Ichabod's son, Jeremy Crane/Henry Parrish (John Noble), is actually another of the Four Horsemen of the Apocalypse (don't ask).

This Hollow is anything but sleepy.

See also: **Mills, Abbie** (*Sleepy Hollow*)

Smith, Mrs. (*Mr. & Mrs. Smith*)

One of two sexy operatives who pose as a suburban couple during their international missions.

See: *Mr. & Mrs. Smith* (1996, 13 episodes, USA)

Smith, Vanessa (*The Most Deadly Game*)

Member of a detective team dedicated to solving only the most unusual crimes.

See: *The Most Deadly Game* (1970–1971, 12 episodes, USA)

Snoop, Ernesta and Gwendolyn (*The Snoop Sisters*)

A pair of elderly sisters who write mysteries and solve crimes in their spare time.

See: *The Snoop Sisters* (1972–1974, 5 episodes, USA)

The Snoop Sisters (1972–1974, 5 episodes, USA)

Created by: Alan Shayne
Production Co.: Universal TV
Originally Aired: NBC
Main Cast: Helen Hayes, Mildred Natwick, Lou Antonio, Bert Convy

Short-lived, but ahead-of-its-time movie series about two spirited, elderly sisters who write mysteries and solve crimes on the side. Ernesta (Helen Hayes) is the actual writer, while Gwendolyn (Mildred Natwick) works as her assistant, although both are in it up to their elbows when they stumble upon an actual crime, much to the consternation of their nephew, police Lt. Steven Ostrowski (Bert Convy). Their long-suffering, ex-con chauffeur Barney (Lou Antonio) is supposed to keep the sisters out of trouble, but poor Barney is at the mercy of the willful, but charming sisters, driving them places they shouldn't be and helping with things they shouldn't be doing. In "The Devil Made Me Do It" (1974), the sisters are targeted by a satanic cult, and must follow a trail of tarot card clues before they become the Satanists' next murder victims. Ernesta and "G" come to the rescue of a has-been horror movie actor (Vincent Price), accused of killing his wife, in "Black Day for Bluebeard" (1974). Whether questioning a demonic rockstar (Alice Cooper), standing on the roof of their vintage 1930s

Amateur sleuth Ernesta Snoop (Helen Hayes) questions a satanic rockstar (Alice Cooper) in *The Snoop Sisters* (NBC/Photofest).

Lincoln to break into a doctor's office, or collecting evidence on the golf links, the Snoop sisters are an unstoppable crime-fighting one-two punch, albeit in velvet gloves.

Snoops (1989–1990, 13 episodes, USA)
Created by: Sam Egan, Tim Reid
Originally Aired: CBS
Main Cast: Tim Reid, Daphne Maxwell Reid, John Karlen, Troy Curvey, Jr.

Real-life marrieds Tim Reid and Daphne Maxwell Reid portray Chance and Micki Dennis, sophisticated amateur sleuths à la *Hart to Hart* in this short-lived series. Chance is a criminologist and professor at Georgetown University, while Micki does protocol work for the State Department. Although it sounds like Chance's encounters with crime should remain in the purely theoretical realm, Lieutenant Akers (John Karlen) often brings unsolved cases to Chance's classroom or students find themselves in trouble (as students do). Then the attractive mates flex their detective muscles in the field, but the Washington, D.C., these sleuths inhabit is witty and urbane rather than gritty and noirish, a place full of high style, diplomacy, and murder.

Snoops (1999, 13 episodes, USA)
Created by: David E. Kelley
Production Co.: David E. Kelley Productions, 20th Century–Fox Television
Originally Aired: ABC
Main Cast: Gina Gershon, Paula Marshall, Danny Nucci, Paula Jai Parker, Edward Kerr

The investigations of Glenn Hall, Inc., a detective agency in the city of Angels, known for its young, sexy operatives. Led by savvy rule-breaker Glenn Hall (Gina Gershon), the staff includes by-the-book ex-cop Dana Plant (Paula Marshall) and brazen go-getter Roberta Young (Paula Jai Parker), three distinct personality types destined for conflict. But none of these ladies likes murder, so they overcome their differences to help clients, working undercover as prostitutes to prevent a political scandal in "Higher Calling" and investigating a homicide revealed under hypnosis in "A Criminal Mind." Manny Lott (Danny Nucci) adds zest (and testosterone) as the firm's technology whiz, but this formidable foursome ultimately can't make a go of it, disbanding in the series finale, "Swan Chant" (unaired in the U.S.).

Sommers, Jaime (*The Bionic Woman*)

Lindsay Wagner stars as Jaime Sommers, a former tennis star who suffers critical injuries during a skydiving accident and is saved by the addition of some computerized body parts. Jaime becomes a schoolteacher by day, but moonlights as an operative for the Office of Scientific Investigations under the watchful eye of Oscar Goldman (Richard Anderson). She uses her exceptional abilities, such as massive strength and lightning speed, for the cause of good around the globe, as in "Angel of Mercy" (1976), when she must rescue a U.S. ambassador and his wife from a collapsed building in Costa Brava. In the three-part "Kill Oscar" (1976), the bionic woman must fight other cyborgs, called Fembots, to save Oscar and the world from a weather-control device. The series concludes with the *Prisoner*-esque "On the Run" (1978), where Jaime learns it's not easy to retire from secret government work, but staying on the job may finally give her what she needs.

See also: *The Bionic Woman* (1976–1978, 58 episodes, USA)

Sommers, Jaime (*Bionic Woman*)

Bionic woman for the new millennium, this time using her enhanced abilities for a private intelligence firm.

See: *Bionic Woman* (2007, 8 episodes, USA)

South Beach (1993, 7 episodes, USA)
Created by: Dick Wolf, Robert De Laurentiis
Production Co.: Universal TV, Wolf Films
Originally Aired: NBC
Main Cast: Yancy Butler, Eagle Eye Cherry, John Glover, Patti D'Arbanville

Yancy Butler portrays Kate Patrick, a beautiful con artist/thief (is there any other kind?), blackmailed into working for the government in return for staying out of jail. Kate receives her assignments from mysterious Agent Roberts (John Glover), and works with a local named Vernon (Eagle Eye Cherry) to bring down bad guys, while using her unique, if not completely legal, skill set. In "Pirates of the Caribbean" (1993), Kate uses her grifter experience, equipped with a luxurious yacht in an undercover operation, to trap hijackers off the Florida coast.

Alas, this second collaboration between Butler and the Wolf/De Laurentiis creative team was even more short-lived than the prior year's *Mann & Machine*, but Butler would go on to achieve cult status with *Witchblade*.

Southland (2009–2013, 43 episodes, USA)
Created by: Ann Biderman
Production Co.: John Wells Productions, Warner Bros. Television
Originally Aired: NBC (2009), TNT (2010–2013)
Main Cast: Michael Cudlitz, Shawn Hatosy, Regina King, Michael McGrady, Ben McKenzie, Tom Everett Scott, C. Thomas Howell, Kevin Alejandro, Arija Bareikis

Police procedural with a "day in the life" flavor, following cops of various stripes throughout their rounds in the City of Angels. Unlike most procedurals, which focus on the work of one unit or precinct, *Southland* casts a wide net, covering several geographic areas, such as Hollywood Division and Alvarado Division, and multiple aspects of police work, from street patrol, to gangs and narcotics, to robbery and homicide. Long-termers amongst the large cast include Michael Cudlitz as John Cooper, training officer for rookie Ben Sherman (Ben McKenzie), Shawn Hatosy as Detective Sammy Bryant, a member of the gang squad, and Regina King as Lydia Adams, a robbery-homicide detective. While tracking down killers, Lydia must adjust to a succession of very different partners after her original partner, Russell Clarke (Tom Everett Scott), is shot and seriously injured by one of his neighbors. As Russell's case shows, the personal is never far from the professional in *Southland*. Sammy's confrontation with his ex-wife Tammi (Emily Bergl) leads to an investigation by Internal Affairs, where Sammy lies about some evidence. Lydia copes with life-and-death issues, the birth of her baby and the passing of her mother, while still trying to be fully present on the job. It's SouthLAnd, where life should be sunny, but isn't always, especially if you're a cop.

Space Precinct (1994–1995, 24 episodes, UK)

Created by: Gerry Anderson
Production Co.: Gerry Anderson Productions, Grove Television Enterprises, Mentorn Films
Originally Aired: In Syndication
Main Cast: Ted Shackelford, Rob Youngblood, Simone Bendix, Mary Woodvine, Jerome Willis

In 2040, the place to be if you're a cop who enjoys a challenge is Demeter City, "the crime capital of the galaxy," located on the planet Altor. Former NYPD detective Patrick Brogan (Ted Shackelford) moves his wife and kids to the distant solar system, and tackles cases where humans or one of several alien races may be the perpetrators. Assisting Brogan is his partner from the old days back on earth, Jack Haldane (Rob Youngblood), and another human officer, Jane Castle (Simone Bendix), who later becomes Haldane's love interest. Other police at the precinct are from alien races, including Aurelia Took (Mary Woodvine), a Tarn, who possesses telepathic and telekinetic abilities. Together, this motley crew investigates murders, counterfeiting, jewelry heists, and illicit drugs, because there is nothing new under the sun (or any sun) when it comes to crime.

Spade, Samantha (*Without a Trace*)

Poppy Montgomery portrays Samantha Spade, Special Agent for the FBI's Missing Persons Squad in New York City. Samantha works with team members, such as **Vivian Johnson** (Marianne Jean-Baptiste), to locate runaways, kidnap victims, hoaxers—anyone who's gone missing seemingly "without a trace." Sometimes the job is dangerous, as in "Fall Out, Part 1" (2003), when a ransom drop goes sour and Sam is wounded with her own gun. After Sam's rescue, work continues as usual for the team, when they search for a missing teenage violinist in "Prodigy" (2003), while Samantha resists psychological counseling after her kidnapping and shooting. She bears the scars of a troubled and violent past, but is grace under pressure in "Thou Shalt Not" (2004), when she quickly removes a bomb that's been strapped to an immobilized woman. Her relationship with unit supervisor Jack Malone (Anthony LaPaglia), which includes an on-again-off-again extramarital affair, leads to repercussions in their professional and personal lives, but Sam seems to find happiness and a new start with her baby's father in series finale "Undertow" (2009).

See also: *Without a Trace* (2002–2009, 160 episodes, USA)

Special Unit 2 (2001–2002, 19 episodes, USA)
Created by: Evan Katz
Production Co.: Paramount Television, Rego Park Productions
Originally Aired: UPN
Main Cast: Michael Landes, Alexondra Lee, Danny Woodburn, Richard Gant

Special Unit 2 is a secret division within the Chicago Police Department, tasked with handling cases which involve "Links," missing links between apes and humans, traditionally thought of as the monsters of mythology, but in actuality quite real and living in Chicago. Nick O'Malley (Michael Landes) is the unit's maverick, tortured by guilt over the loss of his partner to a Link called The Chameleon. Alexondra Lee portrays Detective Kate Benson, Nick's new partner, who has known since childhood about the things that go bump in the night, so is the perfect recruit for SU2. Nick and Kate battle gargoyles, werewolves, spider-women, the Sandman, and Medusa, while relying upon a kleptomaniac gnome named Carl (Danny Woodburn) to feed them information about the Link community. These detectives surely have their hands full, especially when Links can form even from the discarded fat of liposuction patients ("The Waste," 2001).

Spy Game (1997, 13 episodes, USA)
Created by: John McNamara, Ivan Raimi, Sam Raimi
Production Co.: McNamara Paper Production, Inc., MCA Television
Originally Aired: ABC
Main Cast: Linden Ashby, Allison Smith, Bruce McCarty

Stylish spy spoof about a retired secret agent who is called back into service when the end of the Cold War leaves operatives out of work and ready to cause trouble for the U.S. Linden Ashby portrays Lorne Cash, an old-school spy out of his element in the new world of high-tech gadgets and shifting world alliances. Allison Smith is Maxine "Max" London, his forward-thinking rookie partner at the Emergency Counter-Hostilities Organization (E.C.H.O.), the secret agency tasked with policing all the unemployed spies. Along the way, Lorne and Max must thwart a plot to blow up the president, foil a defense contractor's plans to start an android-provoked war, and otherwise save the U.S. each week— easier duty than expected, given this show's short run.

Standoff (2006–2007, 18 episodes, USA)

Created by: Craig Silverstein
Production Co.: Sesfonstein Productions, 20th Century–Fox Television
Originally Aired: Fox
Main Cast: Ron Livingston, Rosemarie DeWitt, Gina Torres, Michael Cudlitz, Raquel Alessi, José Pablo Cantillo

Matt Flannery (Ron Livingston) and Emily Lehman (Rosemarie DeWitt) are negotiators par excellence. At work, the two are agents for the FBI's Crisis Negotiation Unit in Los Angeles. At home, they are lovers, negotiating not only the intricacies of romantic relationships, but also the terra incognita of working with a lover in a dangerous profession. Although their affair is supposed to be secret, Matt reveals it to create empathy with a hostage-taker, much to the consternation of both Emily, and CNU chief Cheryl Carrera (Gina Torres). When Matt and Emily deal with standoffs on the subway and even over the airwaves, as a hostage-taker contacts a radio personality, Emily's cerebral, analytical style contrasts, but complements, Matt's propensity to go with his gut. Other personal issues intrude into the professional realm, when Emily's sister, who is incarcerated in federal prison, seems to be involved with a hostage-taker.

Too bad Matt and Emily couldn't negotiate a second season for this offbeat police procedural.

Stanhope, Vera (*Vera*)

Brusque, but caring Detective Chief Inspector of the Northumberland & City Police Department.
See: *Vera* (2011– , 16 episodes, UK)

Stanton, Lynn (*Sirens*)

Black single mother who doubles as a rookie cop in Pittsburgh.
See: *Sirens* (1993–1995, 35 episodes, USA/Canada)

Stanwyck, Carole (*Partners in Crime*)

Former socialite turned photographer turned private investigator after inheriting a detective agency.
See: *Partners in Crime* (1984, 13 episodes, USA)

Starrett, Jane (*Dick and the Duchess*)

Trouble-prone noblewoman who gets involved in the cases of her insurance-investigator husband.
See: *Dick and the Duchess* (1957–1958, 26 episodes, USA/UK)

Stickney White, Sarah (*Tales of the Gold Monkey*)

American spy working undercover as a sultry singer on a Pacific island in 1938.

See: *Tales of the Gold Monkey* (1982–1983, 21 episodes, USA)

Stone Undercover (2002–2003, 26 episodes, Canada)

Created by: Andrew Wreggitt
Production Co.: Alberta Filmworks, Canadian Broadcasting Corp., Tom Stone Productions Inc.
Originally Aired: In Syndication
Main Cast: Chris William Martin, Janet Kidder, Stuart Margolin, Natascha Girgis

Known as *Tom Stone* in Canada, this crime series stars Chris William Martin in the title role, an ex-cop and ex-con who takes a job with the Royal Canadian Mounted Police in Calgary. Stone works as an undercover investigator with RCMP Corporal Marina Di Luzio (Janet Kidder), a specialist in commercial crime from Toronto, who is none too happy about her reassignment to the former Cowtown. Neither is she thrilled with fast-talking new partner Tom or his larcenous buddy Jack Welsh (Stuart Margolin), but the three need each other for their disparate ends, so this unholy alliance wages war against money launderers, crooked real estate developers, insider traders, and corporate spies. While the crimes they solve are mostly white-collar, even white collars get dirty, and they find themselves pulled into the darker, more dangerous world of drug dealers, mad bombers and professional killers.

Strange Report (1969–1970, 16 episodes, UK)

Production Co.: Arena Productions, Incorporated Television Company
Originally Aired: NBC
Main Cast: Anthony Quayle, Kaz Garas, Anneke Wills

Adam Strange (Anthony Quayle) investigates bizarre and baffling cases using the latest forensic techniques in his own home laboratory. Assisted by American grad student Hamlyn Gynt (Kaz Garas) and artist/model Evelyn McLean (Anneke Wills), Strange navigates London during the swinging 60s, using his criminology skills to assist the authorities when they require his unique perspective. In "Cover Girls: Last Year's Model" (1969), Strange becomes involved in neighbor Evelyn's world of fashion, when a designer's collection is stolen. Other "Strange Reports" involve the occult in "Hand: A Matter of Witchcraft" (1969) and distant relations in "Sniper: When Is Your Cousin Not?" (1969).

How very Strange.

Strike Force (1981–1982, 20 episodes, USA)
Created by: Lane Slate
Production Co.: Aaron Spelling Productions
Originally Aired: ABC
Main Cast: Robert Stack, Dorian Harewood, Trisha Noble, Richard Romanus, Michael Goodwin, Herb Edelman

Action-packed police procedural starring Robert Stack as Captain Frank Murphy, head of an elite LAPD unit which takes on only the toughest cases, one at a time, to get results. Murphy's neo–*Untouchables* team includes family man Paul Strobber (Dorian Harewood), womanizer Charlie Gunzer (Richard Romanus), and nice guy Mark Osborne (Michael Goodwin). Balancing (or bubbling) all that testosterone is Sgt. Rosie Johnson (Trisha Noble), a beautiful, but tough (there's a switch) detective, who joined the police force after her husband went missing in Vietnam. The team deals with every type of serious crime imaginable, from serial decapitations to kidnappings, from hijackings to rapes, with their signature hail-of-bullets style.

While *Strike Force* did not have the longevity of Stack's *The Untouchables*, it did have the dubious distinction of being the most violent show on the air at that time.

Sue Thomas: F.B.Eye (2002–2005, 56 episodes, Canada/USA)
Based on: The real-life experiences of Sue Thomas
Created by: Dave Alan Johnson, Gary R. Johnson
Production Co.: Pebblehut Productions, Paxson Entertainment
Originally Aired: PAX
Main Cast: Deanne Bray, Yannick Bisson, Rick Peters, Enuka Okuma, Marc Gomes, Ted Atherton, Tara Samuel

Based on a true story, this inspiring series stars Deanne Bray as title character **Sue Thomas**, a deaf woman whose lip-reading ability lands her on an FBI surveillance team. Members of the elite unit include boyish Jack Hudson (Yannick Bisson), the man in charge and a big believer in Sue's abilities, affable Bobby Manning (Rick Peters), a transplanted Australian and the office jokester, and dour Myles Leland (Ted Atherton), a condescending know-it-all, who initially gives Sue all kinds of grief because he feels she is unqualified. Sue navigates this new world with the help of Lucy Dotson (Enuka Okuma), the unit's office manager, who soon becomes Sue's roommate and confidante. Levi (Jesse), a hearing ear dog, is indispensable to Sue, alerting her when there is something she needs to hear, such as a doorbell, and always accompanying her to the office and out on field assignments. Together, this unique team searches for assassins, investigates bomb threats, and chases drug smugglers, while managing to maintain a fun and positive office environment and idealized friendships.

If you like dark, gritty tales, this series probably won't be up your alley, but if you prefer nice people and uplifting messages, this one's for you.
See also: **Thomas, Sue** (*Sue Thomas: F.B.Eye*)

Sullivan, Caitlyn "Cat" (*Taxi Brooklyn*)

NYPD detective who solves crimes with the help of a Brooklyn taxi driver.
See: *Taxi Brooklyn* (2014– , 12 episodes, France/USA)

Sweating Bullets (1991–1993, 66 episodes, Canada)

Created by: Sam Egan
Production Co.: IO International, SafriTel, Accent Entertainment Corp., et al.
Originally Aired: CBS
Main Cast: Rob Stewart, Carolyn Dunn, Ian Tracey

Former DEA agent Nick Slaughter (Rob Stewart) establishes a detective agency in the resort town of Key Mariah, Florida, but soon realizes life in paradise isn't all piña coladas and pink sunsets. Dead bodies, arms dealers, and drug smugglers seem as plentiful as beach umbrellas on the key, so Nick has his work cut out for him. In "Death's a Beach" (1991), travel agent Sylvie Girard (Carolyn Dunn) hires Nick to find one of her clients, a man who has disappeared with an expensive yacht. Sylvie and Nick go on to become partners in crime-solving, tracking parrot-smugglers, searching for pirates' treasure, and investigating a rapist who leaves behind tattoos.

Shown as part of the CBS *Crimetime After Primetime* lineup in the United States, *Sweating Bullets* is known as *Tropical Heat* elsewhere in the world, and was a surprise hit in Serbia.

Tales of the Gold Monkey (1982–1983, 21 episodes, USA)

Created by: Donald P. Bellisario
Production Co.: Belisarius Productions, Universal TV
Originally Aired: ABC
Main Cast: Stephen Collins, Jeff MacKay, Caitlin O'Heaney, Roddy McDowell, Marta DuBois

Stephen Collins stars as Jake Cutter, a freelance pilot whose odd jobs on the South Pacific island of Boragora lead to mystery and adventure in 1938. Boragora is a hotbed of intrigue (treasure! Nazis!), drawing the attention of the U.S. government, which plants a spy, Sarah Stickney White (Caitlin O'Heaney), to keep an eye on its interests. Sarah works undercover as a sultry chanteuse at the Monkey Bar, owned by slippery island magistrate "Bon Chance" Louie (Roddy McDowell). In "Black Pearl" (1982), the Nazis are trying to create a super bomb on a nearby island, so Jake poses as a defecting U.S. scientist, while Sarah searches for the bomb and a famed black pearl. Jake seems to have feelings for Sarah, but has trouble admitting them in "Trunk from the Past" (1982), when a mysterious trunk from Sarah's late father leads to a lost civilization. Other members of Jake's motley crew include his alcoholic mechanic Corky (Jeff MacKay) and his one-eyed-dog-with-an-attitude Jack. The Nazis don't stand a chance!

Taxi Brooklyn (2014– , 12 episodes, France/USA)
Based on: The film *Taxi* directed by Gérard Pirès.
Production Co.: EuropaCorp Television, Gary Scott Thompson Productions
Originally Aired: NBC
Main Cast: Chyler Leigh, Jacky Ido, James Colby, José Zúñiga, Jennifer Esposito, Bill Heck, Ally Walker, Raul Casso

  Chyler Leigh stars as NYPD detective Caitlyn "Cat" Sullivan, a woman not known for her diplomatic or driving skills, especially when a crash after a reckless pursuit finds her demoted to foot patrol. Enter Leo Romba (Jacky Ido), a French-African from Marseille, who drives a Brooklyn taxi and has an immigration situation. Problem solved! Cat will help Leo with immigration, and Leo will become Cat's personal driver. In the course of Cat's investigations, which include her off-the-books probe into the murder of her NYPD detective dad, Leo becomes not just her driver, but her crime-solving partner and friend.

Taylor, Susan (*Touching Evil*)
  Detective Inspector with a reckless partner in a unit devoted to organized and serial crime.
  See: *Touching Evil* (1997–1999, 16 episodes, UK/USA)

Team Knight Rider (1997–1998, 22 episodes, USA)
Based on: The TV series *Knight Rider* created by Glen A. Larson
Created by: Rick Copp, David A. Goodman
Production Co.: Sterling Pacific Films, Universal TV, MCA Television
Originally Aired: In Syndication
Main Cast: Brixton Karnes, Christine Steel, Duane Davis, Kathy Trageser, Nick Wechsler and the voices of Tom Kane, Nia Vardalos, Kerrigan Mahan, Andrea Beutner, John Kassir

  Based on the popular *Knight Rider* series from the 80s, *TKR* multiplies *KR* by five, giving us five crimefighters instead of one and five talking supercars à la KITT from the previous show. Led by Kyle Stewart (Brixton Karnes) and his vehicle, "Dante" (voiced by Tom Kane), the team, under the aegis of the Foundation for Law and Government (FLAG), hunts terrorists, assassins, and other evildoers, bringing them to justice in high-octane style. Girls want to have fun as well, so two of the team members are female—four, if you count the vehicles they drive. Jenny Andrews (Christine Steel), a former Marine and possibly the daughter of Michael Knight (David Hasselhoff) from the original series, burns rubber in "Domino" (voiced by Nia Vardalos), a gossipy Ford Mustang. Erica West (Kathy Trageser), a former con artist (there seems to be one in every law enforcement crowd), rides Kat (voiced by Andrea Beutner), a motorcycle with a rules fetish. With additional members of FLAG and a long list of villains, including Mobius (voiced by David McCallum), it's hard to tell the players without a scorecard.

Perhaps it was character clutter that led to the early demise of this one.

Teeger, Natalie (*Monk*)

Successor to **Sharona Fleming**, Natalie serves as assistant and companion to obsessive-compulsive detective Adrian Monk (Tony Shalhoub). Unlike Sharona (Bitty Schram), Natalie calls her employer "Mr. Monk" and generally takes a softer approach in dealing with Monk's needs and phobias. As portrayed by Traylor Howard, Natalie is spunky and tenacious, venturing into a killer's home when Monk is under the weather in "Mr. Monk Stays in Bed" (2005). She sticks by her guns, pointing to the real murderer when no one believes her in "Mr. Monk and the Critic" (2009). Mother to Julie (Emmy Clarke), she is heir to a toothpaste fortune from her wealthy parents, who make an appearance in "Mr. Monk Goes to a Wedding" (2005), but she chooses to live her life simply and away from the country club set.

See also: *Monk* (2002–2009, 125 episodes, USA)

Tennison, Jane (*Prime Suspect*)

Detective Chief Inspector who battles male chauvinism and her own personal demons in London.

See: *Prime Suspect* (1991–2006, 15 episodes, UK/USA)

Theroux, Nina (*Alphas*)

Defense Department consultant with the enhanced ability to "push" people into doing her bidding.

See: *Alphas* (2011–2012, 24 episodes, USA)

The Thin Man (1957–1959, 72 episodes, USA)

Based on: The novel by Dashiell Hammett
Production Co.: Clarington Productions, MGM Television
Originally Aired: NBC
Main Cast: Peter Lawford, Phyllis Kirk

Peter Lawford stars as Nick Charles, a former private investigator now living in luxury on New York's Park Avenue. Phyllis Kirk is his wife, Nora, a beautiful socialite prone to jealousy, since Nick appears to be a magnet for the attention of females, especially those of the floozy variety. Together the marrieds stumble upon crimes in amateur sleuth fashion, while trading quips, exuding charm, and overseeing the comic antics of their dog Asta. In "Paris Pendant" (1957), Nora becomes the focus of thieves who wish to possess her newly acquired prize necklace. Nora is targeted again in "The Fashion Showdown" (1957), when she fills in for a model on the runway, unaware that the gown she wears identifies her as the murder victim-to-be. Other cases find the pair solving a homicide via an acrostic puzzle, investigating a robot murder suspect, and discouraging the stalker of singer Vic Damone (as himself).

The Charleses follow *Mr. & Mrs. North* in a long line of adorable, crime-solving TV couples, including *Hart to Hart* and *McMillan and Wife*.

Thomas, Andrea (*Isis*)

High school science teacher who can transform herself into the goddess Isis via an Egyptian amulet.

See: *Isis* (1975–1976, 22 episodes, USA)

Thomas, Sue (*Sue Thomas: F.B.Eye*)

Deanne Bray portrays the title character, a deaf woman who accepts a position with the FBI, in this series based on the experiences of the real Sue Thomas. Sue arrives in Washington with her hearing ear dog Levi (Jesse) and is promptly assigned the task of analyzing fingerprints, not the career choice energetic Sue has in mind. When she meets Special Agent Jack Hudson (Yannick Bisson), Sue demonstrates her lip-reading ability and lands a job on Jack's surveillance team, where she reads suspects' lips when no audio is available. Sue, who is able to communicate in both English and American Sign Language, interrogates a suspect who cannot hear or speak in "The Signing" (2002), and helps the man turn his life around while gaining information which leads to the capture of a notorious criminal. Sue is not always office-bound, often making it into the field, as in "Simon Says" (2004), when a serial killer leads her through his own warped version of Simon Says. There isn't much time for romance in this dangerous, high-pressure work, but pretty Sue and handsome Jack are certainly attracted to each other. They keep it all business to abide by bureau policy, leaving fans' wishes for them unfulfilled when PAX abruptly pulled the plug on this series in 2005.

See also: *Sue Thomas: F.B.Eye* (2002–2005, 56 episodes, Canada/USA)

Thorson, Dottie and Brandi (*The Huntress*)

The Thorson women, mother Dottie and daughter Brandi, are fledgling bounty hunters. As portrayed by Annette O'Toole and Jordana Spiro, Dottie and Brandi enter the business reluctantly, having inherited it from their late husband and father Ralph "Papa" Thorson (Craig T. Nelson). Brandi is cynical and headstrong, and in "Scattered" (2000), she quits college, partnering with a different bounty hunter after a falling-out with her mother. In "The Two Mrs. Thorsons" (parts one and two, 2001), Dottie confronts a woman who claims to be the late Ralph's real wife, but when the second Mrs. Thorson turns up dead, Dottie is charged with murder. Later adventures involve teaming up with a self-styled superhero and questing for millions in lost ransom money.

See also: *The Huntress* (2000–2001, 29 episodes, USA)

Thyme, Laura (*Rosemary & Thyme*)

Former policewoman turned gardener who stumbles upon murders in people's backyards.

See: *Rosemary & Thyme* (2003–2007, 22 episodes, UK)

Timoney, Jane (*Prime Suspect*)

Reckless, but brilliant detective with the elite Manhattan East Homicide Squad.

See: *Prime Suspect* (2011–2012, 13 episodes, USA)

T.J. Hooker (1982–1986, 91 episodes, USA)

Created by: Rick Husky
Production Co.: Spelling-Goldberg Productions, Columbia Pictures Television
Originally Aired: ABC (1982–1985), CBS (1985–1986)
Main Cast: William Shatner, Heather Locklear, Adrian Zmed, Richard Herd, James Darren

William Shatner is Sgt. T.J. Hooker, a plainclothes detective who opts for duty as a uniformed beat cop after his partner is killed while on patrol. With 15 years of police experience, tough-guy Hooker is assigned as a training officer for academy recruits, including Vince Romano (Adrian Zmed), who becomes Hooker's brash rookie partner on the street. Back at the station, Vicki Taylor (April Clough) mans (or, more correctly, womans) the front desk, while resisting Romano's insistent come-ons. Vicki is quickly replaced by Officer Stacy Sheridan (Heather Locklear), the daughter of the precinct's captain, Dennis Sheridan (Richard Herd). After almost a year (season), Hooker unshackles Stacy from her desk in "Payday Pirates" (1983), assigning her to field duty with Jim Corrigan (James Darren), thereby pairing the best-looking partners ever to break donuts in a black and white. After that, there's lots of "pretty girl" undercover work for Stacy, including posing as an exotic dancer, fashion model, and masseuse (shades of *Charlie's Angels* and *Police Woman*). In the equal-work department, however, Vince Romano also poses as a stripper to flush out a cocaine ring in "Death Strip" (1984).

The things they teach in the modern police academy!

Tom Stone
See: *Stone Undercover* (2002–2003, 26 episodes, Canada)

Took, Aurelia (*Space Precinct*)
Telepathic alien on the planet Altor, using her skills as a member of Demeter City's police force.
See: *Space Precinct* (1994–1995, 24 episodes, UK)

Touching Evil (1997–1999, 16 episodes, UK/USA)
Created by: Paul Abbott
Production Co.: United Productions, Coastal Productions, Anglia Television
Originally Aired: Public Television
Main Cast: Robson Green, Nicola Walker, Michael Feast, Shaun Dingwall

Dark, disturbing police procedural starring Robson Green as Detective Inspector Dave Creegan, who displays an uncanny ability to connect with the criminal mind after recovering from a gunshot wound to the head. Creegan joins the Organized and Serial Crime unit, where he works with Detective Inspector Susan Taylor (Nicola Walker) to flush out England's most twisted criminals. While Taylor and the OSC prefer to use the latest police techniques, Creegan would rather rely on his instincts, which seem infallible, even if he is often reckless. But the team also employs time-honored investigative tools such as undercover stings, as when Susan and DC Rivers (Shaun Dingwall) pose as an infertile couple to break a child-selling operation in "What Price a Child/Paedophile Ring, Part 1" (1998). Whatever the methods, these cops, in their pursuit of serial killers and psychopaths, are always touching evil.

Touching Evil (2004, 13 episodes, USA)
Based on: The TV series *Touching Evil* created by Paul Abbott
Production Co.: Cheyenne Enterprises, Lexington Films
Originally Aired: USA Network
Main Cast: Jeffrey Donovan, Vera Farmiga, Zack Grenier, Brian Markinson, Kevin Durand

Remake of the British series about a detective whose gunshot wound to the head leaves him with a sixth sense about criminals. This American reboot adds lack of impulse control to the list of new personality traits David Creegan (Jeffrey Donovan) experiences after recovering from the shooting, making him a brilliant but eccentric investigator for the FBI's Organized and Serial Crime Unit. His partner, Susan Branca (Vera Farmiga), tries to stay connected to Creegan in his new world, where he can be dreaming while awake. Susan bears her own scars, albeit the emotional kind, from the suicide of her fiancé. They work through this personal darkness to find more darkness in their work, but when they deal with killers and psychopaths, it leaves a little more light for the rest of us.

Towne, Christina (*Diamonds*)

Former star of a TV detective series, who turns to real-life sleuthing with her ex-husband.
See: *Diamonds* (1987–1989, 44 episodes, Canada)

Towne, Elizabeth "Foxfire" (*Codename: Foxfire*)

Former CIA operative carrying out undercover assignments for the brother of the U.S. president.
See: *Codename: Foxfire* (1985, 8 episodes, USA)

Tropical Heat

See: *Sweating Bullets* (1991–1993, 66 episodes, Canada)

Tucker, Amanda (*Tucker's Witch*)

Half of a married sleuthing couple, the half that also happens to be a witch.
See: *Tucker's Witch* (1982–1983, 12 episodes, USA)

Tucker's Witch (1982–1983, 12 episodes, USA)

Created by: William Bast, Paul Huson
Production Co.: Hill/Mandelker Films
Originally Aired: CBS
Main Cast: Tim Matheson, Catherine Hicks, Bill Morey, Alfre Woodard, Barbara Barrie

Rick and Amanda Tucker are a pair of married sleuths with a twist—Amanda is a bona fide witch. With a detective agency in the Laurel Canyon area of Los Angeles, Rick (Tim Matheson) and Amanda (Catherine Hicks) solve cases, often with the help of Amanda's special gifts, and sometimes in spite of them, since Amanda is still learning how to control her powers. In "Abra Cadaver" (1982), the Tuckers investigate when a conductor's dead body disappears from a funeral home and leads to smuggled diamonds. Other only-in-La-La-Land cases involve a rockstar's missing girlfriend and a celebrity hairdresser targeted by an international assassin. The Tuckers are assisted by Amanda's cat Dickens, who has a Lassie-esque ability to help out in times of trouble.

Turner, Beth (*Moonlight*)

Sophia Myles stars as Beth Turner, investigative reporter for *Buzzwire*, an Internet tabloid with a taste for sensational stories. Beth hits the jackpot in "No Such Thing As Vampires" (2007), when a college coed turns up dead with two puncture marks on her neck, and a brooding Los Angeles detective may hold the key to solving the crime. Soon Beth and the P.I., Mick St. John (Alex O'Loughlin), are teaming up to solve cases, and Beth learns that they share a past that she doesn't quite remember, a past in which vampire Mick saved her life. As Beth is introduced to the world of undead L.A., she and Mick fight their romantic longings, while the murder of Beth's fiancé (Jordan Belfi) causes a rift in "Love Lasts Forever" (2008). But Beth's fate is intertwined with Mick's, at least for the duration of this short-lived series.

See also: *Moonlight* (2007–2008, 16 episodes, USA)

24 (2001–2010, 194 episodes, USA)

Created by: Joel Surnow, Robert Cochran
Production Co.: Imagine Television, 20th Century–Fox Television, Real Time Productions, Teakwood Lane Productions
Originally Aired: Fox
Main Cast: Kiefer Sutherland, Leslie Hope, Sarah Clarke, Elisha Cuthbert, Dennis Haysbert, Mary Lynn Rajskub, Carlos Bernard, James Morrison, Reiko Aylesworth, Jude Ciccolella

Taut, high-concept espionage series where each one-hour program runs in real time and every 24-episode season comprises a single day in the life of Jack Bauer (Kiefer Sutherland). Bauer is an agent for the fictional Counter Terrorist Unit (CTU) in Los Angeles, and he races against the clock to thwart terrorists and traitors in their plots to assassinate presidential candidate David Palmer (Dennis Haysbert) on Day 1, detonate a nuclear bomb on Day 2, release a biological weapon on Day 3, and so on throughout the eight days/seasons. In the meantime, Jack must protect his loved ones, who are exceedingly trouble-prone, especially especially his teenage daughter Kim Bauer (Elisha Cuthbert), who later becomes a computer analyst at CTU. Jack rushes around Los Angeles, using whatever means necessary to extract information from suspects, while receiving support from the skilled, if not always loyal, agents back at CTU.

Second-in-command Nina Myers (Sarah Clarke) is helpful and supportive when a terrorist kidnaps Jack's wife, Teri Bauer (Leslie Hope), and daughter Kim, but Nina is later revealed to be a double agent, even killing Teri before trying to flee. Nobody "doubles" better than nefarious Nina, who has appeared on many lists of best TV villains, including *TV Guide*'s in March 2013.

On the other end of the fidelity spectrum is Chloe O'Brian (Mary Lynn Rajskub), a CTU senior analyst and computer nerd, who is always loyal to Jack, even risking her job and reputation at times, but always in her trademark whining and pouting way. Chloe even shows up in the miniseries sequel, *24: Live Another Day*, now a renegade hacker, but still assisting Jack, who is also on the lam. That's one loyal woman and one indestructible man who never seems to run out of lives.

21 Jump Street (1987–1991, 103 episodes, USA)

Created by: Patrick Hasburgh, Stephen J. Cannell
Production Co.: 20th Century–Fox Television, Patrick Hasburgh Productions, Stephen J. Cannell Productions
Originally Aired: Fox (1987–1990), In Syndication (1990–1991)
Main Cast: Johnny Depp, Holly Robinson, Peter DeLuise, Dustin Nguyen, Richard Grieco, Steven Williams, Frederic Forrest

Quintessentially 80s series about a gang of youthful cops who work undercover at high schools, colleges, and other places where kids gather to solve crimes from the inside. Johnny Depp is Tom Hanson, who wasn't taken seriously by perps on the street due to his boyish good looks, and is given a second chance with the Jump Street brigade. Holly Robinson portrays **Judy Hoffs**, who not only adds gender and racial balance to the team as an African American woman, but also brings intelligence and professionalism to the sometimes immature group. Peter DeLuise plays Doug Penhall, a leather-jacketed, updated Fonzie, who thinks he's a ladies man. Dustin Nguyen rounds out the original unit as Harry Truman Ioki, a Vietnamese refugee passing himself off as Japanese to avoid painful questions. The responsible adults at 21 Jump Street, an abandoned chapel where the unit is headquartered, are Captain Richard Jenko (Frederic Forrest), an ex-hippie who still seems to live in the 60s, replaced after his untimely death by Captain Adam Fuller (Steven Williams), a stern fellow who seems to have skipped the 60s altogether. The crew pursues drug dealers, rapists, pornographers, arsonists, and even murderers, some of whom are barely out of puberty.

These cool cops are a *Mod Squad* for the 80s. "Say jump, 21 Jump Street!"
See also: **Hoffs, Judy (*21 Jump Street*)**

Two (1996–1997, 22 episodes, Canada)

Created by: Charles Grant Craig
Production Co.: New World Television Productions, Telegenic Programs, Two Television Productions
Originally Aired: In Syndication
Main Cast: Michael Easton, Barbara Tyson, Lochlyn Munro

This short-lived Canadian drama riffs on the classic 60s series *The Fugitive*, but brings us an evil twin brother in place of the one-armed man. The man falsely accused of murdering his wife in this case is Gus McClain (Michael Easton), a college professor leading the good life in Seattle until everything falls apart when his twin comes to town. Gus and brother Booth Hubbard (Easton in a dual role) had been separated at birth, and now Booth is out for vengeance, having drawn the short straw in both the parental and health lotteries. Booth frames Gus for the murder of Sarah McClain (Allison Hossack) and for other homicides around the country, leaving Gus on the run from the FBI. The "Gerard" of the piece is FBI agent Theresa "Terry" Carter (Barbara Tyson), convinced that Gus had killed her partner as well as his wife, and obsessed with his capture. Carter follows McClain around the country, while his evil twin, as evil twins do, leaves a trail of dead bodies to blame on his brother.

Alas, *The Fugitive* this wasn't, and while Richard Kimble was exonerated after four seasons, Gus McClain was left in evil-twin limbo when *Two* was canceled after its first season.

Tyler, Alice (*Whiz Kids*)

Amateur detective who solves crimes with three boys and a computer named Ralf.

See: *Whiz Kids* (1983–1984, 18 episodes, USA)

Udinov, Alexandra "Alex" (*Nikita*)

Mole planted in a rogue spy organization in hopes of foiling its operations.

See: *Nikita* (2010–2013, 73 episodes, USA)

Under Cover (1991, 13 episodes, USA)

Created by: William Broyles, Jr.
Production Co.: Sacret, Warner Bros. Television
Originally Aired: ABC
Main Cast: Anthony John Denison, Linda Purl, Josef Sommer, John Rhys-Davies

Short-lived, but intriguing series, a cross between a family drama and an action-adventure/thriller. Dylan and Kate Del'Amico (Anthony John Denison and Linda Purl) work as covert operatives for the National Intelligence Agency under the supervision of erudite section chief Stewart Merriman (Josef Sommer). The couple travels to world hot spots like Kuwait, where they face capture by Iraqi soldiers, or take meetings with KGB agents at the local elementary school. When they are not engaging in car chases and gun battles, Dylan and Kate try to maintain a blissful domestic existence, juggling their kids' Little League games or their own opportunities for romance at home.

The spy stuff is played seriously here, so seriously, in fact, that the show's timely handling of Middle Eastern themes brought about reschedulings when the Persian Gulf War broke out, contributing to its early cancellation.

Under Suspicion (1994–1995, 18 episodes, USA)

Created by: Jacqueline Zambrano
Production Co.: Lakeside Productions
Originally Aired: CBS
Main Cast: Karen Sillas, Philip Casnoff, Paul McCrane, Seymour Cassell, Michael Beach, Richard Foronjy, Natalie Shaw

Karen Sillas stars as Detective Rose "Phil" Phillips, the only female detective in a Portland police precinct. Phil finds herself with two jobs: solving homicides and fighting the sexist attitudes of many of her colleagues. Investigating serial killers, arsonists, wife abusers, drive-by shooters, and cop killers, Phil confronts the pressures of her work with professionalism, retaining her compassion while trying to be one of the boys. One of those boys, Internal Affairs detective Jimmy Vitelli (Philip Casnoff), does catch Phil's eye, sparking a romantic involvement, but it's not smooth sailing when their departments clash in "Sex Harassment/Corruption Case" (1995). Phil is shot in series finale "Wrongful Shooting" (1995), and with no second-season resurrection for this series, the wound is apparently fatal.

Undercovers (2010, 11 episodes, USA)

Created by: J. J. Abrams, Josh Reims
Production Co.: Warner Bros. Television, Bad Robot Productions, Good Butter Productions
Originally Aired: NBC
Main Cast: Gugu Mbatha-Raw, Boris Kodjoe, Ben Schwartz, Mekia Cox, Carter MacIntyre, Gerald McRaney

Caterers or spies? Steven and Samantha Bloom are enjoying a happy (and youthful) retirement from the CIA, when they are pressed back into service to locate a missing operative and friend. Enjoying the return to intrigue, the Blooms stay on with the company to tackle special missions, which take them from Berlin to Peru, and from Tuscany to Tel Aviv. Samantha (Gugu Mbatha-Raw) and Steven (Boris Kodjoe) retrieve code-breaking devices, thwart assassinations, and search for biological weapons, while Samantha's sister Lizzy (Mekia Cox), who does not know about their secret lives, helps back home in Los Angeles with their catering business. With only 11 missions (which made it to air), it's a good thing that these great-looking retirees have another career to fall back on.

Unforgettable (2011–2014, 48 episodes, USA)

Based on: The short story "The Rememberer" by J. Robert Lennon
Created by: John Bellucci, Ed Redlich
Production Co.: Timberman-Beverly Productions, CBS Television Studios, Sony Pictures Television
Originally Aired: CBS
Main Cast: Poppy Montgomery, Dylan Walsh, Jane Curtin, Dallas Roberts, Tawny Cypress, James Hiroyuki Liao

"Only a few people in the world have the ability to remember everything. I'm one of them."

Carrie Wells (Poppy Montgomery) has a rare medical condition which allows her to remember everything she ever saw or heard. The only lacuna in her otherwise perfect archive is the memory of what happened on the childhood day when her sister was murdered. As a homicide detective for the NYPD, Carrie still seeks her sister's killer or at least the memory of what happened that day. Working with her ex-partner and former boyfriend, Lt. Al Burns (Dylan Walsh), Carrie scans crime scenes and suspects' homes or workplaces like a human camera, snapping vital information she can retrieve later in the blink of an eye. Carrie and Al travel to Syracuse in "The Man in the Woods" (2012), where they investigate a possible link to the murder of Carrie's sister, and find some answers, but also (not surprisingly) more questions.

CBS canceled the show after this episode, the first season finale, then apparently forgot it was canceled, ordering new episodes for two subsequent summer seasons. Then it remembered to cancel the show again in 2014. That's *Unforgettable*.

An Unsuitable Job for a Woman (1997–2001, 9 episodes, UK/USA)

Based on: The novel by P.D. James
Production Co.: Ecosse Films, WGBH Boston
Originally Aired: Public Television
Main Cast: Helen Baxendale, Annette Crosbie

Cordelia Gray (Helen Baxendale) inherits a floundering detective agency from her boss, who committed suicide, and decides to run the business on her own, even though she is only an apprentice investigator. Cordelia dives feet-first—literally—into her maiden case, "Sacrifice" (1997), when her faltering investigation into the death of a prominent scientist's son gets her thrown to the bottom of an abandoned well. Her office assistant, long-suffering Mrs. Sparshott (Annette Crosbie), constantly frets over Cordelia's safety, and never more so than when a very pregnant Cordelia agrees to follow a mysterious man around London in "Living in Risk" (1999).

Cordelia Gray is not the typical, smarter-than-everyone-in-the-room detective that viewers have come to know in shows like *Agatha Christie's Marple* or *The Mentalist*. Though brave and intelligent, Cordelia still has a lot to learn about her new profession, and sometimes she gets things wrong, as in "Playing God" (2001), when she's a generation off as to the identity of the murderer.

But if you like realistic, albeit somber, depictions of detective work, then *An Unsuitable Job for a Woman* will be just your cup of Earl Grey tea.

V (2009–2011, 22 episodes, USA)

Based on: The TV mini-series *V* created by Kenneth Johnson
Created by: Scott Peters
Production Co.: The Scott Peters Company, HDFilms, Warner Bros. Television
Originally Aired: ABC
Main Cast: Elizabeth Mitchell, Morris Chestnut, Joel Gretsch, Logan Huffman, Laura Vandervoort, Morena Baccarin, Scott Wolf

A reimagining of the 1983 miniseries of the same title, *V* again brings us "Visitors," the extraterrestrial type, who seemingly come in peace, but actually have planetary conquest on their (reptilian) minds. Led by the luscious Anna (Morena Baccarin), the visitors look like humans, incredibly beautiful humans, and offer their technological and medical advances to the people of our planet. But FBI agent **Erica Evans** (Elizabeth Mitchell) quickly learns that extraterrestrial beauty is only skin deep (literally), and that the aliens' intentions aren't very pretty either. While keeping her day job and ostensibly protecting the aliens against terrorist attacks, Evans secretly joins a resistance movement, sabotaging Anna's plans at every turn.

See also: **Evans, Erica (*V*)**

Van Buren, Anita (*Law & Order*)

Anita Van Buren (S. Epatha Merkerson) has the distinction of being the longest-running character (by episode count) during the 20 seasons of TV titan *Law & Order*. Van Buren is a lieutenant for the NYPD, and serves as commander of the 27th Precinct Detective Squad, supervising the work of field detectives, such as Lennie Briscoe (Jerry Orbach) and Ed Green (Jesse L. Martin). Van Buren instructs the detectives on which leads to follow, interrogates suspects, and consults with the various assistant district attorneys, including Jack McCoy (Sam Waterston). Since only the first half of most episodes focuses on the police investigation, and, at that, mostly outside the station, Van Buren gets only a few short scenes per episode. Over the years, however, she makes an impact as a black woman of strength and substance, working among a group of predominantly white males. In "Ritual" (1997), Van Buren makes the difficult decision to file a discrimination lawsuit against the department, when she is passed over for promotion to captain in favor of a white woman with less seniority. In her personal life, she deals with cervical cancer and uses medical marijuana to ease the side-effects of treatment, even though the practice is illegal in the state of New York. The series ends on an up note for Van Buren with seemingly good news about her health and the announcement of her engagement to Frank Gibson (Ernie Hudson) in "Rubber Room" (2010).

This character deserves a happily ever after.

See also: *Law & Order* **(1990–2010, 456 episodes, USA)**

Van Doren, Paige (*Line of Fire*)

Rookie agent in the FBI's Richmond, Virginia office.
See: *Line of Fire* **(2003–2004, 13 episodes, USA)**

Van Loween, Sybil (*The Delphi Bureau*)

Washington, D.C., socialite who doubles as a handler in a secret government intelligence agency.
See: *The Delphi Bureau* **(1972–1973, 8 episodes, USA)**

Van Pelt, Grace (*The Mentalist*)

Rookie member of a California Bureau of Investigation team working with a former con man.
See: *The Mentalist* **(2008– , 138 episodes, USA)**

Vargas, Tess (*Beauty & the Beast*)

New York homicide detective and keeper of "beastly" secrets.
See: *Beauty & the Beast* **(2012– , 44 episodes, USA/Canada)**

Vasco, Jane (*Painkiller Jane*)

Operative for a top-secret agency which hunts aberrants with superhuman mental abilities.
See: *Painkiller Jane* **(2007, 22 episodes, Canada/USA)**

Vera **(2011– , 16 episodes, UK)**

Based on: The novels of Ann Cleeves
Production Co.: ITV Studios
Originally Aired: Public Television
Main Cast: Brenda Blethyn, David Leon, Jon Morrison, Paul Ritter, Wunmi Mosaku, Tom Hutch, Sonya Cassidy, Clare Calbraith

Vera Stanhope (Brenda Blethyn) works as Detective Chief Inspector of the Northumberland & City Police Department. Middle-aged Vera is sometimes brusque, often obsessed with her work, and always shabbily dressed, giving Columbo a run for his money, especially in the raincoat division. Vera supervises a team of detectives, but her "you're with me" man is handsome Detective Sgt. Joe Ashworth (David Leon), and the two travel the picturesque countryside in Vera's equally shabby Land Rover, searching for clues and suspects in homicide cases. Their mysteries usually involve dark, tangled personal relationships, as in "Protected" (2014), where the lives and loves of the past lead to murder in a seaside community. Other members of Vera's long-suffering team include her favorite whipping boy, Kenny Lockhart (Jon Morrison), and young detective Holly Lawson (Wunmi Mosaku), who works hard, but never seems to get a nod of approval from her caustic boss. Vera's solitary lifestyle is a wee bit shabby as well, and she vows to clean it up after an angina diagnosis in "The Ghost Position" (2012).

No matter what, though, the raincoat and floppy hat are STAYING.

Veronica Clare (1991, 9 episodes, USA)

Created by: Jeffrey Bloom
Production Co.: Hearst Entertainment, Inc.
Originally Aired: Lifetime
Main Cast: Laura Robinson, Robert Beltran, Christina Pickles, Tony Plana

Veronica Clare (Laura Robinson) is a detective in the classic 40s noir tradition, except, of course, that she's a woman, and a modern one at that. Veronica owns a jazz club in LA's Chinatown, while she plies the PI trade, searching for missing spouses, solving murders, and catching thieves. Even though both jobs keep her busy, she still has time for voice-over narration and verbal sparring with her partner, Duke Rado (Robert Beltran). Although she is non-violent, Veronica always dresses to kill.

Veronica Mars (2004–2007, 64 episodes, USA)

Created by: Rob Thomas
Production Co.: Stu Segall Productions, Silver Pictures Television, Rob Thomas Productions, Warner Bros. Television
Originally Aired: UPN (2004–2006), CW (2006–2007)
Main Cast: Kristen Bell, Enrico Colantoni, Percy Daggs III, Jason Dohring, Francis Capra, Ryan Hansen

High school noir series starring Kristen Bell as the title character, a student and apprentice private investigator in the wealthy, seaside community of Neptune, California. Veronica and her PI dad, Keith Mars (Enrico Colantoni), solve cases big and small in a locale where the sunny beauty of the surroundings belies the dark crimes and motivations shading the lives of all the residents. One of the most sensational crimes is the murder of Veronica's best friend,

Lilly Kane (Amanda Seyfried), which is the catalyst for most of the major events in season one, including Keith's dismissal as sheriff and Veronica's abandonment by her boyfriend and the A-list of cool kids at school. Now less popular, but no less smart and tenacious, Veronica works as Keith's secretary and assistant, but also takes on her own cases from fellow students willing to pay for her exceptional research and sleuthing skills. Murders, disappearances, thefts, infidelities, paternity questions (including Veronica's own) are all in a day's after-school work for Veronica Mars.

Vetter, Tracy (*Forever Knight*)

Tracy Vetter (Lisa Ryder) is a detective for the Toronto police department, newly assigned to work with Nicholas Knight (Geraint Wyn Davies) after the death of Knight's previous partner. Unbeknownst to Tracy, Nick is a vampire, but she quickly learns about the existence of fanged immortals from Javier Vachon (Ben Bass), a vampire who survives the plane bombing she is investigating. Nick places Tracy under Vachon's protection, because her new knowledge makes her a threat to vampires, and she is a "resistor," someone who is not susceptible to mesmerizing by vampires. In the meantime, Tracy must work with Nick in the mortal world to solve crimes, even though the human and supernatural realms often overlap, as in "Blind Faith" (1995), when a vampiric dog may be a vigilante killer. As a police commissioner's daughter, Tracy wants to prove she deserves the job of detective on her own merits, and takes a risky undercover assignment in "My Boyfriend Is a Vampire" (1995). Tracy continues to resist her growing attraction to Vachon, while keeping her secret from Nicholas, still unaware that Nick is hiding an ironic truth of his own.

See also: *Forever Knight* **(1992–1996, 70 episodes, Canada/West Germany)**

Vick, Karen (*Psych*)

Santa Barbara police chief who rides herd over a fake psychic detective and his colleagues.

See: *Psych* **(2006–2014, 121 episodes, USA)**

V.I.P. (1998–2002, 88 episodes, USA/Germany)

Created by: J.F. Lawton
Production Co.: Lawton Entertainment, Sony Pictures Television, Global Entertainment Productions GmbH & Company Medien KG, Lafitte Productions
Originally Aired: In Syndication
Main Cast: Pamela Anderson, Molly Culver, Natalie Raitano, Shaun Baker, Dustin Nguyen, Angelle Brooks, Leah Lail

Pamela Anderson stars in this campy (with a capital C) series about a woman working at a hotdog stand who becomes an accidental and famous celebrity bodyguard. Anderson is Vallery Irons, a beautiful woman on a date at a red carpet event, who manages to foil a shooter, branding her as the hottest (in more ways than one) bodyguard in L.A. Enter Colt Arrow Security, a down-on-its-luck protection firm, whose members approach untrained Vallery to be their figurehead. Re-christened as Vallery Irons Protection or V.I.P., the gorgeous bodyguards promise Val she'll just be the front person, but, like *Remington Steele*, Val gets pulled into cases, often winning the day, even without experience. Other members of the stunning (in more ways than one) team include Tasha Dexter (Molly Culver), a former model and spy (as often happens), Nikki Franco (Natalie Raitano), a weapons and explosives expert, Kay Simmons (Leah Lail), a computer whiz, and Quick Williams (Shaun Baker), a martial arts master. The team chases buff bad guys around L.A., but also tackles undercover assignments, sometimes working for the feds, and even deals with an evil double (as often happens) in "Val Cubed" (2002).

This action-comedy series, at least by judicious choice of initials, has secured its V.I.P. position among TV's female spies and sleuths.

Wainthropp, Hetty (*Hetty Wainthropp Investigates*)

Lancashire postal employee who opens a private detective agency at the age of 60.

See: *Hetty Wainthropp Investigates* (1996–1998, 27 episodes, UK)

Walker, Annie (*Covert Affairs*)

Rookie agent in the CIA's Domestic Protection Division, who speaks seven languages fluently.

See: *Covert Affairs* (2010– , 69 episodes, USA)

Walker, Darcy (*Black Scorpion*)

A police detective in Angel City, who turns into a vigilante superhero at night.

See: *Black Scorpion* (2001, 22 episodes, USA)

Walker, Sarah (*Chuck*)

Sarah Walker (Yvonne Strahovski) is a CIA agent with a unique assignment. Dispatched to Burbank, CA, Sarah must guard Chuck Bartkowski (Zachary Levi), a computer nerd at an electronics superstore, who has accidentally downloaded "The Intersect"—the CIA/NSA's complete database—into his BRAIN. Sarah adopts the cover of Chuck's girlfriend, a fish-out-of-water fast food jockey first at Weinerlicious and later at Orange Orange, an always empty yogurt emporium. Protecting Chuck from evil spies who want to access the information in his head is hard work, especially when Sarah starts to develop romantic feelings for her asset and vice versa. In "Chuck Versus the Broken Heart" (2009), Sarah is reassigned when it appears that her budding relationship with Chuck is impeding her effectiveness, but is reinstated once she rescues Chuck from kidnappers. Their relationship experiences twists and turns as old lovers reappear and disappear, and especially when Chuck decides to train as a full-fledged operative, raising questions of how they could remain spies and share a normal domestic life. Eventually Sarah and Chuck come to believe they can have it all, and are married in "Chuck Versus the Cliffhanger" (2011), deciding to set up shop as freelance operatives. But this is the spy game, so complications ensue, when Sarah loses her memory and can't remember her feelings for Chuck. In series finale "Chuck Versus the Goodbye" (2012), there is a hint that a single kiss may set things to rights.

See also: *Chuck* (2007–2012, 91 episodes, USA)

Warehouse 13 (2009–2014, 64 episodes, USA)

Created by: Jane Espenson, D. Brent Mote
Production Co.: Universal Cable Productions
Originally Aired: Syfy
Main Cast: Eddie McClintock, Joanne Kelly, Saul Rubinek, Allison Scagliotti, Genelle Williams, Aaron Ashmore, CCH Pounder

Warehouse 13 is in South Dakota, but it isn't a wheat storage facility. Located miles from anyone, the warehouse protects the world's supernatural artifacts, which have been collected for thousands of years since the time of Warehouse 1 during the reign of Alexander the Great. Secret Service Agents Pete Lattimer (Eddie McClintock) and **Myka Bering** (Joanne Kelly) are assigned to the warehouse's latest incarnation, number 13, and their task is to acquire new artifacts, which usually come to light after reports of bizarre and unexplained deaths or illnesses. Pete and Myka work under the supervision of the Warehouse's irascible Agent in Charge, Artie Nielsen (Saul Rubinek), and receive tech support from young **Claudia Donovan** (Allison Scagliotti), who later becomes a field agent in her own right. Almost as weird as the warehouse and the wonders it possesses is Mrs. Irene Frederic (CCH Pounder), the warehouse's caretaker, who seems to appear and disappear at will, ages slowly (or not at all), and has a mental link to the warehouse itself. The agents collect seemingly harmless items, such as Catherine O'Leary's Cowbell or Lewis Carroll's Looking Glass, but the quaint appeal of these historical curiosities belies their power as spontaneous firestarters or mysterious soul-swappers. The artifacts are so dangerous, in fact, that sometimes they threaten the very existence of the world. But Pete, Myka, Claudia, and Artie are always on hand with purple goo, neutralizing bags, and sometimes even artifacts themselves to save the world and set things right. We can all rest easy.

See also: **Bering, Myka** (*Warehouse 13*); **Donovan, Claudia** (*Warehouse 13*)

Waters, Samantha "Sam" (*Profiler*)

Forensic psychologist with the psychic ability to "see" a murder after inspecting a crime scene.

See: *Profiler* (1996–2000, 83 episodes, USA)

Watson, Joan (*Elementary*)

Joan Watson (Lucy Liu) is a former surgeon who left medicine because she accidentally killed a patient during a procedure. She finds a new career as a "sober companion" for recovering alcoholics and drug addicts, and her latest assignment is a man called Sherlock Holmes (Jonny Lee Miller). She lives with Holmes in his New York brownstone, and, in the course of monitoring his sobriety, accompanies him on his cases for the NYPD, where he works as a consulting detective. Intelligent and analytical, Watson is every bit a match for the brilliant and eccentric detective, and she soon moves beyond her status as sober companion to become an investigative apprentice to Holmes and later a detective in her own right. In "Dead Clade Walking" (2014), Watson reopens a murder case Holmes had been unable to solve while he was using drugs, discovering that a rare fossil is the key to the crime. Watson manages to have a relationship of respect and trust with Sherlock, despite his anti-social tendencies, although professional and personal disagreements do arise, as when she begins a brief affair with Sherlock's brother, Mycroft (Rhys Ifans), in "Step Nine" (2013). The brothers' complex past leads to Watson's kidnapping in "Paint It Black" (2014), and once she is free of the kidnappers, she moves toward independence from Sherlock as well. But New York is a small town when it comes to private police consultants, and Watson will not be rid of Sherlock that easily or vice versa.

See also: *Elementary* (2012– , 48 episodes, USA)

Welles, Tiffany (*Charlie's Angels*)

One of a trio of beautiful women working as private detectives for a rich, unseen boss.

See: *Charlie's Angels* (1976–1981, 110 episodes, USA)

Wells, Carrie (*Unforgettable*)

NYPD homicide detective with the ability to remember everything she's ever seen.

See: *Unforgettable* (2011–2014, 48 episodes, USA)

Wesley, Mary (*Boston Blackie*)

Girlfriend and assistant of a hardboiled private detective in Los Angeles. See: *Boston Blackie* (1951–1953, 58 episodes, USA)

West, Erica (*Team Knight Rider*)

Former con artist who rides a talking motorcycle for the Foundation for Law and Government.
See: *Team Knight Rider* (1997–1998, 22 episodes, USA)

West, Honey (*Honey West*)

From the opening scene of *Honey West's* first episode, "The Swingin' Mrs. Jones" (1965), where a disguised Honey (Anne Francis) flips a man over her hip in an alley and is left unconscious in the ensuing fracas, it's clear that Honey will not be joining June Cleaver in her 60s kitchen. Honey is the proprietor of her own detective agency, Honey West & Co., working with loyal partner Sam Bolt (John Ericson) in a profession normally reserved for men, especially in the years before the women's liberation movement. In "The Princess and the Paupers" (1965), Honey and Sam enter the swinging 60s rock scene, hired by a millionaire to deliver ransom money for his kidnapped musician son. "A Nice Little Till to Tap" (1965) finds an undercover Honey working as a teller to crack a string of inexplicable bank robberies.

Honey West first appeared

Anne Francis as high-kicking private eye and 60s trailblazer *Honey West* (ABC/Photofest).

on television in the Burke's Law episode, "Who Killed the Jackpot?" Although her tenure in her own series lasted just one season, Honey was a harbinger of better things to come for female detectives and netted Anne Francis a Golden Globe Award for her spirited portrayal of this TV trailblazer.

See also: *Honey West* (1965–1966, 30 episodes, USA)

Wheeler, Megan (*Law & Order: Criminal Intent*)

New York detective, a member of the Major Case Squad, dealing with the worst criminal offenders.

See: *Law & Order: Criminal Intent* (2001–2011, 195 episodes, USA)

Whelan, Molly (*Sirens*)

Second-generation cop, working as a rookie patrol officer in Pittsburgh.

See: *Sirens* (1993–1995, 35 episodes, USA/Canada)

White Collar (2009– , 75 episodes, USA)

Created by: Jeff Eastin
Production Co.: Fox Television Studios, Jeff Eastin & Warrior George Productions
Originally Aired: USA Network
Main Cast: Matt Bomer, Tim DeKay, Willie Garson, Marsha Thomason, Tiffani Thiessen, Sharif Atkins

Neal Caffrey (Matt Bomer) is a charming con artist/forger/thief, who works for the FBI, catching other white-collar criminals in return for a reduced sentence. Neal's watchdog at the Bureau is straight-laced agent Peter Burke (Tim DeKay), who doesn't trust Neal as far as he can throw him, hence Neal's electronic ankle-monitor, which keeps the restless rogue tethered to Manhattan. The two men forge an uneasy alliance, but they prove to be an effective team, retrieving stolen art works, thwarting jewelry heists, and conducting corporate sting operations, sometimes calling upon Neal's con-man friend Mozzie (Willie Garson) for assistance. Backing up the mismatched partners is Diana Berrigan (Marsha Thomason), a dedicated and loyal FBI agent, someone Peter can rely on in his working world of liars and cheats. On the home front, Peter receives support from his understanding wife Elizabeth Burke (Tiffani Thiessen), an event planner, while Diana has a challenging relationship with her physician girlfriend, which ends after a brief engagement. Not surprisingly, Neal is the least domesticated of the group, pursuing an on-again, off-again romance with glamorous insurance investigator Sara Ellis (Hilarie Burton), but his most stable relationship is his friendship with landlady June Ellington (Diahann Caroll), a widow whose husband was also a con man. In the slippery world inhabited by this motley crew, the truth may be the rarest treasure of all, but if they stick together, they will find it.

Whitfield, Eve (*Ironside*)

Plainclothes officer for the SFPD who works with a paraplegic police consultant.

See: *Ironside* (1967–1975, 199 episodes, USA)

Whiz Kids (1983–1984, 18 episodes, USA)

Created by: Philip DeGuere, Bob Shayne
Production Co.: Universal TV
Originally Aired: CBS
Main Cast: Matthew Laborteaux, Todd Porter, Jeffrey Jacquet, Andrea Elson, Melanie Gaffin, Max Gail, A Martinez

SF/adventure series about four teenagers who use their computer (a.k.a. "hacking") skills to solve crimes as amateur detectives. Richie Adler (Matthew Laborteaux) is the leader of the group, who assembles obsolete computer equipment into an advanced system he calls, "Ralf." Assisting Richie and Ralf are friends Ham Parker (Todd Porter), Alice Tyler (Andrea Elson), and Jeremy Saldino (Jeffrey Jacquet), and together this group of whiz kids takes on L.A.'s bad guys, especially corrupt officials in business or government. They even get involved with the KGB, when they learn that Alice's new boyfriend is being sought by Russian agents in "Father's Day" (1984). Making sure that the kids stay out of danger is local reporter Llewellen Farley (Max Gail) and police lieutenant Neal Quinn (A Martinez).

Never has so much been accomplished with floppy disks.

Wild Card (2003–2005, 36 episodes, USA)

Created by: Lynn Marie Latham, Bernard Lechowick
Production Co.: Busiek Productions, Fireworks Entertainment, Lifetime Television
Originally Aired: Lifetime
Main Cast: Joely Fisher, Chris Potter, Vikki Krinsky, Aislinn Paul, Jamie Johnston

Zoe Busiek (Joely Fisher) seems happy in her career as a Vegas blackjack dealer until life reshuffles the cards when her sister dies in a car accident, and Zoe must care for her nieces and nephew. Zoe moves to Chicago so she can be with the kids, but further trouble is in store when her sister's insurance company refuses to pay the family's claim. Not believing her sister was at fault in the accident, Zoe sets out to make things right, and on the way acquires a new career as an insurance fraud investigator. She and partner Dan Lennox (Chris Potter) frequently go undercover, investigating a fog machine explosion at a strip club in "Mimi's Assets" (2003) and pesticides in the mud at a spa in "Sand Trap" (2003). In the meantime, Zoe navigates the new world of sudden motherhood, dealing with bad grades, teen angst, and holiday craziness. Wild card, indeed.

Williams, Holly (*Dangerous Curves*)
Former policewoman working as an operative for a private security firm in Dallas.
See: *Dangerous Curves* (1992–1993, 34 episodes, USA)

Willows, Catherine (*CSI: Crime Scene Investigation*)
Former exotic dancer, now a blood-spatter analyst for a forensics team in Las Vegas.
See: *CSI: Crime Scene Investigation* (2000– , 337 episodes, USA/Canada)

Winfield, Cordelia (*The Baron*)
Secret agent who works for British intelligence with an American antiques dealer.
See: *The Baron* (1966–1967, 30 episodes, UK)

Winstone, Rebecca "Becca" (*Missing*)
Retired CIA agent who gets involved in international intrigue when her son goes missing in Europe.
See: *Missing* (2012, 10 episodes, USA)

The Wire (2002–2008, 60 episodes, USA)
Created by: David Simon
Production Co.: Blown Deadline Productions, Home Box Office
Originally Aired: HBO
Main Cast: Dominic West, Lance Reddick, Sonja Sohn, John Doman, Deirdre Lovejoy, Wendell Pierce, Seth Gilliam, Domenick Lombardozzi, Clarke Peters, Andre Royo

This Peabody Award–winning drama examines the soul of a major metropolitan city, Baltimore, by looking at the relationship between its police and some of the city's major institutions, including the drug trade (season one), the school system (season four), and the print media (season five). As the series opens, hard-drinking and hard-driving officer Jimmy McNulty (Dominic West) instigates an investigation into the Barksdale crime organization, a development which has wide-ranging repercussions for the police, and sets up the many interlaced plot threads of successive seasons. The Barksdale investigation is headed by Lieutenant Cedric Daniels (Lance Reddick), an ambitious detective, who nonetheless jeopardizes his career by pushing forward with the probe when his superiors try to derail it. Also working Barksdale is Detective Shakima "Kima" Greggs (Sonja Sohn), a dedicated professional, who is shot and seriously wounded during an undercover buy gone wrong. Kima later accepts desk duty to appease her worried girlfriend, Cheryl (Melanie Nicholls-King), but hates being a "housecat." She returns to detective work with McNulty and Daniels, whose focus is now human-trafficking on the waterfront.

A large cast populates the broad canvas of the remaining seasons, where political deals and cover-ups are rampant, but some manage to keep their integrity, especially Kima Greggs. When she learns that McNulty has created a fake homicide and the illusion of a serial killer to elicit more funding, Kima reports him to Daniels, which leads to McNulty's retirement from the force. Still, McNulty shakes hands with her at his "wake" (retirement party), and life goes on as usual in crime-ridden Baltimore.

Wire in the Blood (2002–2008, 31 episodes, UK)
Based on: The novels of Val McDermid
Production Co.: Coastal Productions, Ingenious Broadcasting
Originally Aired: BBC America
Main Cast: Robson Green, Hermione Norris, Simone Lahbib, Mark Letheren, Emma Handy, Mark Penfold

Dr. Tony Hill (Robson Green) is a brilliant, if eccentric clinical psychologist who specializes in profiling serial killers. Hill's weird ability to empathize with murderers makes him a valuable asset to Detective Chief Inspector Carol Jordan (Hermione Norris), head of the Major Incident Team at the Bradfield police department in northern England. As the two work together to track down serial killers, feelings develop, as feelings are wont to do, but Tony won't allow his to blossom into romance. When Carol makes an abrupt exit, moving to South Africa, Tony begins working with Detective Inspector Alex Fielding (Simone Lahbib), a workaholic single mother. Others on the team include Detective Constable Paula McIntyre (Emma Handy), who is kidnapped during an operation to catch a serial killer, and is saved by Tony in "Torment" (2006). These folks stare darkness in the face for a living, a darkness which rises from a "wire in the blood."

Witchblade (2001–2002, 23 episodes, USA)
Based on: The comic book series by Marc Silvestri, David Wohl, Brian Haberlin, Christina Z, Michael Turner
Created by: Ralph Hemecker
Production Co.: Blade TV Productions, Halsted Pictures, Top Cow Productions
Originally Aired: TNT
Main Cast: Yancy Butler, David Chokachi, Anthony Cistaro, Will Yun Lee, John Hensley, Eric Etebari

Yancy Butler stars as Sara Pezzini, just another New York City detective on the job until she runs into an ancient, supernatural weapon called the Witchblade, a device which attaches to her hand like a gauntlet, but seems to have a will of its own. "Pez," as she is known, sets out to learn more about the blade, running into wealthy and mysterious Kenneth Irons (Anthony Cistaro), who seems to have a dark connection to the blade and Sara's past. In "Legion" (2001), the Witchblade allows Sara to speak with the dead, both the murder victim in her current case and her deceased partner Danny Woo (Will Yun Lee). She must prove she is worthy to wield the Witchblade in "Periculum" (2001), a test of her mettle, where she meets those who have worn the gauntlet before her, such as Joan of Arc. The Witchblade can manipulate time, and in "Emergence" (2002), Pez uses it to undo the circumstances which led to Danny's death.

Without a Trace (2002–2009, 160 episodes, USA)

Created by: Hank Steinberg
Production Co.: Jerry Bruckheimer Television, Grossman Productions, Jumbolaya Productions, Warner Bros. Television
Originally Aired: CBS
Main Cast: Anthony LaPaglia, Poppy Montgomery, Marianne Jean-Baptiste, Enrique Murciano, Eric Close, Roselyn Sanchez

Gritty procedural drama following the investigations of the FBI's Missing Persons Squad in New York City. Headed by Jack Malone (Anthony LaPaglia), the team follows leads in the field, on the computer, and by phone—whatever it takes to untangle the intricate case histories of the victims. Unit members **Samantha Spade** (Poppy Montgomery), **Vivian Johnson** (Marianne Jean-Baptiste), Danny Taylor (Enrique Murciano), Martin Fitzgerald (Eric Close), and later Elena Delgado (Roselyn Sanchez) interview witnesses and construct a timeline of the victim's 24 hours prior to disappearance, knowing that the next 48 hours will be crucial for a positive outcome. The agents' personal problems, such as serious illness, marital discord, and office romances, sometimes intrude, but this team is relentless in locating the runaways, the hoaxers, the kidnapped, and, yes, the murdered, because there's no such thing as "without a trace" for these professionals.

See also: **Johnson, Vivian** (*Without a Trace*); **Spade, Samantha** (*Without a Trace*)

Women's Murder Club (2007–2008, 13 episodes, USA)

Based on: The novels of James Patterson
Created by: Elizabeth Craft, Sarah Fain
Production Co.: 20th Century–Fox Television, Rat TV
Originally Aired: ABC
Main Cast: Angie Harmon, Laura Harris, Paula Newsome, Aubrey Dollar, Tyrees Allen, Linda Park, Rob Estes

Four professional women in San Francisco—a homicide detective, a deputy district attorney, a medical examiner, and a newspaper reporter—come together to solve murders, while dealing with juicy personal issues on the side. Angie Harmon takes the lead as Inspector Lindsay Boxer, a transplanted Texan who is obsessed with the unsolved "Kiss Me Not" killer case, an obsession which led to the breakup of her marriage. Joining Lindsay in the rarefied sleuthing club are Jill Bernhardt (Laura Harris), the D.D.A., Claire Washburn (Paula Newsome), the M.E., and Cindy Thomas (Aubrey Dollar), a crime reporter. The investigations of this formidable foursome take them from a nursing home, where a drug ring is flourishing, to the drag queen community, where a murderer may lurk. Concerns about babies (accidental/intended) and lovers (past/present/future) are distractions, but everyone is focused, especially Lindsay, when the "Kiss Me Not" killer resurfaces.

Wonder Woman (1975–1979, 59 episodes, USA)

Based on: The comic book series by William Moulton Marston
Created by: Douglas S. Cramer, Stanley Ralph Ross
Production Co.: Warner Bros. Television, Bruce Lansbury Productions, Douglas S. Cramer Company
Originally Aired: ABC (1975–1977), CBS (1977–1979)
Main Cast: Lynda Carter, Lyle Waggoner, Norman Burton

The adventures of the classic superhero move from comic books to the small screen in this campy series, starring Lynda Carter as Wonder Woman and her alter ego, Diana Prince. The action begins in World War II, as Wonder Woman battles the Nazis and defends America with the help of Major Steve Trevor (Lyle Waggoner) and her magic bracelets, tiara, and lasso. The scene shifts to the 70s in season two, where the ageless Amazon princess leaves her island sanctuary again to help Steve Trevor, Jr., the Major's son (Waggoner again), and the U.S., this time in the form of the Inter-Agency Defense Command. The IADC fights contemporary blights such as crime and terrorism, and in "Mind Stealers from Outer Space" (parts one and two, 1977), deals with the ultimate threat, planetary invasion! Ghosts of the Third Reich surface in "Anschluss '77" (1977), when Diana/Wonder Woman must thwart an attempt to clone Hitler! Whatever the threat, diabolical rock star, demented toymaker, or roller coaster phantom, Wonder Woman is forever "putting all her might on the side of right!"

Woo, Shelby (*The Mystery Files of Shelby Woo*)

High school student who solves crimes with her friends in Cocoa Beach, and later Boston.

See: *The Mystery Files of Shelby Woo* (1996–1998, 41 episodes, Canada/USA)

The X-Files (1993–2002, 202 episodes, USA)

Created by: Chris Carter
Production Co.: Ten Thirteen Productions, 20th Century–Fox Television, X-F Productions
Originally Aired: Fox
Main Cast: David Duchovny, Gillian Anderson, Robert Patrick, Annabeth Gish, Mitch Pileggi

"THE TRUTH IS OUT THERE"
Iconic SF/horror/mystery series about a pair of FBI agents who are assigned weird cases with paranormal overtones. Special Agent Fox "Spooky" Mulder (David Duchovny) is the true believer, expecting extraterrestrials around every corner, and suspecting conspiracies and cover-ups at each turn. **Dana Scully** (Gillian Anderson) is the skeptic, a medical doctor who applies scientific analyses to the evidence and whose initial assignment is to debunk Mulder's outlandish theories. As evidence mounts, however, of UFOs, alien abductions, and a global conspiracy, Scully is forced to re-examine her views, and the partners come to trust only each other. In the meantime, they confront all manner of strangeness, including golems, shape-shifters, time travelers, demonic babies, brain-eating mutants, and even genies. In later years, when Agent Mulder goes missing, John Doggett (Robert Patrick) becomes Scully's new partner, and after Scully is assigned to the FBI Academy, Monica Reyes (Annabeth Gish) replaces her on the X-Files project. A resolution of sorts for Mulder and Scully occurs in the series finale, "The Truth" (parts one and two, 2002), including a reunion with series villain "Cigarette Smoking Man" (William B. Davis), but the search for the truth goes on....
See also: **Scully, Dana** (*The X-Files*)

Young, Roberta (*Snoops*)

One of several young, sexy operatives in a Los Angeles detective agency.
See: *Snoops* (1999, 13 episodes, USA)

The Zoo Gang (1974, 6 episodes, UK)

Based on: The novel by Paul Gallico
Production Co.: Incorporated Television Company
Originally Aired: NBC
Main Cast: Brian Keith, John Mills, Lilli Palmer, Barry Morse

The Zoo Gang comes by its moniker via the group's members, all former World War II resistance fighters given the code names of wild animals. Brian

Keith stars as Stephen Halliday a.k.a. "The Fox"; John Mills is Thomas Devon, "The Elephant"; Lilli Palmer portrays Manouche Roget, called "The Leopard"; and Barry Morse is Alec Marlowe, "The Tiger." The gang re-bands 30 years after the war, when The Elephant (who never forgets) spots a former war criminal in his jewelry shop on the French Riviera. The old pros rally to find the man, who had betrayed them to the Nazis, and bring him to justice. Upon completion of the mission, the four decide to stay together, fighting crime, while fleecing the criminals of their ill-gotten gains. They use the money obtained from their exploits to establish a hospital in the name of one of their fallen comrades, Claude Roget, Manouche's husband, killed in front of her by the Gestapo. In later cases, the gang investigates art thieves, thwarts gold smugglers, searches for sunken treasure, and in general comports itself like a band of ex-freedom fighters with cool code names should.

Appendix: The Most Rewatchable Television Shows on DVD (Female Spies and Crimefighters Edition)

The best DVDs in a personal video collection are the ones you watch again and again, rewarding your financial investment. The TV shows listed below, featuring female spies and sleuths, are the author's recommendations for outstandingly "rewatchable" television series. The list is biased in favor of British mysteries and American detective series with a healthy dose of humor, so viewers with a preference for grit and gore probably won't find their favorites selected. In keeping with the focus of this book, the list also tends toward shows with female leads and co-leads, so series like *Monk* and *Psych*, although eminently rewatchable, are excluded because women are not the main crime-solvers there. Other first-rate series, such as *Cold Case*, do not appear because they have not been released on DVD.

DVD availability can change, but all titles on the list were offered for sale by Amazon.com when this appendix was compiled. Titles are listed alphabetically.

Adventures of Superman. Season One. Perf. George Reeves, Phyllis Coates, Jack Larson, and John Hamilton. Warner Home Video, 2006. DVD.

The first season of this 50s adventure, rightly known as the "dark series" because of its noir look and feel, focused on strange mysteries rather than the cartoon criminals of later years. Two *Daily Planet* reporters (George Reeves and Phyllis Coates) vie for scoops while investigating the weird happenings, and Coates is marvelous as the competitive, inquisitive, and feisty newshound, who gets in trouble often, but isn't afraid to take a swing at a bad guy, never content simply to await rescue by Superman. And let's not forget the man of steel himself, different from the comic book vision, but unforgettable due to the winning performance by Reeves. A classic of early television.

Agatha Christie's Marple: Series Four. Perf. Julia McKenzie. Acorn Media, 2009. DVD.

Not the most faithful of the TV Marple adaptations, but certainly the most lavish. All six seasons are good, but this show hits its stride when the wonderful Julia McKenzie comes on board as the famed amateur sleuth in season four, replacing Geraldine McEwan's less traditional Miss Marple. Time and again murderers underestimate the keen intelligence of this unassuming old lady, with delicious results.

The Bletchley Circle: Cracking a Killer's Code. Perf. Anna Maxwell Martin, Rachael Stirling, Sophie Rundle, and Julie Graham. PBS, 2013. DVD.

Four brilliant women who worked as codebreakers at Bletchley Park during World War II (Anna Maxwell Martin, Rachael Stirling, Sophie Rundle, and Julie Graham) become amateur sleuths in this dark, riveting series, which combines history and mystery. When not taken seriously by the police, the friends set off on their own to stop a serial killer, placing their lives in jeopardy. With its intricate plotting and fine performances, *The Bletchley Circle* is a treasure. Too bad the series was so short-lived, but its early demise should not be taken as a comment on its quality. (The title listed above is also known as "Season One.")

Cagney & Lacey: Season One. Created by Barbara Avedon and Barbara Corday. Perf. Tyne Daly, Sharon Gless, Al Waxman, and John Karlen. MGM, 2007. DVD.

It's hard to overestimate the influence of this series about two female detectives (Tyne Daly and Sharon Gless) who work in a man's world, also known as the NYPD of the 1980s, while trying to maintain happy and stable personal lives. The actresses locked up Emmy Awards for six years (four awards for Daly and two for Gless) with their gritty and moving portrayals of women who had no mentors or examples to follow, so had to become their own role models. A true television gem. (The title above is technically season two, but is the first season with Gless, who replaced Meg Foster after a series reboot.)

Honey West: The Complete Series. Created by Gwen Bagni and Paul Dubov. Perf. Anne Francis, John Ericson, and Irene Hervey. VCI Entertainment, 2008. DVD.

Anne Francis received a Golden Globe Award for her spirited portrayal of Honey West, a woman who would rather wrestle crooks in an alley than join June Cleaver in the kitchen during the 60s. Honey heads her own detective agency, working with a hotheaded, but loyal partner (John Ericson), some nifty gadgets, a phenomenal wardrobe budget, and a whole lot of attitude. Ahead of its time, *Honey West* lasted just one season, but its half-hour episodes, with their jazzy scores and Honey's quintessential noir cool, live again on DVD.

McMillan and Wife: Season One. Created by Leonard Stern. Perf. Rock Hudson, Susan Saint James, John Schuck, and Nancy Walker. Universal Studios, 2005. DVD.

If you like your mysteries with a generous helping of wit and charm, you'll love this classic series about a police commissioner (Rock Hudson) and his kooky, but perceptive wife (Susan Saint James) who solve crimes together, while engaging in various 70s fashion excesses. Always snappy dialogue here, and a great supporting performance from Nancy Walker as the couple's faithful housekeeper, who has a love/hate relationship with "the commish." Don't miss it.

The Mentalist: Season One. Created by Bruno Heller. Perf. Simon Baker, Robin Tunney, Tim Kang, Owain Yeoman, and Amanda Righetti. Warner Home Video, 2009. DVD.

Engaging, but occasionally dark series about a former "psychic" (Simon Baker), who uses his keen skills of observation to help the police. Keeping this con man in line is a petite, but formidable California Bureau of Investigation agent (Robin Tunney), and the interplay between the blond bad boy and the brunette spitfire keeps this series fresh year after year, even when the Red John (serial killer) arc grows a bit stale.

Miss Fisher's Murder Mysteries 1. Created by Deb Cox and Fiona Eagger. Perf. Essie Davis, Nathan Page, Ashleigh Cummings, and Hugo Johnstone-Burt. Acorn Media, 2013. DVD.

A free-spirited, beautiful detective (Essie Davis) sashays her way through 20s Melbourne in this intelligent and lavish Australian production. There's a bit of everything here: mystery, history, social commentary (with a left-leaning slant), romance, humor, and plenty of good-looking people, including a handsome police inspector (Nathan Page) and an adorable maid/companion (Ashleigh Cummings). A sumptuous treat.

New Tricks: Season One. Created by Nigel McCrery and Roy Mitchell. Perf. Amanda Redman, Alun Armstrong, James Bolam, and Dennis Waterman. BBC Home Entertainment, 2009. DVD.

Long-running British police procedural, starring Amanda Redman as a Detective Superintendent who must assemble a squad from amongst retired detectives to solve open cases. The retirees, as portrayed by Alun Armstrong, James Bolam, and Dennis Waterman, are a complete handful, but they get the job done, as they learn about technological innovations and complain a lot. Laugh-out-loud-funny at times, even while presenting taut, believable mysteries.

Remington Steele: Season Two. Created by Robert Butler and Michael Gleason. Perf. Stephanie Zimbalist, Pierce Brosnan, and Doris Roberts. 20th Century Fox, 2005. DVD.

A private detective (Stephanie Zimbalist) invents a male superior to conform to clients' expectations, but things get deliciously complicated when a charming con man (Pierce Brosnan) stands in for the imaginary boss. The two strangers form a partnership that leads to mystery, adventure, and romance in this wise and well-written series, that benefits from the addition of Doris Roberts as a mature gal Friday in season two. Still fresh 30 years later.

Rizzoli & Isles: Season One. **Perf. Angie Harmon, Sasha Alexander, Lorraine Bracco, Jordan Bridges, Bruce McGill, and Lee Thompson Young. Warner Home Video, 2011. DVD.**

A *Cagney & Lacey* for the new century, but with the twist that one-half of the female crime-fighting duo is a coroner, the procedural flavor of the month (or decade). Angie Harmon is outstanding as the beautiful working-class cop and Sasha Alexander ably assists as the brainy, but glamorous medical examiner. Colleagues and best friends, these two constantly deal with death, but find humor in their conflicting styles, intuitive vs. scientific, impatient vs. plodding. With Lorraine Bracco and the city of Boston in supporting roles, this one's a winner.

Rosemary & Thyme: The Complete Collection. **Created by Brian Eastman and Clive Exton. Perf. Felicity Kendal and Pam Ferris. Acorn Media, 2011. DVD.**

Two women (Felicity Kendal and Pam Ferris) join forces in a professional gardening business, but stumble upon murder wherever they go. Not the most believable premise, but it works with these two fine actresses, crisp writing, and stunning gardens across both England and Europe. A modern spin on the British cozy mystery.

Scarecrow and Mrs. King: Season One. **Created by Brad Buckner and Eugenie Ross-Leming. Perf. Kate Jackson, Bruce Boxleitner, Beverly Garland, Mel Stewart, and Martha Smith. Warner Home Video, 2010. DVD.**

A divorced housewife (Kate Jackson) is handed a mysterious package by a handsome spy (Bruce Boxleitner) and begins a wild ride of adventure, intrigue, and romance in this classic 80s series. Placing a homespun newcomer among the worldly spies was a comic masterstroke, and the crackling chemistry between the leads transitions beautifully from humorous exasperation to something deeper. With a stellar supporting cast, including Beverly Garland, who sparkles in the domestic scenes, this one never grows old.

Vera. **Perf. Brenda Blethyn, David Leon, Wunmi Mosaku, and Paul Ritter. Acorn Media, 2011. DVD.**

British police procedural about a middle-aged Detective Chief Inspector (Brenda Blethyn) who solves dark, tangled crimes with her handsome young associate and long-suffering staff. Blethyn thoroughly inhabits the role of the solitary, caustic, but caring, and shabbily dressed DCI, making the title character one of the most memorable TV detectives in many a year. The beautiful Northumberland settings are icing on the multi-layered cake. (The title listed above is the first set in the series.)

A Note on Sources

Information contained in the work comes from a variety of sources, an individual listing of which might comprise a book on its own.

The most important sources, of course, were the TV shows themselves, viewed over the decades via broadcast TV, cable, VHS tapes, satellite and DVR. DVDs were pivotal to the research for this book, providing the opportunity both to revisit old programs and to discover new shows that can be easily missed in an increasingly crowded TV environment. Series descriptions and episode blurbs included on DVD menus and packaging provided additional information.

Two comprehensive guides to TV programming were invaluable in compiling the list of series to be included in this book: *The Complete Directory to Prime Time Network and Cable TV Shows: 1946–Present* by Tim Brooks and Earle Marsh (Ballantine Books, 2007) and *The Complete Encyclopedia of Television Programs: 1947–1979* by Vincent Terrace (A.S. Barnes, 1979). *The Encyclopedia of TV Spies* by Wesley Britton (BearManor Media, 2009) helped to solidify the list of spy shows to be covered.

Two scholarly books provided feminist perspective with chapters on TV's female detectives, *The Female Investigator in Literature, Film, and Popular Culture* by Lisa M. Dresner (McFarland, 2006) and *Hardboiled and High Heeled: The Woman Detective in Popular Culture* by Linda Mizejewski (Routledge, 2004).

It's the information age and this book would not have been completed without the extensive reach of the Internet. Valuable Internet resources, particularly for more recent series, include *Wikipedia* (en.wikipedia.org), *IMDb* (imdb.com), and TV.com, all of which contain articles on individual series, including cast lists, production credits and episode summaries. Also helpful were product descriptions and professional reviews for DVDs at Amazon.com, wikis for individual TV shows at Wikia.com, and official websites for the series, where available.

Specialized sites, such as *The Thrilling Detective Web Site* (www.thrillingdetective.com), *Mystery*File* (mysteryfile.com/blog), *For Your Eyes Only* (www.

for-your-eyes-only.com), *The Classic TV Archive* (ctva.biz) and *TV Acres* (www.tvacres.com) were useful in tracking down information about older series. The *BFI/British Film Institute* website (bfi.org.uk) was a good source for esoteric production credits.

At least three sources were consulted for each entry, and inconsistencies between sources were resolved wherever possible.

Index

Abercrombie, Ian 36
Acevedo, Kirk 88, 167
Acker, Amy 164–165
Adams, Don 5, 21, 90–91
Adams, Jonathan 40
Adams, Julie 149
Aiello, Danny 115
Akinnuoye-Agbaje, Adewale 102
Alden, Norman 77
Alejandro, Kevin 195
Alessi, Raquel 198
Alexander, Khandi 62
Alexander, Sarah 110
Alexander, Sasha 14, 107, 151, 176–178, 232
Ali, Mahershalalhashbaz 87
Allen, Laura 87
Allen, Tyrees 225
Allman, Jamie Anne 112
Alonso, Laz 66
Amos, John 103
Anderson, Barbara 106
Anderson, Gillian 10, 184, 227
Anderson, Loni 162
Anderson, Melody 127
Anderson, Nicole Gale 32
Anderson, Pamela 10, 216–217
Anderson, Richard 35, 58–59, 194
Andes, Keith 92
Andrews, David 127–128
Andrews, Tige 142
Angarano, Michael 58
Anholt, Tony 169
Annis, Francesca 19–20
Anton, William 189
Antonio, Lou 73, 192
Anwar, Gabrielle 43–44, 91
Arison, Amir 37
Arkin, Adam 120

Armitage, Alison 15
Armstrong, Alun 153–155, 231
Armstrong, Curtis 144
Arquette, Patricia 75, 135
Ashby, Linden 197
Ashley, Elizabeth 149
Ashmore, Aaron 74, 218
Asner, Ed 67
Atherton, Ted 200
Atkins, Sharif 221
Aycox, Nicki 65
Aykroyd, Dan 170
Aylesworth, Reiko 208

Baccarin, Morena 79, 101, 213
Badler, Jane 140
Bailey, G.W. 54, 126
Bain, Barbara 4–5, 46, 140, 176
Baird, Jenni 87
Baker, Kathy 17
Baker, Shaun 216–217
Baker, Simon 121, 136, 231
Bakula, Scott 141
Baldwin, Adam 53, 105
Balfour, Eric 95–96
Ballard, Alimi 157–158
Barber, Glynis 68
Bareikis, Arija 195
Bari, Lynn 3, 70
Barrie, Barbara 207
Barry, Thom 55
Bartley, Adam 122
Basinger, Kim 73
Basis, Austin 32
Bass, Ben 86, 134, 179, 216
Bastedo, Alexandra 49–50
Baur, Elizabeth 106
Baxendale, Helen 212
Baxter, Meredith 180
Beach, Michael 211

Bean, Noah 156
Bean, Sean 139
Beasley, Allyce 98, 144
Bedelia, Bonnie 12, 72
Beharie, Nicole 13, 137, 191
Belfi, Jordan 208
Belknap, Anna 63
Bell, Coby 43
Bell, Kristen 215
Bell, Michael 75
Bell, Tom 167
Bellamy, Bill 81
Bellamy, Ralph 103, 145
Bello, Maria 141, 167
Bellows, Gil 20
Beltran, Robert 215
Belzer, Richard 118–119
Ben-Victor, Paul 105
Bendix, Simone 196
Benfield, Derek 98
Bennet, Chloe 21–22
Bennett, Cle 123
Bennett, Nigel 86–87, 170
Bent, Lyriq 27
Benz, Julie 70
Benzali, Daniel 20
Berenger, Tom 127
Bergl, Emily 196
Berkeley, Xander 156
Berman, David 61
Bernard, Carlos 208
Bernard, Ed 166
Bernsen, Corbin 171
Beutner, Andrea 202–203
Bhaneja, Raoul 74
Bibb, Leslie 121
Bishop, Nic 59
Bisson, Yannick 200, 204
Blackman, Honor 4, 28, 88
Blackthorne, Paul 74
Blacque, Taurean 99
Blake, Kayla 159

Blake, Madge 30
Blethyn, Brenda 13, 214, 232–233
Bligh, Richard 138
Blucas, Marc 112
Bogosian, Eric 118
Bolam, James 153–155, 231
Bomer, Matt 221
Boone, Megan 37–38
Boreanaz, David 40, 42
Bosley, Tom 8, 81, 149, 159
Bosson, Barbara 99
Bowers, Chris 36
Boxleitner, Bruce 8, 42–43, 69, 113, 182–183, 232
Boyd, Guy 37
Boyer, Lombardo 148
Bracco, Lorraine 176, 178, 232
Brandon, Michael 68
Bratt, Benjamin 117
Bray, Deanne 12, 200, 204
Brenner, Dori 48
Brewster, Paget 60
Bridges, Beau 20
Bridges, Jordan 176, 178, 232
Bright, Cameron 146
Brill, Charlie 189
Brimble, Ian 19
Britton, Barbara 3, 141
Brolin, James 49
Brook, Jayne 72, 189–190
Brooks, Angelle 216
Brooks, Martin E. 35
Brooks, Roxane 4, 176
Brosnan, Pierce 7, 101, 114, 174–175, 231–232
Brown, Blair 88
Brown, Clancy 191
Brown, Delroy 184
Brown, Max 32
Brown, Olivia 9, 137
Brown, Roger Aaron 72
Brown, Sophina 157
Brown, Wes 66
Bruno, Dylan 157
Bryant, Lucas 95–96
Buckley, A.J. 63
Bullmore, Amelia 184
Burgi, Richard 159
Burr, Raymond 106
Burrows, Saffron 118
Burton, Hilarie 221
Burton, LeVar 164
Burton, Norman 226
Busch, Adam 150
Butler, Chris 113

Butler, Yancy 127–128, 195, 224
Byrnes, Edd 97

Caan, Scott 96
Cahill, Eddie 63
Calbraith, Clare 214
Calf, Anthony 153
Calpakis, Gregory 56
Camargo, Christian 70
Cameron, JoAnna 107
Campbell, Billy 87, 112
Campbell, Bruce 43–44, 108
Campbell, Conchita 87, 190
Campbell, Nicholas 71
Campbell-Martin, Tisha 169
Cantillo, José Pablo 198
Capra, Francis 215
Caroll, Diahann 221
Carpani, Rachael 17–18
Carpenter, Jennifer 70
Carroll, Leo G. 91
Carroll, Pat 188
Carroll, Rocky 20, 151
Carter, John 29
Carter, Lynda 6, 162, 226
Cartwright, Ryan 23–24
Caruso, David 11, 62–63
Casey, Dillon 156
Casnoff, Philip 211
Cassell, Seymour 211
Cassidy, Joanna 55
Cassidy, Shaun 94
Cassidy, Sonya 214
Casso, Raul 202
Cate, Field 172
Caviezel, Jim 47, 164–165
Cayne, Candis 78
Cerra, Erica 79, 125
Chalk, Garry 56
Chan, Michael Paul 54, 126
Chapman, Kevin 164–165
Charles, Lewis 82
Chase, Bailey 122, 182
Chenoweth, Kristin 172
Cherry, Eagle Eye 195
Chestnut, Morris 213
Cho, John 84
Chokachi, David 224
Christie, Morven 102
Christie, Warren 23, 146
Christopher, Dennis 11, 168
Cibrian, Eddie 31
Ciccolella, Jude 208
Cioffi, Charles 90
Cistaro, Anthony 224–225

Clair, Cyrielle 57
Clark, Matt 73
Clarke, Emmy 203
Clarke, Melinda 156
Clarke, Patrick James 119
Clarke, Sarah 208
Clennon, David 20
Close, Eric 50, 225
Clough, April 205
Coates, Conrad 74
Coates, Phyllis 17, 116–117, 229
Cobden, Joe 27
Cochrane, Rory 62–63
Colantoni, Enrico 215
Colby, James 202
Cole, Christina 50
Cole, Michael 5, 30, 142
Cole, Taylor 80
Colin, Margaret 119
Collier, Lois 41
Collins, Clifton, Jr. 80
Collins, K.C. 123
Collins, Joely 56
Collins, Stephen 201
Conlin, Michaela 40
Connors, Mike 128
Conrad, Michael 99
Conrad, Robert 97
Conrad, William 29
Consuelos, Mark 139
Convy, Bert 192
Conway, Russ 176
Cook, A.J. 60
Cook, Perry 103
Cook, Rachael Leigh 164
Cooper, Alice 192–193
Cooper, Bradley 23
Cord, Alex 48
Court, Hazel 71
Courtemanche, Michel 185
Cox, Christina 12, 39
Cox, Mekia 211
Cox, Ronny 20
Coyne, Jonny 22
Coyote, Peter 87, 105
Craig, Yvonne 30–31
Cromwell, James 148
Crosbie, Annette 212
Cross, Roger 57, 146
Cruz, Gregory Norman 182
Cruz, Raymond 54, 126
Cruz, Valerie 74
Cubitt, David 135
Cudlitz, Michael 195, 198
Culver, Molly 216–217
Cummings, Ashleigh 83, 138, 231

Curtin, Jane 212
Curtis, Cliff 139
Curtis, Donald 70
Curvey, Troy, Jr. 193
Cuthbert, Elisha 208
Cutler, Brian 107
Cutter, Lise 64
Cypress, Tawny 212

Dacascos, Mark 96
Daddo, Cameron 187
Daggs, Percy, III 215
Dale, Ian Anthony 80, 148
Daley, John Francis 40
Dalton, Brett 21–22
Daly, James 86
Daly, Tyne 7, 44–45, 115, 230
Damon, Stuart 49–50
Damone, Vic 203
Danby, Noah 161
Danes, Claire 13, 101–102
Danson, Ted 61
D'Arbanville, Patti 155, 195
Darren, James 205
Darrow, Henry 134
Davenport, Jack 84
Davi, Robert 168
David, Ellen 150, 189
Davidson, Jim 160
Davies, Alan 110, 126
Davies, Geraint Wyn 86, 216
Davies, John Graham 98
Davis, Duane 202
Davis, Essie 83, 138, 231
Davis, William B. 227
Davison, Bruce 103
Dean, Ron 26
De Caestecker, Iain 21–22
DeKay, Tim 221
Delaney, Kim 62
Delfino, Frank 82
DeLorenzo, Michael 155
DeLuise, Peter 100, 209
DeMay, Janet 174–175
Demetral, Chris 185
Denier, Lydie 15
Denison, Anthony John 210
Denison, Tony 54, 126
Denning, Richard 141
de Pablo, Cote 151–152
Depp, Johnny 9, 100, 209
D'Errico, Donna 31
Deschanel, Emily 40, 41
Devenie, Stuart 108
Dever, Seamus 48–49
DeWitt, Rosemarie 198

Dickinson, Angie 5, 25–26, 48, 166
Diehl, John 137
Dierkop, Charles 166
Dietzen, Brian 151
Diggs, Taye 148
Dillane, Stephen 102
Dingwall, Shaun 206
Dinsdale, Reece 19
Disher, Catherine 86–87
Dobson, Peter 58
Dohring, Jason 143, 215
Doig, Lexa 57
Dollar, Aubrey 225–226
Doman, John 107, 223
Donahue, Troy 97
Donat, Richard 95
D'Onofrio, Vincent 11, 76, 118
Donovan, Jeffrey 43, 91, 206
Donovan, Tate 66
Dorff, Stephen 159
Dormer, Natalie 78
Dotchin, Angela 108
Dotrice, Roy 141
Dourdan, Gary 61
Doyle, David 51–52
Dryer, Fred 103–104, 130
Dube, Desmond 157
DuBois, Marta 201
Duchene, Deborah 86
Duchovny, David 10, 184, 227
Dudek, Anne 59
Dudgeon, Neil 146–147
Duke, Bill 111
Dunbar, Rockmond 136
Dungey, Merrin 23, 43
Dunn, Carolyn 201
Dunsworth, John 95
Dupuis, Roy 10, 83
Durand, Kevin 206
Dzundza, George 117

Eads, George 61
Easton, Michael 209–210
Ebsen, Buddy 29, 129
Echikunwoke, Megalyn 62–63, 87
Edelman, Herb 200
Edwards, Preslaysa 150
Eggold, Ryan 37–38
Eilbacher, Lisa 134
Eisley, Anthony 97
Ejogo, Carmen 50
Ellis, Nelsan 105
Elson, Andrea 222
Emerson, Michael 47, 164

Emery, Julie Ann 121
Emmerich, Noah 24
Enos, Mireille 112
Enriquez, Rene 99
Erbe, Kathryn 11, 76, 118
Ericson, John 102, 220, 230
Eriksen, Kaj-Erik 87
Erwin, Jhene 152
Esposito, Jennifer 202
Estes, Rob 189, 225
Etebari, Eric 224
Evans, Linda 103
Eversman, Nick 139
Evigan, Greg 170
Ezer, Sarah 16–17

Fabiani, Joel 68
Facinelli, Peter 81
Falk, Peter 67
Farmer, Gary 86
Farmiga, Vera 206–207
Farr, Diane 157–158
Faust, Chad 87
Fawcett, Farrah 6, 51–52, 75, 89, 147
Feast, Michael 206
Feldon, Barbara 5, 21, 90–91
Felton, Tom 148
Ferguson, Colin 79, 125
Ferguson, Matthew 83
Ferlito, Vanessa 63, 92–93
Fernandez, Alex 112
Ferraez, Marcos 160
Ferreira, Louis 146
Ferrer, Miguel 36, 61, 169
Ferris, Pam 12, 180, 232
Ferris, Paul 30
Ferris, Samantha 87
Fiennes, Joseph 84
Filippo, Fab 120
Fillion, Nathan 32, 48
Findlay, Katie 112
Finn, John 55
Finneran, Katie 105
Fisher, Gail 128
Fisher, Joely 222
Fitts, Rick 160
Flack, Enya 37
Fletcher, Brendan 16
Florek, Dann 117–119
Flueger, Patrick 87
Fonseca, Lyndsy 156
Forbes, Michelle 112
Foronjy, Richard 211
Forrest, Frederic 209
Forrest, Steve 30
Forster, Robert 22, 111

Forsythe, John 51–52, 75, 89
Foster, Meg 44, 46, 230
Fowley, Douglas 69
Fox, Colin 170
Fox, Jorja 61–62
Fox, Vivica A. 13, 139
Francis, Anne 3, 102, 220, 230
Franciscus, James 103
Francks, Don 83
Frechette, Peter 168
Freeman, Cassidy 122
Frewer, Matt 170
Friederlcy, Bonita 53
Friel, Anna 172
Friend, Rupert 101

Gabel, Seth 88
Gaffin, Melanie 222
Gail, Max 222
Gaines, Boyd 27
Gallagher, Peter 59
Galloway, Don 106
Gant, Richard 197
Garas, Kaz 199
Garber, Victor 12, 23, 52, 66
Garcia, Aimee 70
Garcia, Jorge 22–23
Garland, Beverly 3, 8, 67, 182, 232
Garner, Jennifer 12, 23, 43
Garson, Willie 221
Garth, Jennie 150
Gaunt, William 49–50
Gautier, Richard 90
George, Lynda Day 140, 146, 188
George, Melissa 102–103
Gerety, Peter 167–168
German, Lauren 96
Gershon, Gina 194
Getz, John 125
Ghanizada, Azita 23–24
Giacomo, Laura San 182
Giannini, Adriano 139
Gianopoulos, David 72
Gibson, Thomas 60
Giddish, Kelli 53
Gidley, Pamela 26–27
Gilbert, Chris Payne 169
Gilliam, Seth 223
Gimpel, Erica 168
Giovanni, Kearran 126
Giovinazzo, Carmine 63
Girgis, Natascha 199
Gish, Annabeth 227

Givens, Robin 26–27
Glaudini, Lola 60
Glazer, Eugene Robert 83
Gleason, Paul 159
Gleaves, Nicholas 184
Gless, Sharon 7, 43–46, 115, 230
Glover, Brian 27–28
Glover, John 195
Goldblum, Jeff 118
Gomes, Marc 200
Gomez, Joshua 53
Good, Meagan 66
Goodman, Brian 121
Goodwin, Michael 200
Gordon, Colin 30
Gordon, Matt 179
Gorham, Christopher 59
Gorn, Lev 24
Gorshin, Frank 31
Gossett, Robert 54
Gould, Harold 82
Govich, Milena 117
Gracen, Elizabeth 98
Graham, Julie 38–39, 230
Graves, Peter 46, 140
Graves, Rupert 184
Graves, Teresa 90
Gray-Stanford, Jason 85, 143
Grayston, Neil 79
Green, Robson 206, 224
Greene, Ellen 172
Greenwood, Joan 64
Greenwood, Lyndie 138, 156, 191
Gregg, Clark 21–22
Gregory, Dorian 31
Gregory, James 69
Grenier, Zack 206
Gretsch, Joel 87, 190, 213
Grieco, Richard 209
Griffin, Tim 167
Griffith, Melanie 137
Gubler, Matthew Gray 60
Gugino, Carla 111
Guilfoyle, Paul 61, 186
Gunn, Janet 189
Gupton, Damon 167

Hack, Shelley 51–52, 76
Hadyn, Lili 147
Hagman, Larry 67
Hahn, Kathryn 61
Haid, Charles 99
Hale, Alan, Jr. 34
Hale, Lucy 36
Hall, Diedre 77

Hall, Michael C. 70
Hall, Robert David 61
Hallahan, Charles 103–104
Hamel, Veronica 99
Hamilton, Antony 58–59
Hamilton, John 17, 229
Hamilton, Neil 30–31
Hamilton, Tony 140
Hamm, Jon 72
Hampshire, Susan 64
Handy, Emma 224
Hansen, Ryan 215
Hardin, Melora 58
Hardwick, Omari 65
Harewood, David 101
Harewood, Dorian 200
Hargitay, Mariska 33, 118–119
Harmon, Angie 14, 31, 107, 117–118, 176–178, 225–226, 232
Harmon, Mark 11, 151–152
Harner, Jason Butler 22
Harper, Hill 59, 63
Harrington, Desmond 70
Harrington, Jay 105
Harris, Jo Ann 145–146
Harris, Laura 225–226
Harrison, Noel 4, 91
Harrold, Kathryn 125
Hartley, Mariette 146
Hasselhoff, David 31, 203
Hatosy, Shawn 195
Hauser, Cole 53
Hayes, Helen 192–193
Haysbert, Dennis 208
Heck, Bill 202
Heckart, Eileen 162
Heitmeyer, Jayne 189–190
Helfer, Tricia 112
Helgenberger, Marg 61–62
Henderson, Meredith 16
Hendrix, Leslie 117–118
Hendry, Ian 28
Hennessy, Jill 61, 117–118
Hennings, Sam 135
Hensley, John 224
Hensley, Pamela 129–130
Henson, Taraji P. 13, 47, 72, 164–165
Henstridge, Elizabeth 21–22
Henstridge, Natasha 187
Herd, Richard 205
Hernández, Maximiliano 24
Hervey, Irene 102, 230
Hewitt, Jennifer Love 60
Hexum, Jon-Erik 58–59

Hicks, Catherine 207
Hickson, Joan 8, 19
Hill, Dulé 171
Hill, Jon Michael 77
Hill, Steven 117, 140
Hiltz, Nichole 105, 186
Hinkle, Marin 66
Hinson, Jordan 79
Hinton, J.D. 109
Hirsch, Judd 157
Hodge, Kate 120
Hogan, Michael 56
Holden, Gina 39
Holden-Ried, Kris 123
Holliman, Earl 25, 166, 170
Holly, Lauren 146, 151
Holm, Celeste 109
Hope, Barclay 170
Hope, Leslie 121, 208
Horovitch, David 8, 19
Horsley, Lee 129
Hossack, Allison 210
Howard, Ken 61
Howard, Traylor 143, 203
Howell, C. Thomas 195
Howland, Rick 123
Howze, Leonard Earl 135
Hudson, Ernie 214
Hudson, Rock 6, 132–133, 231
Huertas, Jon 48–49
Huffman, Alaina 161
Huffman, Logan 79, 213
Humphreys, Chris 16
Hunt, Francesca 185
Hunt, Gareth 153
Hunt, Helen 25
Hunter, Amy 160
Hunter, Holly 182
Hurd, Michelle 118
Hurst, Ryan 113–114
Hutch, Tom 214

Ice-T 118–119
Ido, Jacky 202
Ifans, Rhys 219
Iglehart, Jamie 187
Ilonzeh, Annie 52
Innes, Laura 80
Irby, Michael 121
Ireland, John 48
Ivanek, Željko 80

Jackson, Joshua 88
Jackson, Kate 6, 8, 51–52, 69, 75, 89, 113, 182–183, 232
Jacott, Carlos 187

Jacquet, Jeffrey 222
Jagger, Bianca 137
James, Liam 112
Jameson, Susan 153
Janssen, David 4, 67, 176
Jean-Baptiste, Marianne 109, 196, 225
Jeffreys, Anne 67
Jenkins, Noam 179
Jerald, Penny Johnson 48–49
Johansson, Paul 98
Johns, Glynis 92
Johnson, Adrienne-Joi 189–190
Johnson, Amy Jo 72
Johnson, Bob 140
Johnson, Chris 17
Johnson, Don 9, 137
Johnson, Eric 134, 179
Johnson, Janet Louise 94
Johnson, Kenny 167, 182
Johnson, Robin 55
Johnston, Jamie 222
Johnstone-Burt, Hugo 138, 231
Jones, Henry 55, 147
Jones, James Earl 134
Jones, Orlando 191
Jones, Renée 109
Jones, Sarah 22
Jones, Suranne 184
Jones, Tamala 48
Joy, Robert 63
Judd, Ashley 139
Jury, Chris 124

Kanakaredes, Melina 63
Kane, Tom 202
Kang, Tim 136, 231
Kapelos, John 86–87
Kapoor, Ravi 61
Kapture, Mitzi 189
Karlen, John 44, 115, 193–194, 230
Karnes, Brixton 202
Karvelas, Robert 90
Kassir, John 202
Katic, Stana 32, 48–49
Keene, Phillip P. 54, 126
Keith, Brian 227–228
Kelly, Brendan 15
Kelly, Jack 90
Kelly, Joanne 34, 218
Kelly, Michael 120
Kelly, Minka 52
Kendal, Felicity 12, 180, 232
Kennedy, Oscar 102

Kerr, Edward 194
Kidder, Janet 199
Kilpatrick, Lincoln 129
Kim, Daniel Dae 96
King, Regina 195
Kinnaman, Joel 112
Kirk, Phyllis 3, 203
Klar, Noah 150
Klattenhoff, Diego 37, 101
Kneebone, Tom 57
Knighton, Zachary 84
Knudsen, Erik 57
Kodjoe, Boris 211
Kokotakis, Nick 189
Koock, Guich 188
Kopell, Bernie 90
Kove, Martin 44
Kramer, Stepfanie 103–104, 130
Kravitz, Steven 37
Kreuk, Kristin 32
Krinsky, Scott 53
Krinsky, Vikki 222
Krumholtz, David 11, 157, 173
Kurtz, Swoosie 172
Kusatsu, Clyde 42–43

Laborteaux, Matthew 222
Ladd, Cheryl 51–52, 148, 159
Ladin, Eric 112
Lahbib, Simone 224
Lail, Leah 216–217
Lamb, Larry 153
LaNasa, Katherine 66
Lancaster, Sarah 53
Landau, Martin 46, 140
Lander, David 160
Landes, Michael 197
Landis, Monte 82
Lane, Lauren 103
Lane, Rusty 60
Langham, Wallace 61
Langrishe, Caroline 124
Langton, Brooke 120
Lansbury, Angela 9, 85, 149
Lanzoni, Fabio 15
LaPaglia, Anthony 109, 197, 225
Lark, Maria 135
Larson, Jack 17, 229
LaRue, Eva 62–63
Lawford, Peter 203
Lawrence, Mark Christopher 53
Lawson, Denis 153
Lawson, Maggie 158, 171

Layton, Tyler 189
Lee, Alexondra 197
Lee, C.S. 70
Lee, Jason 135
Lee, Will Yun 36, 224–225
Lehman, Kristin 112, 146
Leigh, Chyler 202
Lennix, Harry 37–38
Leon, David 214–215, 232
Letheren, Mark 224
Letts, Tracy 101
Levi, Zachary 53, 217
Levine, Ted 143
Lewis, Damian 101, 120
Liao, James Hiroyuki 212
Lightfoot, Leonard 188
Linn, Rex 62
Lintel, Michelle 37
Lipton, Peggy 5, 30, 142
Lisandrello, Nina 32
List, Peyton 84
Liu, Lucy 13, 77–78, 219
Livingston, Ron 198
Lloyd, Sue 30
Lobbin, Peggy 60
Lo Bianco, Tony 109
Lobo, Stephen 57, 161
Locklear, Heather 205
Logan, Phyllis 124
Logue, Donal 120
Loken, Kristanna 161
Lombard, Karina 87
Lombard, Louise 61
Lombardozzi, Domenick 223
Looney, Peter 160
Lopez, Jennifer 111
Lopez, Mario 160
Lord, Jack 96
Louis, Justin 139
Lovejoy, Deirdre 223
Luckenbill, Laurence 67
Lumbly, Carl 23, 44
Lumley, Joanna 19, 153
Lundy, Jessica 160
Luner, Jamie 11, 168
Lupus, Peter 140
Lyndhurst, Nicholas 153

MacCorkindale, Simon 57, 127
Machado, Justina 139
MacIntyre, Carter 211
MacKay, Jeff 201–202
Macnee, Patrick 4, 28, 88, 153, 163
MacNeill, Peter 134, 179
MacNicol, Peter 157–158

Maffia, Roma 168
Magdane, Roland 71
Maguire, Sean 184
Mahan, Kerrigan 202
Maharis, George 145
Mahendru, Annet 24
Majors, Lee 35
Malahide, Patrick 102–103
Malco, Romany 120
Mandylor, Costas 186
Mankuma, Blu 86
Mann, Terrence 74
Mantegna, Joe 60
Mantooth, Randolph 69
March, Stephanie 118
Margolin, Stuart 199
Markinson, Brian 57, 206
Marshall, Paula 194
Marshall-Green, Logan 65
Martin, Anna Maxwell 38, 230
Martin, Anne-Marie 190–191
Martin, Chris William 199
Martin, Graham Patrick 126
Martin, Jesse L. 117, 213
Martin, Kellie 151
Martin, Kiel 99
Martin, Pamela Sue 94
Martinez, A 48, 222
Martini, Max 120
Marvel, Elizabeth 72, 162
Masak, Ron 149
Massey, Ilona 175
Mastrantonio, Mary Elizabeth 118
Matchett, Kari 59
Matheson, Tim 207
Mathews, George 92
Matter, Niall 79, 125
Mayers, Andre 57
Mbatha-Raw, Gugu 211
McBride, Chi 172
McCallum, David 151, 203
McCarty, Bruce 197
McClintock, Eddie 34, 218
McCook, John 55
McCormack, Eric 164
McCormack, Mary 105, 186
McCrane, Paul 211
McDermott, Dean 139
McDermott, Dylan 65
McDonnell, Mary 13, 126
McDormand, Frances 119
McDowell, Roddy 201
McEwan, Geraldine 13, 18

McGill, Bruce 176, 178, 232
McGoohan, Patrick 64
McGrady, Michael 195
McHattie, Stephen 56
McKenzie, Ben 195
McKenzie, Jacqueline 87, 190
McKenzie, Julia 13, 18–19, 230
McKeon, Nancy 12, 72–73
McKinney, Gregory 64
McLaren, Brandon Jay 92–93
McMahon, Julian 168
McMahon, Travis 138
McPartlin, Ryan 53
McRaney, Gerald 211
McShane, Ian 124, 137, 146
Meloni, Christopher 118–119
Mennell, Laura 23–24
Meredith, Burgess 31
Meriwether, Lee 29
Merkerson, S. Epatha 117, 127, 213
Merrow, Jane 64
Metcalfe, Jesse 53
Metrano, Art 25
Meyer, Dina 36, 186
Michaud, Sophie 57
Michele, Michael 64
Milans, Marta 112
Millegan, Eric 40
Miller, Danny 184
Miller, Jonny Lee 77–78, 219
Miller, Kristen 187
Miller, Paul 170
Milligan, Stuart 110
Mills, Donna 108
Mills, John 227–228
Milne, Travis 179
Mimieux, Yvette 145
Minnette, Dylan 182
Mirren, Helen 10, 54, 167
Misner, Susan 24
Mison, Tom 137, 191
Mitchell, Don 106
Mitchell, Elizabeth 79, 213
Moakler, Shanna 160
Mohr, Gerald 86
Monaghan, Dominic 84, 98
Montana, Manny 92–93
Montgomery, Poppy 13, 110, 196, 212, 225
Mooney, Peter 179
Mooney, Tony 184

Moore, Mary Tyler 4, 176
Moore, Shemar 36–37, 60
Moore, Stephen Campbell 102
Morahan, Hattie 38–39
Morey, Bill 207
Morgan, Cindy 42
Moriarty, Michael 117
Morita, Pat 150
Morris, Garrett 103
Morris, Greg 140
Morris, Kathryn 11, 55, 180–181
Morris, Phil 140
Morrison, James 208
Morrison, Jon 214–215
Morrow, Rob 11, 157
Morse, Barry 227–228
Morton, Greg 182
Morton, Joe 79
Mosaku, Wunmi 214–215, 232
Moses, William R. 108
Mount, Anson 121
Msamati, Lucian 157
Mulgrew, Kate 147
Munro, Lochlyn 209
Murciano, Enrique 225
Murphy, Kim 120
Murray, James 50
Murray, Sean 151
Myles, Sophia 143, 208

Nagra, Parminder 22, 37
Napier, Alan 30
Natwick, Mildred 192
Naud, Melinda 69
Neal, Dylan 39
Needham, Tracey 72–73
Neeson, Liam 137
Negron, Taylor 69
Neill, Noel 17, 117
Neill, Sam 22
Nelson, Craig T. 72, 80, 104, 162, 205
Nelson, Ed 188
Nelson, Kirsten 158, 171
Nelson, Tim Blake 50
Nelson, Tracy 8, 81, 159
Nevin, Brooke 87
Newmar, Julie 31
Newsome, Paula 225–226
Newton, Omari 57
Ng, Irene 150
Nguyen, Dustin 209, 216
Nguyen, Mayko 17
Nicholls, Anthony 49
Nicholls-King, Melanie 224

Nichols, Rachel 57, 60, 105
Nicholson, Julianne 118
Nicole, Jasika 88
Nicols, Rosemary 68
Nimoy, Leonard 140
Noble, John 88, 191–192
Noble, Trisha 200
Nolan, Tom 109
Nolasco, Amaury 53
Nordling, Jeffrey 112
Norris, Hermione 224
Noth, Chris 117–118
Novack, Shelly 145–146
Nucci, Danny 194

Obonsawin, Annick 16
O'Byrne, Brian 167
O'Byrne, Brían F. 84
O'Connell, Jerry 61
Ohama, Natsuko 86–87
O'Hara, David 72, 162
O'Heaney, Caitlin 201
O'Keefe, Michael 113–114
Okuma, Enuka 179, 200
Olin, Lena 12, 23
Olkewicz, Walter 162
Olmos, Edward James 137
O'Loughlin, Alex 96, 143, 208
O'Mara, Jason 20
Omundson, Timothy 158, 171
O'Neal, Patrick 71
O'Neal, Ron 42–43
O'Neill, Dick 44
O'Neill, Jennifer 58–59
Orbach, Jerry 117, 213
Orth, Frank 41
Osoba, Tony 68
O'Toole, Annette 104, 204
Outhwaite, Tamzin 153
Oxenberg, Catherine 15

Pace, Jackson 101
Pace, Lee 172
Page, Harrison 190–191
Page, LaWanda 69
Page, Nathan 83, 138, 231
Palmer, Lilli 227–228
Palmer, Zoie 123
Parish, Diane 124
Park, Grace 96
Park, Linda 225
Park, Susie 120
Parker, Nathaniel 106
Parker, Nicole Ari 148
Parker, Paula Jai 194
Patinkin, Mandy 60, 101

Patrick, Robert 227
Patterson, Scott 80
Patton, Will 20
Paul, Aislinn 222
Paymer, David 121
Peck, Ella Rae 66
Penfold, Mark 224
Penghlis, Thaao 140
Penny, Brendan 146
Penny, Joe 108
Perabo, Piper 13, 59
Peregrym, Missy 133, 179
Perrette, Pauley 11, 151–152
Peters, Clarke 47, 223
Peters, Dennis Alaba 68
Peters, Rick 200
Petersen, Luvia 57
Petersen, William 61–62
Phillips, Lou Diamond 122–123
Picatto, Antoinette 58
Pickles, Christina 215
Pierce, Wendell 223
Pierson, Geoff 70
Pileggi, Mitch 227
Pino, Danny 55
Pinzon, Miguel 150
Plana, Tony 215
Platt, Edward 90
Pleshette, Suzanne 67
Plummer, Christopher 57
Pogue, Ken 16
Ponce, Poncie 97
Popowich, Paul 27
Porter, Nyree Dawn 169
Porter, Todd 222
Potter, Chris 189, 222
Pounder, CCH 74, 218
Powell, Esteban 120
Powers, Stefanie 4, 6, 82, 91, 94–95
Praed, Michael 185
Preville, Anne 86
Price, Molly 36
Price, Vincent 31, 192
Procter, Emily 11, 62–63
Proft, Pat 69
Prosho, David 184
Purl, Linda 210
Purnick, Steve 150

Q, Maggie 13, 156
Qualls, DJ 135
Quayle, Anthony 199
Quentin, Caroline 110, 125
Quinn, Aidan 77, 167
Quinn, Brandon 17

Quinn, Ed 79
Quinn, Molly 48–49

Raitano, Natalie 216–217
Rajskub, Mary Lynn 208–209
Ralph, Sheryl Lee 55
Ramamurthy, Sendhil 32, 59
Ramirez, Marisa 17–18
Ramos, Luis Antonio 104
Rasche, David 190–191
Ratchford, Jeremy 55
Rawat, Navi 157–158, 173
Rawls, Lou 31
Rayner, Adam 102
Read, James 174–175
Reddick, Lance 88, 223
Redman, Amanda 153–155, 171, 231
Reeves, George 17, 116, 229
Reid, Daphne Maxwell 193–194
Reid, Tim 193–194
Rekert, Winston 16
Remar, James 70, 104
Repp, Stafford 30
Reuben, Gloria 20, 139
Reynolds, Corey 54
Rhodes, Hari 145
Rhys, Matthew 24
Rhys-Davies, John 210
Richards, Lou 188
Richardson, Cameron 58
Richardson-Whitfield, Salli 79
Rifkin, Ron 12, 23, 43
Rigg, Diana 4, 28, 146–147, 163
Righetti, Amanda 136, 231
Rippy, Leon 182
Ritter, Jason 80
Ritter, Paul 214, 232
Roberts, Dallas 212
Roberts, Doris 114, 174–175, 231–232
Roberts, Michael D. 127
Roberts, Pernell 146
Roberts, Rick 27
Roberts, Sean O. 161
Roberts, Tanya 51–52
Robertson, Kathleen 148
Robinson, Christina 70
Robinson, Holly 9, 100, 209
Robinson, Laura 215
Robinson, Thomas 169
Rochon, Lela 72–73

Roday, James 158, 171
Rodrigues, Percy 188
Rodriguez, Adam 62–63
Rodriguez, Elizabeth 167
Rodriguez, Freddy 50
Rodriguez, Ramon 52–53
Roemer, Sarah 80
Rollins, Rose 53
Romanus, Richard 200
Romero, Cesar 31
Romijn, Rebecca 113
Ronin, Costa 24
Rosato, Tony 71
Rose, Anika Noni 157
Rose, Emily 95
Rose, Jamie 115
Rossi, Leo 162
Rossovich, Rick 160
Routledge, Patricia 98
Rowan, Kelly 164
Rowe, John 27
Royo, Andre 223
Rubinek, Saul 74, 218
Rundle, Sophie 38–39, 230
Russell, Keri 24
Ryan, Jay 32
Ryan, Michelle 36
Ryan, Sage 169
Ryan, Tracy 152
Ryder, Lisa 86–87, 216

Sackhoff, Katee 122
Sahay, Vik 53
Saint James, Susan 6, 132–133, 231
Sakovich, Nancy Anne 170
Sales, Francis De 141
Sams, Jeffrey D. 121
Samuel, Tara 200
Sanchez, Roselyn 225
Sandoval, Miguel 135
Santiago, Saundra 9, 137
Santiago-Hudson, Ruben 48
Santoni, Reni 127
Sara, Mia 36–37
Sauls, Christa 15
Sawa, Devon 156
Sawahla, Julia 110
Saxon, John 146
Saylor, Morgan 101
Sbarge, Raphael 148
Scagliotti, Allison 73, 218
Schallert, William 94
Schiff, Richard 148
Schmid, Kyle 12, 39
Schram, Bitty 84, 143, 203
Schram, Jessy 108

Schuck, John 132, 231
Schwartz, Ben 211
Sciorra, Annabella 118
Scorsone, Caterina 139
Scott, Ashley 36
Scott, Jill 157
Scott, Sydna 86
Scott, Tom Everett 195–196
Seatle, Dixie 16
Sedgwick, Kyra 13, 54, 126
Sellati, Keidrich 24
Sellecca, Connie 170
Seven, Johnny 25
Sexton, Brent 112, 120
Seyfried, Amanda 216
Shackelford, Ted 196
Shada, Zack 108
Shahi, Sarah 120, 164–165
Shalhoub, Tony 85, 143, 203
Sharp, Lesley 184
Sharpe, Anthony 138
Shatner, William 205
Shaw, Natalie 211
Shawlee, Joan 82
Shayne, Robert 17
Shellen, Stephen 57
Shepherd, Cybill 7, 98, 144
Shera, Mark 29
Sheridan, Jamey 102, 118
Shrapnel, Lex 102
Shue, Elisabeth 61
Sikking, James B. 99
Silk, Anna 123
Sillas, Karen 211
Silva, Trinidad 99
Silver, Ron 66
Simmons, J.K. 54
Sinise, Gary 63
Sisto, Jeremy 117
Skarsten, Rachel 36–37
Slater, Blair 16
Small, Sharon 106
Smith, Allison 197
Smith, Arjay 164
Smith, Gregory 179
Smith, Jaclyn 6, 51–52, 75, 89
Smith, Kurtwood 50
Smith, Martha 69, 182, 232
Smith, Ray 68
Smith, Sheridan 110
Smithhart, Peggy 71
Smitrovich, Bill 80
Snipes, Wesley 137
Snyder, Arlen Dean 66
Snyder, Liza 189–190
Sohn, Sonja 223

Solo, Ksenia 123
Somers, Suzanne 188
Sommer, Josef 210
Sossamon, Shannyn 143
Spader, James 37
Spano, Joe 99
Speight, Richard, Jr. 20
Spelling, Tori 150
Spence, Jennifer 57
Spencer, Abigail 27
Spiro, Jordana 104, 204
Stack, Robert 145–146, 200
Stahl, Lisa 31
Stander, Lionel 94–95
Stanford, Aaron 156
Stearns, Jeff 160
Steel, Christine 202
Stephens, James 81
Stevens, Connie 97
Stevenson, Parker 94
Stewart, Julie 56
Stewart, Mel 182, 232
Stewart, Rob 161, 201
Stirling, Rachael 38–39, 230
Stout, Paul 182
Strahovski, Yvonne 53, 217
Strangis, Judy 77
Strathairn, David 23
Stuart, Randy 3, 34
Stubbs, Imogen 27
Sullivan, Charlotte 179
Sullivan, Susan 48–49
Sumika, Aya 157
Sunjata, Daniel 92–93
Sutherland, Kiefer 208
Sutton, Dudley 124
Swan, Serinda 92–93
Szmanda, Eric 61

Talbott, Michael 137
Tanner, Joy 56, 152
Tawfiq, Hisham 37
Taylor, Holland 134
Taylor, Holly 24
Taylor, Kent 41
Taylor, Rachael 52
Taylor, Robert 122
Taylor, Tamara 40
Tenney, Jon 54, 113
Terry, John 52
Theroux, Justin 72
Thiessen, Tiffani 81, 221
Thigpen, Lynne 72, 80
Thomas, Betty 99
Thomas, Philip Michael 9, 137

Thomas, Richard 24
Thomas, Sean Patrick 72
Thomason, Marsha 221
Thompson, Fred Dalton 117
Thompson, Lea 108
Thoms, Tracie 55
Thor, Jerome 86
Thorson, Linda 28
Thyne, T.J. 40
Tian, Valerie 146
Tilford, Terrell 169
Togo, Jonathan 62
Toomey, Regis 176
Torres, Gina 198
Torv, Anna 88
Toussaint, Lorraine 182
Tracey, Ian 201
Tracy, Jill 160
Trageser, Kathy 202–203
Travanti, Daniel J. 99
Trickey, Paula 160
Tripplehorn, Jeanne 60
Trucco, Michael 112
Tunie, Tamara 118
Tunney, Robin 121, 136, 231
Turco, Paige 20
Tveit, Aaron 92–93
Tyson, Barbara 209–210

Underwood, Blair 80

Vaccaro, Brenda 66
Valentine, Scott 37
Valentine, Steve 61
Valley, Mark 88
Vance, Chris 178
Vance, Courtney B. 84, 118
Vander, Musetta 186
Vandervoort, Laura 79, 213
Vangsness, Kirsten 60
Vardalos, Nia 202–203
Varley, Beatrice 71
Vartan, Michael 12, 23, 43
Vassey, Liz 61
Vassilieva, Sofia 75, 135
Vaughn, Robert 91, 169
Vélez, Lauren 70, 155
Vernon, John 15
Vidal, Lisa 72–73, 80
Vogel, Darlene 160

Wachs, Caitlin 168
Waggoner, Lyle 226
Wagner, Lindsay 6, 35, 109, 194
Wagner, Robert 6, 94–95

Walger, Sonya 84
Walker, Ally 10–11, 168–169, 202
Walker, Andrew W. 17
Walker, Nancy 132, 231
Walker, Nicola 206
Walsh, Dylan 212
Walter, Jessica 25
Ward, Burt 30–31
Ward, Sela 63
Warren, Lesley Ann 105
Warren, Michael 99
Warwick, James 19–20
Waterman, Dennis 153–155, 231
Waterston, Sam 117–118, 213
Watson, Alberta 27, 83
Watson, Tamara Marie 56
Wattis, Richard 71
Waxman, Al 44, 230
Weatherly, Michael 151–152
Weber, Jake 75, 135
Weber, Steven 148
Webster, Victor 57
Wechsler, Nick 202
Weigert, Robin 120–121
Weisman, Kevin 23
Weitz, Bruce 99
Weller, Frederick 105, 186
Welsh, Jonathan 16
Wen, Ming-Na 21–22
West, Adam 30–31
West, Dominic 223
West, Shane 156
Weston, Celia 135
White, Brian 32
White, John 16–17
Whitfield, Dondre 186
Whitman, Stuart 146
Wickersham, Emily 151
Wickes, Mary 81
Wight, Peter 27
Wilkinson, Tom 167
Williams, Clarence, III 5, 30, 142, 151
Williams, Genelle 218
Williams, Grant 97
Williams, Gregory Alan 31
Williams, Natashia 187
Williams, Steven 100, 209
Williams, Treat 17–18
Williamson, Bree 66
Willis, Bruce 7, 98, 137, 144
Willis, Jerome 196

Wills, Anneke 199
Wilson, Peta 10, 83
Windom, William 149
Wint, Maurice Dean 170
Winter, Edward 82
Winter, Katia 191
Witt, Alicia 118
Wolf, Scott 164, 213
Wong, Anna May 13, 89
Wong, BD 118
Wood, Ward 128
Woodard, Alfre 135, 207

Woodburn, Danny 197
Woods, Christine 84
Woodvine, Mary 196
Woodward, Edward 160
Worth, Michael 15
Wright, Alison 24–25
Wyner, George 129, 188
Wyngarde, Peter 68

Yenque, Jose 72
Yeoman, Owain 136, 231
Yoba, Malik 23–24, 155

Young, Lee Thompson 176, 178, 232
Youngblood, Rob 196

Zayas, David 70
Zimbalist, Efrem, Jr. 97, 149
Zimbalist, Stephanie 7, 101, 114, 174–175, 231–232
Zmed, Adrian 149, 205
Zulu 96
Zulueta, Ogie 159
ZúZiga, José 202

www.ingramcontent.com/pod-product-compliance
Ingram Content Group UK Ltd.
Pitfield, Milton Keynes, MK11 3LW, UK
UKHW041938140426
5217IPUK00014B/538